Baseball Forever
Reflections on 60 Years in the Game

Ralph Kiner with Danny Peary

TRIUMPH
BOOKS
CHICAGO

*I met my wife DiAnn 26 years ago while I was doing radio
coverage of the Bob Hope Desert Classic in Palm Springs,
California. One afternoon when I was in the clubhouse,
people who recognized me began to stop at my table to say
hello or ask for an autograph or to be photographed with
me. As DiAnn talked, I knew she didn't know who I was,
other than that I appeared on TV and radio. After an hour
or so, she finally turned to me and said: "Who are you,
anyway?" She believes this book answers that question.
It is to DiAnn that it is dedicated.*

Library of Congress Cataloging-in-Publication Data

Kiner, Ralph.
    Baseball forever : reflections on 60 years in the game / Ralph Kiner with
Danny Peary.
        p. cm.
    ISBN 1-57243-597-6
    1. Kiner, Ralph, 1922– 2. Baseball players—United States—Biography.
I. Peary, Danny, 1949– II. Title.

GV865.K53A3 2003
796.357'092—dc22
[B]

                                                              2003063404

This book is available in quantity at special discounts for your group or
organization. For further information, contact:
    Triumph Books
    601 South LaSalle Street
    Suite 500
    Chicago, Illinois 60605
    (312) 939-3330
    Fax (312) 663-3557

Printed in USA
ISBN 1-57243-597-6
Design by Patricia Frey

Contents

Foreword

The first autograph I ever received from a big-league baseball player was from Ralph Kiner, one of the great hitters of all time and one of the nicest gentlemen you would ever want to meet.

It must have been 1956 or 1957, after Ralph had retired as an active player, that my father approached him while they were competing in the Bing Crosby Pro-Am Golf Tournament in Pebble Beach, California. My father told Ralph that he had a son who one day was going to be a big-league ballplayer and that he would love an autograph for me. Ralph signed the back of my junior high school class picture:

To Tom,
Work hard and good luck,
Ralph Kiner

They were wonderful words of encouragement from one of the great power hitters in major league baseball history to one of the great power hitters in the North Fresno Little League. (Upon my introduction to the curveball, I realized there was no way I was going anywhere in baseball as a hitter.) That treasured autographed picture still rests in the family album at my father's home in Pebble Beach. How ironic that we would one day become teammates at the Baseball Hall of Fame in Cooperstown, New York.

To give you a peek at the wry humor that is so much a part of Ralph Kiner, I'll take you back to the very first day I walked into the major league training camp of the New York Mets. Ralph, of course, was one of the broadcasters of a great three-man team, along with Bob Murphy and Lindsey Nelson, and when I entered the locker room I ran into him. He looked at me, said hello and introduced himself, and then asked, "What took you so long?" He had waited about 10 years to deliver that line. I probably uttered some foolish, nervous response.

Ralph and I would become friends in and outside of baseball. The times I have enjoyed most with him have been the occasions we have had for leisurely conversation—like a dinner on a road trip or a postgame broadcast meeting. When Ralph talks about baseball (as when he writes about it in this book), his very deep respect and love for the game are contagious. Moreover, his unparalleled wealth of knowledge on every aspect of its history makes him a joy to listen to. He moves seamlessly from Babe Ruth to Henry Aaron, from Willie Mays to today's players, and from facing Bob Feller to laying the groundwork for today's Players Association (not to mention all the other intriguing topics that are contained in this book). All issues are fair game and invariably lead to lively banter late into the evening.

Ralph has always been strong in his convictions, and that naturally leads to some very "energetic" discussions. For instance, who wouldn't want to have been a fly on the wall at the Hall of Fame and listened to Ralph and Ted Williams in deep conversation on the art of hitting and how dumb we pitchers are. A simple question like, "What is the best pitch in baseball?" might lead them to asking, "Should a hitter look middle of the plate in or middle out?" which of course would have them wondering, "But what if he has two strikes on him?" Well into the night they carried on their animated, quite healthy arguments as everyone else eavesdropped and learned what it took to be a great major league hitter.

Mets fans will always remember Ralph as the longtime host of *Kiner's Korner*, his postgame televised interview show. The individuals who have been guests read like a who's who of baseball from 1962 to the present, as the show, which had a brief hiatus, was brought back on the air by Fox Sports New York a few years ago.

Going on *Kiner's Korner* was a delight as a player for three reasons. One, you must have done something good. Two, you got paid 50 bucks. And three, Ralph seemed to enjoy the show as much as his guests. It was a postgame "event" that was enjoyed by players, their families, and friends, and it didn't go unnoticed by me that Ralph always went out of his way to say hello to my wife, Nancy, our children, and our guests at the ballpark.

In the industry of professional sports, "civilians" always ask us, "What is so-and-so like?" In the case of Ralph Kiner, my response has not changed in what is now—if you count that initial autograph—closing in on 50 years. From that first meeting in spring training, it has been a 35-year friendship that I cherish. In fact, every time I think of it—or see Ralph at the "office" or away from work—it brings a warm smile to my face. That's because of the kind of gentleman he is. My mother's favorite expression when she described a special person was *a jewel*—it was the highest honor she could bestow on anyone. Ralph Kiner is a precious jewel.

On my bookshelf in my home I have an earlier book titled *Kiner's Korner*, which is signed to Tom Seaver from Ralph Kiner. I got that autograph all by myself. I will be sure to get my copy of this special book autographed as well. Enjoy it.

—Tom Seaver

Acknowledgments

If I were younger, this book would have been much shorter. But because my life and career in baseball have spanned many decades, I needed a great deal of help in assembling this volume, which includes everything I have to say about the game I have lived and loved.

First of all, I thank my coauthor, Danny Peary, who pushed me to tell my story as I never have before. Through the interview process, the writing, and the editing, we evolved from being longtime acquaintances to close and trusting friends.

I wish to express my sincere and very personal gratitude to Tom Seaver, who graciously wrote his Foreword between our seasons together in the New York Mets broadcast booth. His kind, heartfelt words have so much meaning to me because of my own deep admiration for him.

Danny and I would like to thank our mutual agent Robert L. Rosen for bringing us together to write this book, as well as for his friendship. We are equally indebted to Jennifer Unter, the literary agent at RLR Associates, Ltd., for introducing us to Triumph Books and for being there for us every step of the way. Her support has been much appreciated. Other people at R.L.R. who deserve special recognition are Tara Mark, Gail Lockhart, Maury Gostfrand, and Barbara Hadzicosmas.

We have enjoyed our relationship with Triumph Books, where everyone has made us feel secure from the start. We wish to acknowledge in particular Tom Bast, the editorial director (who has Ernie Harwell on his answering machine!); Blythe Hurley, the managing editor; and Linc Wonham, the developmental editor. We were in good hands.

Other individuals who deserve to be singled out are Yogi Berra, Tim McCarver, Bob Murphy, Fran Healy, Nancy Seaver, Carol Summers, Robert Fowler, Jeanie Dooha, Melissa Kay Rogers, Laura Peary, Ezra Fitz, and Janet Suarez, my "girl Friday," who spent hours searching through dozens of boxes of memorabilia for the photos that are included in this book.

I want to acknowledge the continual inspiration I received from my family, old and young alike. I thank Michael Kiner, his wife Maria, and their daughter Nancy, who was born as I began working on this book; Scott Kiner, his wife Lea, and their daughters Carly, Shawn, Lindsey, and Kasey;

K.C. (Kathryn Chafee) and her husband Robin Freeman, and their sons Chase and Kyle; Tracee, her husband Gary Jansen, and their children Ali, Lauren, and Chase; Kimberlee, her husband Bob Mazzone, and their children Samantha and Kasey; and Candice, her husband Michael Beck, and their children Matthew, Andrew, Katie, Josiah, Bethany, Nathaniel, and Benjamin.

Most of all, Danny and I are grateful to our wives, Suzanne and my DiAnn, for their endless encouragement and dedication to helping us finish this book. They did not stay in the background.

—Ralph Kiner

Introduction

When I was about to graduate from high school, during an unexpected burst of maturity and practicality, I opened a small bank account. Down at the ballfield, scouts were waiting to court me, and it was clear I'd soon realize my dream of becoming a professional baseball player, but I wanted something to fall back on if I didn't succeed. I wasn't able to save any money, but my brief moment of gazing into the future was an indication that I understood baseball wouldn't last forever.

Ironically, in my case, it would. Since I signed a contract with the Pittsburgh Pirates in 1940 and reported to their camp the following spring, I have worked continuously in baseball—as a player, minor league general manager, and major league broadcaster. In 1869, the Cincinnati Reds became the first team to play for money, and it occurs to me that if you combine the years I was a young fan with the more than 60 years I have been employed in baseball, that total represents more than half the lifetime of America's pastime as a professional sport. That's a long time.

Baseball immortal Rogers Hornsby, who played 23 major league seasons, once said, "People ask me what I do in winter when there's no baseball. I'll tell you what I do. I stare out the window and wait for spring." I certainly understand how most kids could relate to that marvelous quote. But I grew up in Alhambra, California, where there was no winter. There were three hardly distinguishable seasons that you could conjugate as nice, nicer, and nicest. The weather was always conducive to being outside, and from the time I was 10, I played baseball and other sports throughout the year, including almost every day after school.

In whatever sport I participated, I wanted to be like the athletes I admired. So when I played football I wanted to play like the stars of college powerhouses USC and Stanford, whose games I'd listen to on the radio while hanging out at the gas station. My Saturday afternoons included the great Stanford runners Bones Hamilton and 175-pound fullback Bobby Grayson, and Trojans backs Orv Mohler and "Cotton" Warburton. Mohler preceded me at Alhambra High and had a dad, Kid Mohler, who made it to the major leagues for three games in 1894 as a left-handed second baseman. When I played tennis I wanted to be like the dominating Bill Tilden, whom

I read about in the sports pages. And having been taken by my mother to the 1932 Olympics in Los Angeles, I wanted to dive like Sammy Lee, swim like Buster Crabbe, and run like such sprinters as Mac Robinson, Jackie Robinson's older brother. (When I became a professional baseball player I was one of the few players who included running in his off-season regimen—actually I was one of the few players back then who *had* an off-season regimen.)

All those guys were great, but my biggest hero by far was Babe Ruth, who played baseball three thousand miles away. Despite accumulating the two highest batting averages in history, Ty Cobb and Rogers Hornsby didn't interest me. Finesse wasn't a quality kids admired much. But home-run hitters delivered knockout punches. I hit the ball farther than any of my friends did, so I had no intention of becoming a singles hitter. I wanted to be a home-run hitter like the most famous athlete in the world.

I played a lot of touch and tackle football, basketball, tennis, and fast-pitch softball, which was a big sport in southern California. But I played baseball most of all. It was the sport I played best and for which I cultivated an ever-lasting attachment as I played it and thought about it endlessly. As a young fan, I'd buy *Baseball* magazine, which had 8-by-10-inch photos of baseball stars, and I read accounts in the newspapers. I also got to see major league exhibition games during spring training. And I'd listen to Hal Berger and the "Old Scotsman" Gordon McClendon do thrilling re-creations on the radio.

I played in hundreds of pickup sandlot games, which lasted until it got too dark to see. I played in school. I played American Legion ball. I played in a Sunday morning league with men, and I played afternoons with a team sponsored by a local merchant. I played with a team backed by the New York Yankees called the Yankee Juniors. I would estimate that I played more than 200 games a year for six or seven years. Few kids play that much anymore, but that's what it took to make the big leagues back then, when every young athlete wanted to be a baseball player.

Baseball was the only sport then that you could continue to play and make a decent living. But it was more than that. Even on the West Coast, where there was no major league baseball until 1958, we realized that it was part of the fabric of America. There were teams in mining towns, fishing villages, and farm communities, and it was the sport adopted by immigrants in the teeming urban centers in the East and Midwest. They played and watched it and learned about America.

My father had loved baseball. He was a steam-shovel operator where I was born, in Santa Rita, a copper-mining town of about five thousand in New Mexico. His only son would someday become the only Hall of Fame baseball player ever born in New Mexico—and be voted by *Sports Illustrated* a couple of years ago as the best athlete the state has produced.

Yet my dad wasn't considered good enough to play on the local team with some of the former White Sox players who had been banned from baseball for throwing the 1919 World Series. But he was well liked and considered honest enough to be entrusted with the important job of holding the money that was bet on the games.

When I was four, my father died, and my mother packed us up and moved us to Alhambra, where she took a job as an office nurse for an insurance and trust company, making $125 a month. A tiny lady at 4'11", she spent almost all of her time working and keeping house. Everyone admired how on a small income she always kept a fine, clean home for the two of us, with nice furniture and elegant china and silverware. She had an aura of gentility and culture. Her friends asked her to teach them how to keep their houses as prim and proper as ours was.

My mother was old school and believed in work and responsibility. She thought I was too obsessed with baseball because I was getting some Cs on my report card, so I had to apply myself and get my grades up. She could see that I had the potential to play baseball for a living, but that didn't impress her because she didn't think professional baseball was a worthy profession. Like most mothers in those days, mine didn't consider ballplayers to be as reputable as doctors and lawyers. They didn't have much stature in social circles.

Wanting me to get a good sense of business and money, she made me take a job selling the *Saturday Evening Post* door-to-door in the afternoons. I got five cents a copy, of which I had to pay the dealer four cents. I didn't like that this small enterprise cut into my time playing ball, so I figured out a way to get back my afternoons without angering my mother. On the sly, I mowed lawns for a quarter apiece and earned enough money to pay off my boss. Then I took the magazines and buried them in my backyard. But I wasn't as good with a shovel as I was with a baseball bat, because my mother saw one of the magazines sticking out of the ground. She had the incriminating evidence and judged me guilty of shirking my responsibility to play a silly game. She sent me off to military school in Long Beach for a semester. I hated that, particularly because I couldn't play ball with my friends. Did I learn a lesson? Yes. I never buried another magazine in my life.

Because my mother was so busy working, cooking, and tending to the house, I didn't spend much time with her. In fact, I was raised to a large degree by our friends across the street, Bob and Rose Bodkin. Bob and his teenage son Robert got me into playing baseball. When I was about 11, I started shagging balls for them, standing in a vacant lot across the street from where Robert would hit the balls his father pitched. We did this many times. Hitting looked like more fun than what I was doing, so I finally asked if I could grab a bat, too. It took me a little while before I hit with any confidence or consistency, but I was good enough—or they needed a ninth player—to be included in the organized, merchant-sponsored games Robert and other older kids played. That was the beginning of my becoming a baseball player.

No one knows that I batted left-handed when I played softball. I did it because I didn't want to screw up my right-handed swing, which I hoped would lead me to the promised land. I could hit the ball just as far from that side, but I never batted left-handed playing hardball. In those days, it wasn't considered a real advantage to be a switch-hitter because almost all pitchers were righties, and nobody had figured out yet that, if you go strictly by statistics, left-handed batters are better than right-handed batters at hitting right-handed pitchers. Except for Ruth and Lou Gehrig, most sluggers of the thirties were right-handed, and there was no such thing as platooning. My future manager Frankie Frisch was the only great switch-hitter of the day.

My close friend Lefty Johnson, who did bat left-handed, was also obsessed with baseball, and his father drove us all around the area to play (and also to see an occasional Pacific Coast League game). Without that, I wouldn't have been able to play competitively except in Alhambra. Because of Lefty's dad, I got to play at Gilmore Field in Hollywood (the home of the Pacific Coast League's Stars), Wrigley Field (the home of the PCL's Angels—yes, there really was a second Wrigley Field), and playgrounds in Griffith Park, Brookside Park, La Cienega Park, and elsewhere. Both Lefty and I developed into good players. Lefty would be signed and play in the minor leagues, though he eventually found security as a banker.

The older I got, the more I thought of playing in the major leagues. There was an earlier graduate from Alhambra High named Max West who had made it, breaking in as an outfielder with the Boston Braves in 1938. Max was the first player to homer in his first All-Star Game at-bat, so his name was mentioned during the 2003 All-Star Game when Hank Blalock hit the game-winning pinch-homer in the American League's comeback victory. I got to know Max and his friend Red Ruffing, the future Hall of Famer, so playing in the major leagues didn't seem like an impossible dream anymore. I was getting close to my goal.

What convinced my mother that baseball might not be such a bad career for me was that I received an offer of a $3,000 signing bonus from the Pirates. She didn't say no. With that money we were able to pay off the mortgage on our house. From that day forward, she referred to herself as "Cinderella" and had a different attitude toward the sport that had changed our fortunes overnight. When I went off to play ball professionally, I sent her a wire every time I homered.

Most young players run into rough spots along the way to the major leagues and contemplate quitting. But things went well for me right from the beginning, and I never considered giving up the game and living on what was left of the $150 salary I received each month my first year. In my first professional game, at Brookside Park, the White Sox spring-training field in Pasadena, I played first base and went 4-for-5 with two homers against two good pitchers, Bill Dietrich and Thornton Lee. That was an encouraging way to begin, and my spring was so hot in 1941 that instead of being assigned to Class C or Class D, where most kids I played ball with started, I was sent to Albany in A ball. That was the third-highest designation, behind A1 and the highest minor league, Double A (which comprised the International League, the American Association, and the Pacific Coast League). I had only a fair year and wasn't advanced. But in my second season at Albany I led the Eastern League with 14 home runs. It was a pitchers' league, in which only one batter hit .300.

The next year I was promoted and spent six weeks with Toronto, in the International League, before enlisting in the navy. I was one of thirty-five hundred minor leaguers who went into the service. The two and a half years I was in uniform was the only time I didn't play ball for an extended period. During that time as a flyer, I matured and learned what life was all about.

When I got out of the service in 1946, instead of sending me back to Toronto, Pittsburgh kept me on the major league roster after I hit 13 homers in spring training. Perhaps they should have sent me back to the minors because I was extremely rusty despite lighting it up during the spring. My rookie year was a rude awakening. I was able to lead the league in home runs, but in other ways I struggled and realized that there were players who were as good as I was. That made me work even harder to improve. Baseball was a continuation of a fantasy. I didn't think of putting together a great career and setting home-run records. I just wanted to play and do well. And fortunately I was able to play well enough for 10 major league seasons (1946–55) that I would be bestowed baseball's highest honor—induction into the Hall of Fame, in 1975.

By that time, I was well into my second career in baseball—broadcasting. After five years as the general manager (GM) of the San Diego Padres in the Pacific Coast League, I spent one year as a radio broadcaster for the Chicago White Sox before I began working for the New York Mets, first on TV and radio, and then television only. Unlike with baseball, I had no training and no help; I just did it, learning on the job. For my first five years with the Mets I was given one-year contracts, so I never knew from year to year if I'd be rehired. Apparently I was doing something right because I'm still here. I take tremendous pride in the fact that I have been with the Mets now for 42 years. For the first 17 years I worked with Hall of Fame broadcasters Lindsey Nelson and Bob Murphy—the longest time a three-man team has ever been together.

Broadcasting, which came unexpectedly to me, was my way to continue to stay in baseball. It has been the ideal way for me to convey my knowledge and appreciation for the game itself and teach the history that is more significant in baseball than in any other sport. I have tried to call games with expertise, candor, and humor and to mix play-by-play and analysis with on-air stories about the past. I know my passion for the game has come across. It has never been just saying words.

I continue to broadcast in the manner I do for the same reason I have written this book. I want to honor the game I love by telling the true story of what it was like to be a ballplayer in my time, so fans can see how the game progressed over often-bumpy roads to where it is today. I want to give the players' side of post–WWII baseball, rather than have it told once again by a sportswriter, and to talk about baseball after I retired, from the perspective of a former player who started watching the game from high above the field. As Yogi Berra might say, this book is half memoir, half history, and half personal observations—both serious and humorous—about America's pastime after World War II and today, with a busy bridge between those two great times that is my 43-year broadcasting career. I write about personalities, life off the field and the game on it, and major issues; I also write about movie stars and golf, another passion. And I write about my own relationship to baseball, as a kid, as a player, and as a broadcaster.

With no false modesty, I can say that I have a unique perspective on baseball from the thirties to now. No one else has seen baseball from my vantage point. I participated in so much that happened, as both a player and a player representative for the Pirates and then the entire National League. And I have witnessed so much that has transpired ever since while still being a part of the game in the booth. The change in baseball—the progress—has been stunning. We went from buses and trains to prop planes and jets and cross-country travel. We saw the introduction of the pension plan, the breaking down of the color barrier, the advent of television (leading to pay-TV and vast revenues), and the revolution that brought the downfall of the reserve clause and the birth of a powerful players' union that has brought about enormous salaries, free agency, arbitration, and agents. (I spin a tale of avarice and madness only when the reserve clause and owners are the topic.) I have seen team movement, expansion, ugly labor conflicts and strikes, fallen records, controversy, young stars and then their sons play their entire careers, and even the computer threaten to take too much of the human element out of baseball.

It is an important story because it is the history of baseball at a time when the entire world changed just as dramatically. And baseball is, to me, a carbon copy of life. Success is rewarded and failure is too often accepted. It is a team game, but as an individual you are limited only by ability and the amount of work you are willing to do. I know that whatever you give to baseball, it will give you back far more in return. I know it has with me. I think that's an important message to get across.

At times as a broadcaster, it gets discouraging when your team isn't winning—just as it did playing for losing teams—and you read that ratings are down, see that attendance isn't where it was, and hear that many young and uneducated baseball fans find the game so dull that they are turning to other activities. You worry that nobody is watching, nobody is listening, and nobody cares about baseball anymore. But it's not true. I'll be paying my check in some roadside diner in the middle of nowhere, and strangers will turn around and say, "Ralph Kiner! I'd recognize that voice anywhere!" Then they grab my hand and start shaking.

So many people say they grew up listening when Lindsey, Bob, and me broadcast the Mets in their formative years and through their two miracle pennants, in 1969 (when they magically won the world title) and 1973. Others say they became baseball fans when Tim McCarver, Steve Zabriskie, and I broadcast a reenergized Mets team in the eighties, highlighted by their second world championship in 1986. I think it's quite wonderful that because of the many different phases of my career in baseball, I am remembered by fans from several distinct time periods—and cities.

Some people I run into aren't Mets fans, but baseball fans, who just want to talk to someone who has experienced what they did. Recently an 84-year-old man came up to me in a restaurant and started rattling off the New York Giants infield from the thirties. I just nodded and smiled. He could have said anybody and I wouldn't have known the difference. I filed away a few names for future research. I never stop being a student of baseball history.

I returned to Pittsburgh on Opening Day in 2003 to be honored in a ceremony at PNC Park. They dedicated a statue of a bat to me and placed it by the gate in left field, which is where I played for the Pirates in Forbes Field from 1946 to 1953. Twenty-five thousand fans came out in bad weather, and they treated me great. I was reminded of the big crowds that turned out to watch us play in the postwar years despite our poor records. I had my family with me, and I was proud when longtime fans came up and told me how much it meant to have seen me play.

But surely one of my fondest memories of that day is meeting a young man who *never* saw me play. He was a paraplegic, having been wounded in the service. He had come from West Virginia to be in Pittsburgh for Opening Day because his life was baseball. At such moments, you realize what baseball means to so many people, still. As it does with that young man, baseball fills a big part of their lives. It meant a lot to me to be reminded that the passion I had for baseball as a boy almost 70 years ago still lives on in others. That is why I have written *Baseball Forever*.

Chapter **1**
The **Players**

Recently a veteran sportswriter who was armed with a lethally sharp pencil cornered me after he thought he heard me make some negative comments during a New York Mets broadcast about the attitudes of current ballplayers. Having grown up in the late forties and fifties, he hoped to push me into saying that the players of that unique era when I played 10 major league seasons had much better character than their counterparts of today. But I said, "Hey, wait a minute. All I alleged is that *some* of today's players don't seem to have much passion for the game. But that was also true of some of the players in my time. Sure, I wouldn't want to hang out with some current players, but there were a number of guys I wasn't crazy about being around when I played. In fact, in those first few years after the war, I thought some of them should have been behind bars."

The disappointed writer was about to pocket his weapon, when I stopped him. "But," I conceded, "I was fortunate to have played exactly when I did and with the players of my day." *Because it was a great brand of baseball?* "Yes, and also because of the camaraderie." *But what about those players who were more suited for convict garb than baseball uniforms?* I grinned and said, "At least they are part of my stories."

What made the postwar players special was an esprit de corps, an astonishing sense of unity that, regrettably, has diminished with each generation since, until we see few traces of it among present-day players. Whereas players of today don't even have their teammates' cell phone numbers, we were joined at the hip. In groups of 25, we were thrown together for hours on end in clubhouses, hotel lounges and lobbies, restaurants following day games, and overnight trains; and we talked endlessly about baseball. This reinforced the strong connection that already existed because we all had lived through two harrowing events in world history: the Depression and then World War II.

We forged a tight bond because we were all in the same boat. Because of the reserve clause, we were bound for life to the teams that first signed us. We had the same kinds of deals, the same measly meal money, and the same travel hardships. We had the same makeup and the same goals in life. Also, on the positive side, we felt lucky to be playing baseball for a living

1

at even the minimum salary when the guy working down at the bank was making less than $150 a month. And we felt patriotic being participants in America's pastime—which at the time was the only popular professional sport other than boxing. President Franklin Roosevelt knew it was so vital to the country's morale that he had issued his famous "green light" letter to make sure baseball stayed in business for the duration of the war.

WWII had been traumatic for all of us who had been through it, either overseas or on the home front, and the great majority of the thirty-eight hundred professional ballplayers who had enlisted came back to baseball like a thundering herd, happy to be alive and back in civilian life. We were so eager to play ball, break with the past, and make a little money that the 16 major league training camps were packed in 1946.

For that one year only, teams were allowed to increase their rosters from 25 to as many as 30 players. Because of the Veterans Act, jobs were supposed to be given back to the players who had gone into the service, at the same professional level. That accounted for approximately three hundred of the major league roster spots. The remaining positions were vied for by us minor leaguers and those players who got 4-Fs and had remained in the big leagues during the war years. The returning vets were the best players, but many had lost their skills due to inactivity or had committed the unpardonable sin for athletes of reaching their midthirties (though numerous players took a couple of years off their ages). Consequently, despite the law, more than 140 players with big-league contracts when the war began were released or demoted to the minors by midseason—sparking a number of court cases.

I wasn't scheduled to make the Pirates in '46 when I reported to spring training in San Bernardino, California, which was near where I lived with my mother in Alhambra. Having spent little more than two years in Pittsburgh's farm system prior to joining the navy, I was earmarked for the Hollywood Stars in the Pacific Coast League. But I had a terrific spring with a lot of homers, and they kept me. At the age of 23, I began my major league career.

As I discovered, the men who populated major league baseball during the postwar era were as diverse as they are today, but in different ways. We didn't have players from all over the world back then, and the integration of African Americans and Hispanics would be slow, but in the days before television and extensive travel, guys from the Northeast, South, Midwest, Southwest, and West were as distinct from one another as night and day. Their one common thread, other than their dirty, hot, ill-fitting uniforms, was toughness. I liken them to the Teamsters during Jimmy Hoffa's time in power.

Baseball was fun, but many factors made it a difficult lifestyle, especially for the married players. These men were willing to spend much of their lives on trains and in cramped hotel rooms in order to play a game that was much rougher than it is today—in fact, they were responsible for making it that way. The style of play was so aggressive that by the end of a game, all uniforms were covered with dust and bodies had new cuts, bruises, and other badges of honor. Having lived through a time when there were literally no jobs, these men played through injuries and ailments—as well as an occasional crabs outbreak when the attendant who washed all the jockstraps from the team's common laundry bin didn't use the proper dose of disinfectant.

Some of the old ballparks were tough to play in. Crosley Field in Cincinnati and Sportsman's Park in St. Louis were the worst in the National League. They were so hot that when you came off the field you'd have to soak your feet in buckets of ice. Crosley had a sharp incline as you approached the outfield fence that made running treacherous. Sportsman's Park was shared by the Browns and Cardinals, so there were no days off and the grass virtually disappeared. It was like playing on dirt. Besides the heat, we had to endure a cramped dugout with a bench that had room for only about 12 players.

The worst situation was when you played an aggressive team in a lousy ballpark and their fans were hostile. At Shibe Park in Philadelphia, even the male fans in suits, ties, and hats would use rubber bands to shoot staples at our backs. That stung worse than a bee, so we'd constantly move around in the outfield. Meanwhile in the stands, they were dropping beer and mustard from the bleachers onto the visiting players' wives. Home players on the Phillies and the Athletics weren't immune—after the final out, Phillies outfielder Del Ennis sometimes went after hometown fans who had hassled him during the game. He also planted pals in the stands to beat up anyone who really got on his case. Those Philly fans were so mean that in the fifties, when the Athletics' star player, Gus Zernial, was carried off the field with a broken collarbone, they booed him.

Most players of the era smoked, drank, chewed tobacco, bet on horses, played cards, and, particularly if single, prowled the bars at night in search of dates. If they played day games and had a little money, they could take in the nightlife, especially in big cities like New York and Chicago. If they played night games, they went to the movies or the racetrack during the day. I saw fewer movies than most players because I agreed with Rogers Hornsby and Ted Williams that you could strain your eyes. As it was, many players were already terribly nearsighted but, like the umpires, wouldn't even consider wearing glasses because that was considered wimpy. Years earlier, Paul Waner was a great hitter despite not even being able to read the scoreboard. I had played in the minors for Specs Toporcer, who in the twenties became the first major league infielder to wear glasses. He was a good manager, but would fine players $5 if he caught them eating hot dogs.

3

Some players went to church. The most religious were the Southern Baptists, although many Catholics and even non-Catholics attended Mass. The only division I saw in regard to religion was that occasionally some players would make some passing remarks about Jews, although I had noticed more of that in the minor leagues. However, bench jockeys on opposing teams were not above insulting a player's religion or ethnicity, as well as his physical characteristics. When Jackie Robinson and other African Americans entered the majors beginning in 1947, the hecklers, primarily those from the rural South, showed them little mercy.

Players then were far more superstitious than they are today. For instance, anytime a player saw a truck with a load of hay, he knew he'd have a good day. Even guys who wore crosses might have a lucky charm or rabbit's foot in their pockets. I wore a St. Christopher's medal, and I wasn't even Catholic. As a young player, I kept a four-leaf clover. I didn't consider myself super-stitious, but I did it *just in case.* If something was working, you were afraid to not do it. So players would repeat patterns if they were doing well or their team was winning. For example, you made sure to drive the same way to the ballpark until you had a change of fortune. And if you were on a hitting streak, you might not wash your socks or underwear until it ended. It could get a little raunchy after a few games, which is why nobody would have been thrilled if a teammate approached Joe DiMaggio's 56-game hitting streak. The degree of superstition after the war was probably related to a lack of education, but nobody was immune.

There were more college graduates playing ball than there had been in the past, but even on the long train rides there wasn't much reading other than of sports pages, and when we arrived in a city, nobody rushed off to a museum or to see a performance of *Swan Lake.* There wasn't much culture. In fact, most players couldn't come up with ways, other than seeing movies and indulging in the usual vices, to spend their free time. We were ordered not to swim or lift weights because managers insisted we'd get too bulked up in our shoulders and chests to swing smoothly. That was non-sense. I was one of the few players who lifted weights anyway. I worked out after I got out of the service, but I did it mostly in the off-season and nowhere near the degree to which players do it today. I mostly tried to strengthen my hands, as did Ted Williams when he did push-ups on his fingers. (When I became better known, I lent my name to a spring-filled gripper that you squeezed and twisted to make your hands and wrists stronger—somebody insisted we should market it, but "Ralph Kiner's Hand-Twisters" didn't catch on.)

There weren't many coaches around in those days to encourage players to come up with a good conditioning program, so most didn't do it. Players knew that if they arrived at camp with a good tan, the coaches would assume they were in great shape. I thought it was important to really be fit, so each year I began working out and running in February, about a month before spring training. I also improved my quickness by using a punching bag and, for a brief time, taking fencing lessons from the man who dueled in the movies with Errol Flynn—I was pretty fast with a sword.

Golf was also prohibited during the season because management insisted it would mess up our swings. Wrong again. It was so stigmatized that when Louisville Slugger offered players a choice between receiving $25 or a brand-new set of golf clubs for signing a lifetime contract with their company, the players invariably took the money. Undeterred, I took up the sport in the off-season in Alhambra, even joining a club. Apparently I knew what other ballplayers didn't: Babe Ruth and Ty Cobb were avid golfers! So obsessed was Cobb with the sport that in the fifties, he once played through on a hole without caring that it was President Eisenhower's party that had to wait for him to pass.

What I learned as a rookie is that the superior teams had the most dedicated and disciplined players. The Pittsburgh Pirates were a terrible team, and in my first two years, most of my teammates were crazy, card-playing, heavy-drinking carousers who led the fast life and had good times after games and way past curfews. They were an all-fun-and-games bunch. There was a record player in our clubhouse, and I think it's indicative of who these guys were that their favorite 78 was about how cigarettes, whiskey, and wild women will drive you crazy. They played it over and over. I liked most of these guys, but they were real characters and totally undisciplined. I know that a lot of what went on was the result of the players having just been in the service, where they had lived each day as if it were their last on Earth. Coming back to civilian life, they no longer wanted to follow orders and conventions, and their mantra was "eat, drink, and be merry."

You often hear about how in those days, players on each team policed each other to make sure no one broke the team's rules or the town's laws and wasn't ready to play the next day. The Pirates didn't do this. So while management and members of the media gave nothing more than sidelong glances, everyone was free to get into whatever trouble they wanted to. And they did. It might have been easier to take if we won, but one reason we lost so many games is because of what was going on. Fortunately, I had grown up during the Depression, attended junior college (and would matriculate for three whole days at USC in 1947), and been a pilot and officer during the war, so I was mature for my age and nothing fazed me. I may not have fit in with the older, veteran players, but I knew that I belonged in the big leagues. Still, it wasn't a good situation for a young man who wanted to become a good baseball player and play on a winning team.

One can only imagine how unruly ballplayers earlier in the century had been, because hotels and restaurants wanted nothing to do with them. But after the war, respectable establishments considered ballplayers, even the Pirates, so civilized that they were clamoring for our business. Perhaps it was because the postwar players didn't emulate those from the Roaring Twenties who fired guns at the billboards outside their hotel windows, or the Cardinals' "Gas House Gang" members of the thirties who would drop water balloons onto pedestrians walking below. However, they did keep alive a time-honored tradition by scouting women with binoculars from those windows. Also they requested the same hotel rooms each time they returned to a town because they had drilled peepholes through the walls and doors leading to the adjoining rooms.

Womanizing was one of the vices of choice on our team. The single guys were always out at night. I rarely saw my roommate, outfielder Jim Russell, away from the ballpark—though I often kept company with his bags. You didn't have to be a star to get women; being a ballplayer was enough. Nick Strincevich, for example, was a so-so pitcher who went up and down from the majors to the minors, yet he was out with beautiful women almost every night. Admittedly, Nick was a great-looking guy, but Jack Hallett, another pitcher who got a lot of pretty dates, was anything but handsome—and that is an understatement.

Branch Rickey, who operated the Dodgers before coming to the Pirates, and other general managers preferred married players because they were less likely to stray from the straight and narrow. But some married players ran around on the road, too. Kirby Higbe was a broad-shouldered Southerner we got from the Dodgers in 1947. He wasn't what we needed. He was a good pitcher for us but a wild man who became the most disruptive player on the team, the leader of the group that liked to party nonstop. His favorite expression was, "I'm sicker than a mule." According to a funny story that made the rounds, once Higbe returned from a road trip and his wife, Anne, went through his clothes before sending them out to the cleaners. She found a note in a suit that read:

Dear Kirby,
I never had such a wonderful time in my life!
I look forward to seeing you again!

It was signed "*with love*" by Trixie, Lola, Cha-Cha, whomever. Of course, Anne had a fit and confronted her husband with the evidence. He looked at her with a straight face and said, "It must be some other Kirby."

With good reason, managers didn't trust their players to be in before curfew, so some would make frequent calls to players' rooms. Back when Pirates right-hander Jim Bagby Jr. pitched for the Indians—he and his roommate Al Smith were the ones who halted DiMaggio's hitting streak in 1941— he picked up the ringing phone one night at 2:00 A.M. Bagby, who had a harelip and spoke with a lisp, said, "H'llo, who ith thith?" His manager identified himself and asked, "Are both you guys in the room?" "Yeth, I'm in 'ere," said Bagby, stalling. "What about Smith?" "Juth a minuth, I'll geth 'im." A few seconds later the manager heard, "Thith ith Smittth. I'm 'ere, skippp." (When Bagby would call his wife from the road, his greeting to her was always, "Geth who thith ith?")

There weren't groupies in those days, but there were girls who hung out at some of the bars that the players frequented when they arrived in town. For instance, in Cincinnati there was a big hangout called The Barn. Once authorities shut down the illegal gambling on the Kentucky side of the river, it was one of the few places around that had any action. Players went there specifically because of the women. It already had a notorious reputation, but it wasn't until years later that they made it off-limits to ballplayers so they'd stop breaking curfew. There weren't prostitutes in the bars that players went to, but they were in other places the players knew about— Chicago was loaded with that sort of thing.

We were shocked when Phillies first baseman Eddie Waitkus, a former Cub, got shot by a woman in Chicago. Eddie didn't even know her, but he got a message that she was coming to his room. Ruth Ann Steinhagen wasn't a groupie or a prostitute, just a deranged fan who had been obsessed with him from afar—she even learned Lithuanian because that was his heritage. She apparently hoped to be linked to him forever by killing him, but luckily, he survived and returned to baseball after a year's recuperation. Most teams that visited Chicago stayed at the Stevens Hotel, but Waitkus and the Phillies were at the Edgewater Beach, which was a beautiful hotel with much larger rooms. Red Smith, the legendary sportswriter of the *New York Herald Tribune* and later of the *Times*, wrote that if the Phillies had been staying at the Stevens, it never would have happened. First of all, if Steinhagen left a message for Waitkus, he never would have gotten it. Second, she couldn't have gotten on one of the elevators with a rifle because they were always too crowded. And third, the rooms were so small she couldn't have gotten the rifle inside.

After Waitkus was nearly killed, you couldn't help worrying that such a thing could happen to you, but I doubt if it changed the behavior of any ballplayers. It didn't slow anyone down. It was like when we went into the service and were shown pictures of what could happen if you got a venereal disease from a stranger—the gorgeous women in those pictures made young guys think it was worth it.

Perhaps the players shrugged off the Waitkus incident because they thought Chicago was a dangerous town where such things happened. In fact, years earlier a woman with a gun had come looking for a player in his Chicago hotel room. While the player actually slipped out the window and hid on the ledge, his roommate told the woman he wasn't there. The woman said, "You'll do!" and shot him below the belt. Fortunately, that player also escaped death and returned to baseball.

I would be robbed twice in Chicago hotels. The first time was in 1955, when I was in my final year with the Indians. While we were playing the White Sox at Comiskey Park, a hotel employee entered the room I was sharing with Al Rosen and had the audacity to try on our clothes until he got the right fit. He practiced writing my name on a checkbook that I had left in the room and then strolled into the lobby and tried to pass off a $100 check using my forged signature—at which time he was apprehended. The second time came after I had retired, when I was staying with Hank Greenberg at the Executive House. Someone sneaked into our suite when we were both asleep in our rooms. The next morning we found our wallets on the floor and our money gone. We were grateful we didn't wake up and get shot.

Drinking, which was often a major component of womanizing, was another popular recreation of the post-WWII ballplayer. There was a lot of social drinking on the Pirates, but I can't say there was too much across the board. It depended on the individual. For instance, I would have an occasional beer—in Pittsburgh bars, you'd order a boilermaker, which is a straight shot of whiskey and a bottle of beer—but not much else. At the other extreme were the heavy drinkers who knocked them down hard and fast. They spent entire days in bars and, if they couldn't find a date, entire nights. Casey Stengel had an interesting take on the situation: "Being with a woman all night never hurt no professional ballplayer—it's staying up all night *looking* for a woman that does him in." During games, some guys would hurry down the runways under the stands to sneak a few swigs from their flasks. Nobody openly drank between games of Sunday doubleheaders, but you can bet it was done surreptitiously.

After games, players drank beer in the clubhouse, tipped the clubhouse boy to run out for sandwiches—there were no spreads in those days—and talked baseball. It was a ritual and a good way to wind down and bond with your teammates. But then Rickey and some other GMs tried to ban beer in clubhouses. That made no sense because players just got dressed and went out to some hole-in-the-wall saloon and drank even more.

Players on other teams would imbibe at the ballpark, too. For instance, Ellis Kinder, who was an outstanding relief pitcher for the Red Sox and other teams, occasionally knocked down a few drinks in the bullpen. Once, he was called into the game, threw his arms over his head while making his first warm-up pitch, and promptly fell over backward off the mound. That kind of thing wasn't so unusual in those heavy-drinking days.

Once, some of the Pirates were invited to a national radio broadcast of a tea dance at our hotel in St. Louis. We were sipping tea, but our backup catcher, Dixie Howell, got there late and assumed it was bourbon and Coke. So he went to the bar and ordered a few of those and showed up drunk as a skunk at the ballpark that night. We tried to hide him from our manager, Billy Herman, before the game, which wasn't so easy because he was running around in the outfield, tackling the other players, and having a ball. Late in the game, Higbe pitched in relief and, as was the custom, Dixie was brought in to catch him because he was our only receiver who could handle Higbe's knuckler. But that night he couldn't catch anything. *Every* pitch went to the backstop. Higbe wasn't too happy with Dixie. He hadn't been to the tea dance and didn't know what had happened to his catcher.

Of course, drinking sometimes led to fighting. Players would go to bars and get loaded and, if there weren't any strangers around who annoyed them, start punching each other. Then they'd make up and have another round. The toughest ballplayer I ever saw was another catcher on our team—Clyde McCullough. On hot days he'd catch without a chest protector, and it wouldn't surprise me to learn that he caught a few games without a mask during his career. He wasn't a big guy, but he had a bad temper, and if you got under his skin, you were in trouble because he could go fast and had fists like nine-pound hammers. He'd fight anybody, including his teammates. If there was going to be a brawl, I wanted him on *my* side, so I was particularly generous where he was concerned. I gave him my clothes, including the actual shirt off my back. Really. When he admired something I was wearing, I gave it to him. It never fit him, but he wore it anyway. (The only guy who compared to McCullough was Eddie Mathews, the Hall of Fame third baseman who began playing for the Braves in the early fifties. He was a muscular ex-marine who drank and could fight. He and his imposing roommate, pitcher Bob Buhl, loved to leave anybody who harassed them lying outside bars and in elevators. Mathews saved the life of his smaller teammate, shortstop Johnny Logan, a hundred times. Logan would challenge some big lug to a bar fight, and Mathews would end up clocking the guy.)

Frankie Frisch, our manager in 1946, and Billy Herman, our manager in 1947, were very lax about disciplining players. Having played in the rough-and-tumble twenties and early thirties, they didn't really care about the womanizing, drinking, or fighting, so they didn't bother to stop any of it. Herman even participated when some of the players indulged in a fourth vice—gambling. He was a regular in the team's "illegal" ante-up card games. The Pirates always had heated games going in the clubhouse and on trains, usually in the vestibules of the sleeping cars. Hearts was the most popular game, but only when someone from the front office was looking. At other times, it was poker with pretty high stakes. As a result, some guys lost most of their paychecks, which caused resentment among the players and trouble back home when they walked in without the money needed to support their families. I wasn't asked to join in, but I knew better anyway. In the minor leagues, I was invited to play Red Dog, a three-card game in which you can lose money in the blink of an eye. From that experience, I learned never to play a game I didn't know how to play, especially with somebody who really can shuffle the deck. I never got trapped again.

Herman was only one of many managers who played cards with the players. Baseball's most storied skipper, Leo Durocher, was a notorious cardsharp who at times ran a minicasino in his hotel room. He let players into his games and thought nothing of relieving them of their monthly paychecks. He was like a spider luring prey into his web of iniquity. When he managed the Dodgers, one repeated victim was Kirby Higbe, who, Durocher joked, "couldn't beat my aunt in Duluth." Rickey finally had to order Durocher to not let Higbe into any more games.

Other players were easy prey for Durocher, or so he thought. In the early fifties, the Indians and Giants were barnstorming back from Arizona at the end of spring training. Each day, Luke Easter, the Indians' slugging first baseman, played gin rummy against Durocher, who since 1948 had been the Giants' manager. They'd play till midnight, sleep a few hours, go to the ballpark, and then get back on the train and play more cards. Herman Franks, who spent years in the Giants organization in many capacities, always stood behind Easter, who fell deeper into debt at each stop. This happened for about 10 days. When the trip was over, Easter owed Durocher $10,000! Easter told Leo he would pay him when he got his paycheck. After about four months of waiting for the check in the mail, Durocher called up Hank Greenberg, the Indians' GM, and said, "Easter owes me $10,000. Will you help me get my money?" Hank went to Easter and said, "Do you know that Durocher is one of the great cardsharps of our time?"

Easter said, "Yeah, I know that."

"But do you know that he isn't above getting some aid playing cards?"

"Yeah, I knew Herman Franks was standing behind me signaling him."

"And you owe him $10,000?"

"Yes."

"Why the hell did you play him if you had no way to win?"

"Because I didn't intend to pay."

When Durocher had been the Dodgers' manager, the commissioner, Happy Chandler, suspended him for the 1947 season, purportedly for associating with gamblers—whom he might have met through his association with actor George Raft—and possibly betting on games (as well as for marrying actress Laraine Day in Mexico before her California divorce had gone through). After that there was more pressure put on players to disassociate themselves from gamblers who might try to coax them into betting on games or influencing games for money. We were repeatedly reminded of the "Black Sox" scandal, when eight White Sox players took money to throw the 1919 World Series, and were told to be careful about going to the wrong bars or restaurants because there might be gambling going on. It also was frowned upon for players or managers to go to the racetrack, although they did it anyway. I never saw shady-looking characters whom I presumed were gamblers hanging around players, but I did spot spectators seated in the stands behind third base at Forbes Field who were openly betting during games. It was my impression that there were professional gamblers handling the bets and that it was tolerated by the Pirates organization. At the time numbers games were very big in Pittsburgh, so gambling was quite common in the city—in fact, the owner of the Pittsburgh Crawfords in the Negro League was a numbers czar.

All the things that you could do as a single guy were available to ballplayers. Some of the Pirates certainly took full advantage of it. My own behavior was by no means exemplary, but I didn't want to accompany my teammates on their wild nightly escapades. Nobody resented me for staying behind. I was just a young kid, and they had their own group.

During my rookie season, Al Lopez, a veteran catcher on the Pirates, kept me from falling in with players who thought more about what happened after games than during them. He made sure I went out with him, particularly in New York. He'd say, "I know where to go to eat," and took me to respectable clubs. He was my father figure that year, so I was concerned when he was traded to Cleveland for Gene Woodling after the season. (We would reunite in 1955, when I played my final season with the Indians and he was my manager.)

What saved me in 1947 was Hank Greenberg finishing his career with the Pirates. He became the single biggest influence of my adult life.

Hank had led the American League in homers and RBIs for the Tigers in 1946, but Detroit decided to waive him out of the league rather than continue to pay his high salary. Seeing the rare chance to acquire a superstar, Pittsburgh purchased his contract in January 1947 for $75,000. The trouble was that Hank had a broken elbow that wasn't healing quickly, and he wanted to retire and go into business. (When he did retire, he instead went to work for Bill Veeck and the Cleveland Indians.) They tried to convince him to play one more year by making him the National League's first $100,000 player. As an added inducement, John Galbreath, who was the minority owner of the team and the owner of Darby Dan Farm, promised him a yearling. Galbreath knew that would seal the deal because Hank's new bride, Caral Gimbel of the Gimbel's Department Store family, was an equestrian of renown and because the horse's value in addition to his six-figure salary would let Hank surpass both Ted Williams and Joe DiMaggio as baseball's highest-paid player. So Greenberg signed and Galbreath never gave him a horse!

When Greenberg arrived at the Pirates' facility in Florida on the first day of spring training, it was hard to believe that after all those years of admiring him from afar I was seeing him in the flesh. Because we had both won home-run titles in 1946, we were asked to pose together for a few pictures, but I don't think we said anything to each other. However, when the workout was over and I was following all the other players off the field, I heard him yell to me from the cage, "Hey, kid, do you want to stay and take some extra batting practice?" Of course I was flabbergasted and eagerly said yes. From that day forward, while everyone else showered, dressed, and went out to paint the town red with Kirby Higbe's hell-raisers, I was happy to stay behind and work on baseball. Under Greenberg's watchful and very critical gaze, I became a good, smart power hitter and increased my homer total from 23 to 51. And that was the beginning of a beautiful friendship. I say "friendship," but in truth Hank Greenberg became the brother I never had.

In Pittsburgh, I lived in Webster Hall, but on the road Hank and I often roomed together. So we'd go out for lunches and dinners, and I absorbed everything he had to say. Hank was interested in a wide range of topics, so while baseball was our priority, we talked about almost everything under the sun. The only subjects that he didn't want to get into were his time as a soldier in India and China and how as a Jew he coped with prejudice, particularly after he left New York City and pursued a baseball career.

Hank was different from any ballplayer I ever knew. He was well educated and cultured and spent a lot of time reading (particularly anything that might help him in business) and going to museums. Like debonair characters I saw in the movies, he wore great clothes, dined at the top restaurants, enjoyed steam baths, and knew the proper way to order wine and champagne (which I tasted for the first time). He wanted to be top dog and tried to learn everything he could from people who could help him be successful. I went with him to art museums, to see big bands, and to dinner at such swank places as the "21" Club and Copacabana. He was well aware of his public image and his special responsibility of being the greatest Jewish player ever, and he was very careful about what he did and where he did it. He lived with dignity and class and taught me to do the same.

Despite his gentlemanly bearing, Greenberg was a hard-nosed guy who never started a fight but finished quite a few, even against some of his own teammates. Once Jim Bagby thought Hank should have gotten to a ball that went for a base hit past first base, and they got into a heated argument on the field. Bagby was taken out of the game and went to the clubhouse. Hank made the last out and charged down the right-field line and into the clubhouse by the fence. And he and Bagby went at it. Hank was still in his spikes and couldn't find his footing on the slippery floor, but he got in a few licks. Bagby was fortunate because Hank was tough.

Hank was living proof that the players who were the most dedicated to baseball were also its biggest stars. The game's reigning superstars, Greenberg, Stan Musial, Ted Williams, Joe DiMaggio, and Bob Feller—as well as Pee Wee Reese, Allie Reynolds, Jackie Robinson, Robin Roberts, Yogi Berra, Gil Hodges, and a few others—were classier than the average players and wanted to achieve more. They recognized that baseball afforded them the opportunity not only to have fame but also to make considerably more money than they could in other lines of work. They made a good living doing something they could do well, and I wanted to follow their examples.

Musial, who was the supreme hitter in the National League, was a completely down-to-earth guy. He was always in a good mood, which might have been because he arrived at spring training each year knowing he'd hit .340. Everyone loved him. Williams had trouble with reporters, particularly in Boston, and with some fans, but other players liked him because he'd talk hitting with them no matter their skill levels. Rather than guard his knowledge, he wanted to share it and help every batter get better against their mutual enemies—pitchers. I got to know Ted only slightly during my playing days, but we became quite friendly later on. I liked him very much and admired his genuine enthusiasm for baseball, particularly hitting. Sometime in the nineties, I went to visit him at his museum in Florida and was very honored that he had included me on his list of the 20 top hitters in baseball history. Apparently he liked long-ball hitters because neither his friend Tony Gwynn nor Pete Rose were on it. If Ted had put himself on the list, I might have been crossed off, too.

DiMaggio was adored by reporters, fans, and teammates for the exceptional, dignified way he played ball, but he was aloof off the field. Joe didn't have many friends, but he and Toots Shor were extremely close. Joe ate 80 percent of his meals at Shor's restaurant and had a table of his own in the back. I'm sure Toots picked up the tab each time because Joe was notorious for never doing it. Once my career took off and I was making more money, I'd often go to the restaurant when the Pirates were in New York and find Joe there, eating. He'd say hello but never ask me to join him. Only years later, when Joe and I were no longer players, did I get to know and befriend him. Once I was with him and Mickey McDermott in Phoenix. DiMaggio liked offbeat people, and he liked Mickey because Mickey was insane. Joe loved that Mickey enjoyed complaining about Joe McCarthy, who had managed Joe in New York and Mickey in Boston. Mickey talked about McCarthy's idiosyncrasies. For instance, he remembered how McCarthy would say he hated "pipe-smoking ballplayers because pipes make them *too content*," but he loved "cigar-smoking players because they are aggressive." Few people ever saw DiMaggio crack a smile, but I witnessed him smiling and laughing among friends.

But DiMaggio gave up his safe haven at Toots Shor's. A few years after he retired, he was briefly married to Marilyn Monroe, and one night Shor's wife, Baby—he was big, she was tiny—had a few cocktails and used a derogatory name for Marilyn. And from that day on, Joe refused to come back to Shor's restaurant and never spoke to him again. Many times, I'd be there for dinner or a nightcap after a show, and I'd see Toots trying to call Joe in San Francisco. Joe always hung up on him. Obviously he could carry a grudge and keep his distance. I never could figure him out. He was a strange man whose congenial side was subverted by his simultaneous needs for privacy and adoration that almost bordered on paranoia. If he trusted you and you let him down, he exiled you from his world.

Although Bob Feller was in the American League, I got to know him because I had the opportunity to play ball with him one November. In those days, salaries were so low that players had no choice but to find off-season jobs. For instance, in the minors I worked as a ticket taker at Santa Anita, where I'd make good money and promptly lose it betting on horses. (Once Betty Grable was trying to rush to the first race through the wrong gate, my gate, and I turned her away rather than break the rules. How dumb can one guy be? She was considered one of the most gracious actresses in Hollywood—but she wasn't gracious to me.) After my first two years in the majors, I spent a month on barnstorming major league All-Star teams, the second of which was Feller's.

The first year, I was with a low-rent operation. We split a cut of the gate and drove our own cars to towns like Pocatello, Idaho, to play night ball in cold weather in minor league parks where the lighting was poor and the fields were in terrible shape. Despite the conditions, it was still a great experience and I made good money. However, I was glad that after the 1947 season, Feller offered me a contract to play on his All-Star team. Feller ran a much higher-scale enterprise, where players were paid on a sliding scale and we usually flew to our next destination.

Feller turned out to be an interesting study. There was no question in his mind that he was the greatest pitcher who ever lived. And he might have been right. He had the best stuff of any pitcher I ever saw and surely would have had 300 victories if he hadn't lost so much time in the service. Characteristically, Feller claimed he had no regrets about being one of the first ballplayers to enlist because the only victory he really cared about was winning the war. In contrast to almost all major leaguers of the time, Bob was all business (which is why he would be such a strong advocate for a pension in 1947). He was a straightforward, tough-minded, financially astute individual. He owned his All-Star team, which competed against African-American and Mexican All-Star teams, and piloted his own plane to take him to games. He was a star in every sense of the word. People talk the most about DiMaggio and Williams from that era, yet Feller was more dominant in my mind. He was the only guy who got a piece of the admissions from his team. When he pitched, the Indians got a full house everywhere he went, so he made a lot of money.

When I came into the big leagues, I was happy to be there and more or less followed the crowd. I certainly didn't expect fans to look up to me and come to the park and tell me I was their favorite player or idol. And I never expected to be looked up to by my teammates. I never gave it any thought until Hank Greenberg taught me that I should step forward and accept responsibilities once I became well known, as Musial, Williams, DiMaggio, Feller, and Hank himself did. That's what I did after he retired. What made it easier is that Billy Meyer became the Pirates' manager in 1948 and got rid of all those disruptive players who were there just for a good time. Suddenly everyone had a good attitude and it was much more enjoyable to be on the team. (Over the next few years, baseball in general became calmer, as a lot of the wilder players who had come back from the service got married, started families, and settled down.)

I was never a take-charge guy, but I tried to be a leader by example. As Hank showed me, a ballplayer can be a role model even for other ballplayers. I was available to help anyone who asked me and work with them for as long as it took. I always had close friends on the ballclub, and there was no open hostility toward me once I became the team's lone All-Star beginning in 1948. I think most of the guys liked me because with my success I elevated their positions and salaries. Also, it made a big difference that I eventually became the team's player representative and fought for their rights.

I remembered that when I was at my first training camp, I couldn't even take batting practice unless a veteran player let me take his spot—which was common on other teams as well—so I made sure young players got a fair shake. On occasion I'd go out with a few younger guys, perhaps to a place they couldn't afford. After all, from 1948 on, I was the only high-salaried player on the Pirates, and most of them were getting close to the minimum of $5,000 a year. (In 1952, the four members of Branch Rickey's "kiddie infield" made a total of $20,000.) I would let them take pride in buying me a drink, and I would pick up the big tab for the dinner. For the most part, ballplayers ate steak seven days a week. I got in the habit of eating steak when I was a kid, and my mother, who was a dietary nurse, made me steak and eggs every morning despite our tight budget because that was considered healthy then. I can't remember any players ever going out for French cuisine or more exotic fare, but some of us would order seafood at Locke-Ober in Boston and Bookbinders in Philadelphia. (It was a thrill for me in 1946 when I dined at Bookbinders with my manager Frankie Frisch and had lobster for the first time.)

When we went to New York to play the Dodgers or Giants, I had a regular routine. A few of us would always go to Toots Shor's to have our steaks and hang out. Pitcher Rip Sewell, a smart, literate, well-dressed graduate of the University of Alabama who told risqué jokes, and I always went to Bertolotti's, a supper club in the Village that had great food. It was a big hangout, and whenever the Cardinals were in town, too, we'd often run into Stan Musial and Red Schoendienst there. In 1951, I would propose to tennis champion Nancy Chaffee there. (Somehow Walter Winchell found out about it beforehand, perhaps from the Pittsburgh jeweler, and mentioned it on the radio, so she was expecting it and still showed up.)

While in town, I always went downtown to see Eddie Condon play guitar down at Condon's on West Third Street in the Village, and uptown to see George Shearing play the piano at Amber's. I'd also go to a restaurant that had opera singers at the tables, and I often ran into Feller there, when the Indians were in New York to play the Yankees. After my time with Hank, I'd still go to the "in" places in the city, like the Stork Club, El Morocco, Copacabana, and the Latin Quarter. We had so much fun that it's a wonder we ever won a ballgame in New York. Actually, we didn't win many.

In other road cities as well, four or five of us would go out to a good place for dinner or to a nightclub. We weren't cliquish, so anyone could come along, even the reporters who rode the rails with us and were part of our social lives. (I got along with the reporters, but some players thought they were linked to the owners and mistrusted them.) Because a game usually was scheduled for the following afternoon, there would be a midnight curfew. Very few adhered to it. When you were caught you'd get fined. Anytime managers wanted to catch you, they could do it easily. Some cleverly had the elevator boys ask players who came in after curfew to autograph a ball. Then they would give that ball to the manager as evidence of who came late.

Pittsburgh had a couple of good nightclubs. There was Lenny Littman's, which is where I first saw Sammy Davis Jr. performing as the star of an act with his father and uncle. (He was only 10, but he was such a good dancer and mimic that some people were convinced he was a midget.) And there was the Carrousel, which was run by a fellow named Jackie Heller. Players would hang out with each other, not with girls, in these places, though they might break off and have a date once in a while. I didn't go out much because the fans wouldn't leave me alone.

One of the teammates I palled around with after Greenberg's departure was George Metkovich, who had a great sense of humor. He also was from California and we became very close. We called him "Catfish," "the Cat," "Poor George," and a number of other names. One time he was struck out by Max Surkont of the Braves. I asked him, "What did he throw you?" George said, "He threw me the radio ball." "The radio ball?" "Yeah," he said, "you can hear it, but you can't see it." Once Catfish was lazing by a swimming pool, when a woman who was walking by expressed horror at his ugly feet. He said, "Lady, if you'd fouled as many pitches off your feet as I have, yours would look like these, too."

In 1952, I got an extortion note. I was told I'd be killed during a game if I didn't leave $4,400 at a secret location. An FBI agent dressed up as me and made the drop, but no one showed up. So the potential killer was still at large. We played the game during which I was supposed to get shot. It was on or around the Fourth of July, and people kept setting off firecrackers that made everybody jump. Nobody would sit next to me on the bench. The game ended and, fortunately, nothing had happened. As I came off the field with George, who had played next to me in center field, he said, "Boy, I'm glad that game is over."

I said, "Gee, George, it was nice of you to worry about me."

He said, "I wasn't worried about you. I was worried about me."

"Why you?"

"What number do you wear, Ralph?"

I answered, "4."

"What number do I wear?"

"You wear 44, George."

"What if that guy had double vision?"

The FBI finally arrested the opposing team's batboy, who needed the money to pay off his bookie.

Once I became a high-salaried player, I wanted to be a good role model for kids. But I don't know if I was. Like most players, I did drink beer, but I turned down doing beer ads because I didn't think it was a good idea for kids to see me promoting it. I didn't smoke cigarettes, but in the early fifties, my wife Nancy and I did an ad for Chesterfields for a thousand bucks. I tried chewing tobacco as a boy and was never so sick in my life and never chewed again; I'd even stay away from players who did, which was the great majority because smokeless tobacco kind of went with the uniform in those days. Still, I agreed to endorse Red Man tobacco. I wouldn't do it now, but at the time no one thought about cancer.

We had one pitcher in the late forties, John "Tobacco Chewin'" Lanning, whose nickname was well earned because he not only chewed while pitching but also slept with a wad of tobacco in his mouth. When he'd stir in the night, he'd spit out the juice on newspapers he laid out next to the bed. Players chewed going back to the days of Honus Wagner, but the best chewer of my era was our second baseman Danny Murtaugh, the future Pirates manager. He could hit your shoes with tobacco juice from 30 feet—and he did. Danny was a funny guy who was an expert with double-talk.

Every team had pranksters, guys who would give you a hotfoot, put shaving cream on your cap, or nail a teammate's shoes to the locker room floor. The Pirates had their share, but when I think of pranksters I think of the Chicago Cubs, to whom George Metkovich and I were traded during the 1953 season. That team had a lot of tough players like Hank Sauer and Walker Cooper, but they all had a good sense of humor. Today's fans consider it a strange practice, but until the early fifties, all the fielders left their gloves on the grass when they went up to bat. However, at Wrigley Field I'd throw my glove into our bullpen. When I returned to left field, the guys in there would throw it back. If Cooper was in there, he'd usually fill my glove with peanut shells and I'd spend the next half inning cleaning shells out of the fingers. I considered myself well off because some players found worms in their gloves.

The veterans would pull a much more devious prank on rookies. In the park on the way to the ballpark was a statue of Sherman on a horse that was rearing back. For years, the veterans would tell the rookies that it was a tradition in Chicago to sneak into the park in the dead of night and paint the testicles of the horse red. They'd go out at 2:00 in the morning with a can of red paint, like spies on a secret mission. But that wasn't the end of it. The next day at the ballpark, several men disguised as policemen would storm into the clubhouse and "arrest" the terrified rookies! Meanwhile, people who were strolling leisurely through the park would happen upon a horse with red testicles. They'd complain to the nearest policeman, and the men in city hall would blow up. The city finally put an end to the Cubs' tradition because it cost too much to keep taking the red paint off the horse.

It couldn't be classified as a prank, but several times I pulled a fast one on Al Rosen and Bob Lemon when I played with them in Cleveland in 1955. They were also well-paid players, so we'd go out together to some of the fancier places. That was when they started to introduce credit cards, so I'd suggest that they give me cash for their share of the bill and I'd pay the entire sum on my card. They didn't take into consideration that I could then take the whole thing as a tax write-off. There were high taxes in that era, so such deductions could mount up. I did it for fun and eventually let on to them what I was doing so I could rub it in their faces. Rather than get mad at me, they said they learned to start signing checks when they went out with other guys who didn't know any better. So what would be common practice in baseball became part of my legacy.

My career ended after that year for the same reason many careers ended during that era: I had an injury at a time when there was no adequate medical treatment. My problem was my back. I had periodic pain from strained ligaments and a tender nerve near my spinal column. I would play and reinjure it, and then it was too painful to play as much. Fans today don't understand that players in the days of the reserve clause basically had no choice but to play through injuries. There was so much competition for jobs that if they asked out of the lineup for even one day—as Wally Pipp did when he had a headache, allowing Lou Gehrig to step in for 2,130 consecutive games—they could end up being permanently benched, exiled to the minors, or traded to a worse ballclub. In fact, I played one year with the Cubs with two excruciatingly painful pulled groin muscles without telling my manager because I knew he'd take me out of the lineup. But with my back pain, I just couldn't swing the bat. I went to several doctors, and they said there was only a 50-50 chance that I'd play again after surgery. If salaries were as high as they are today, I would have gone through with it. But as it was, I didn't like the odds and retired.

So I ceased being one of the players who was fortunate to be in the major leagues during that incredible postwar era, which, unfortunately, few of today's players know anything about.

⚾ ⚾ ⚾

I'm often asked which current players I would most want to have as my guests on *Kiner's Korner*, my long-running New York Mets postgame interview show. I immediately reply that I'd more than welcome return visits from National Leaguers like Todd Helton and Chipper Jones, and, if I could talk to American Leaguers during interleague play, I'd book guys like Alex Rodriguez and Derek Jeter in a heartbeat. I would choose players who have a solid perspective on baseball history for the simple reason that the young men who know who I am usually seem excited to come on the show. Often guys who don't know my background as a player consider it a job to be a guest, so I'd much rather not have them on. Don't get me wrong. I don't resent young players who don't know me or other players from my era, or baseball history in general, because the same percentage of players in my time knew next to nothing about baseball's past. However, I do strongly believe that today's players would benefit greatly from knowing how the game once was, particularly in regard to the camaraderie among teammates—something that is sadly lacking in today's game.

Players now have things so much better than we did. They have powerful agents to do their contract negotiations, they sign huge endorsement deals, they have the union to protect them, and they are offered enormous contracts because there is no longer a reserve clause. Moreover, they travel by plane, they check into individual suites in fancy hotels, and they can afford to take their families with them on the road. But these enormous upgrades have come at a heavy price: they don't experience what I think should be, ultimately, the most rewarding experience in baseball—being part of a close-knit team. They used to joke about how the relatively well-paid players on the Boston Red Sox of the seventies would climb into 25 different taxis after a game was over. That seems to be the way it is on all teams now.

On quick flights, you seldom see groups gathered together. More likely, the players are sitting alone and wearing headphones. You wonder where they go after they land, because they all go in different directions. You seldom see several ballplayers—or even two players—running around together. There are no card games or long train rides or, due to a preponderance of night baseball, dinners where a group of players sits around and talks baseball. So, except when unmarried players go to trendy clubs, where the loud music thwarts conversation, and the occasional golf game, it's no longer social. There is much more individuality off the field, and that, I suggest, is reflected by too much selfish play on it. Gone is the idea that you hate the enemy—the other teams in the league—and gone is the 25 musketeers' "all-for-one-and-one-for-all" mentality. In fact, at the ballpark, prior to games, there is a lot of fraternization on the field between players of different teams. We used to be fined if we talked on the field to our opponents, and the league sent one of the umpires to the park early to make sure we didn't do it. The only ones who would talk were the Hispanic players, who would speak Spanish to each other.

My Mets broadcast partner Tom Seaver thinks fraternization between players makes them less competitive—instead of wanting to beat the other team, they just want to exhibit their own skills. There definitely shouldn't be fraternization in the clubhouse. When Boston's Pedro Martinez passed through the Toronto clubhouse and stopped to say hello to his Blue Jays friends, the manager told him to leave. He pointed to his players and said, "Friends? You hit him and you hit him and you hit him . . ."

I don't agree with the jealous old-timers who accuse today's millionaire players of being pampered because they have the money to buy the luxuries in life, and job security, and have no need to work during the off-season. These young men have worked too hard and long developing and refining their talents to be dismissed so easily. And they aren't soft just because they munch on sunflower seeds in the dugout rather than tobacco.

The American-born players today are hungry to succeed, although they have had different histories from those players of my era who hoped baseball was their means to escape the coal mines and cornfields, or poor mill towns and fishing villages. Their histories are different from those of any players, for that matter, from any time before the advent of free agency. In the old days, few players had much education and only a minuscule number had college experiences; most were rough around the edges. Now, almost all American-born players have at least a high school diploma, and a large number have gone to college. They have played organized ball since they were young. The only players with similar backgrounds to those in the majors after World War II have been the ones coming out of the Dominican Republic and other countries in Latin America (as well as a few who have come from America's inner cities). Like many of the players who emerged from the Depression, these players had nothing as kids—not even real gloves in many instances—and found their only outlet was to play sandlot baseball.

Big money wasn't there when I played. It came out of free agency, not an ability to hit or pitch any better. Even the most famous stars of my day couldn't make a whole lot of money because salaries were kept in check, taxes were so high, and there were no meaningful endorsement opportunities—unlike with some current players who look like walking billboards. Today, players often can make more than their salaries by being in television commercials for automobiles, cereals, shoes, and deodorants. There are an infinite number of products: memorably, years after Kansas City Royals superstar George Brett swore Preparation H did wonders for people with hemorrhoids, the Texas Rangers' Rafael Palmeiro told men to ask their doctors if Viagra was right for them, too. For risking embarrassment, I'm sure both players got big sums of money. That's one of the biggest changes in the game. When I signed with Wheaties and was featured on the box, I got $500 and a case of Wheaties for every home run I hit. (What the hell do you do with 51 cases of Wheaties? I had to keep them in my garage until I gave them away in a food drive.) Today, I'd get millions. And they were all pleasant when drawing up contracts for bats, gloves, and trading cards, but they gave us almost nothing. Today, because of the union, players rake in the dough.

Also, players can make large amounts of money today at card shows by selling their autographs and signed memorabilia. In my day, the only player who knew there was value in memorabilia was Dutch Leonard, the great knuckleball pitcher. Yosh Kawano, the Cubs' clubhouse attendant, said Dutch took more baseballs from the park than anyone he ever saw because he intended to use them as barter. After Don Larsen threw his perfect game in the 1956 World Series, he didn't even think of taking home a few balls as souvenirs. Only one guy, first-base umpire Hank Soar, was savvy enough to do it.

It would be hypocritical of me to criticize current players for signing memorabilia for money, because many of us former players take appearance fees to sign at card shows and also have our own websites with signed bats, balls, and photos for sale. It's a bit uncomfortable, but we do it as a source of income and also to counter those promoters and dealers who sell our merchandise and our signatures (some forged) at exorbitant prices and keep all the profits. I think it's fine that players sell their autographs at shows and on websites, but I find it objectionable when they refuse to sign autographs for free when approached by fans at ballparks or some other public places (unless it's a real imposition). As Rogers Hornsby said, any player who doesn't sign autographs "ain't American." When I was a kid, the Cubs and White Sox played an exhibition game at Brookside Park, and before the game I ran out on the field and asked Dizzy Dean for an autograph. And he brushed me off! I shouldn't have been out there, but it still stung. So I told myself I'd try my best to never turn down anyone. And I still don't. There are some things you never forget, and what Dean did still bothers me 65 years later.

When I played, people wanted autographs to keep, not to sell or trade. They didn't make money off them. When I sign autographs for fans now, I often wonder if they will turn around and sell them. Joe DiMaggio was paranoid about that. Once at the Hall of Fame, my daughter K.C. was with me. She knew Joe, and Joe knew her, and we'd all had dinner together, so she wasn't at all shy about asking him to autograph a baseball for a charity auction. He wouldn't sign it. She thought he was kidding. After a bit of cajoling, he reluctantly signed the ball. But he asked her aggressively, "What did your dad do with all the balls I signed for him?" The truth was I never asked him for a ball in my life.

It often takes great patience to sign autographs for fans, but it's important for players to have solid images. Players should do good off the field as well as on. It's part of their job, but too many players have been negligent about it. Granted, athletes may be the least prepared of anyone to carry the burden of being "role models," but at the very least they should project themselves in a positive light. They should realize they make the money they do because the fans have been there. When you insult fans or do things that turn them away, you're jeopardizing your business and hurting the game of baseball.

A ballplayer is not an island. He can't just play baseball and ignore everything else. Players such as Barry Bonds, who are making millions, owe something back. It's not that hard to do. I can't understand why players would act bigger than the game and superior to the fans. The contract that players sign says they are obligated to perform their duties on and off the field. They are supposed to promote the game, and when they don't fulfill their part of the bargain, the owners should exercise their right to make them. Bonds might be the prime culprit. This extremely talented player has diminished his chance to be an ambassador for the game by his negative approach to the media and the public. To me, that takes away from his stature.

Bonds is an ex-Pirate, so he has always talked to me and been very cordial. However, Fox's Tim McCarver says Bonds has walked past him without saying hello for eight years and counting. Filip Bondy of the *New York Daily News* covered the major league All-Star team's tour of Japan after the 2002 season and wrote in his column that he wanted to ask Bonds one question the entire trip but was never allowed near him. Bonds spoke only to Japanese reporters. I think such behavior will hurt him in the end, unless he is content having a fan base of people who adore front-runners and don't care at all about character.

Another guy who had a terrible reputation with the media is Hall of Famer Eddie Murray, whom the baseball writers voted into the Hall of Fame in 2003. When Murray was traded from the Orioles to the Dodgers for the 1989 season, L.A.'s revered broadcaster Vin Scully introduced himself and said, "I'd like to do a short interview with you so the fans can learn something about you." Murray said, "No way, I'm taking batting practice. I'll talk to you sometime later." Scully, who to the fans *is* the Dodgers, got mad and never asked him again. When Murray joined the Mets three years later, then–Mets broadcaster Tim McCarver, who seems to have a lot of bad experiences with baseball's malcontents, went on the field and introduced himself and welcomed him to New York. Murray wouldn't talk to him. When Tim related that experience to me, I said, "Well, I'm not going to bother going up to him." Oddly, later in spring training, my wife DiAnn and I were at a sponsors' dinner with Murray and a couple of other players. She went over and said, "My husband Ralph broadcasts the Mets games; he admires you and would like to meet you." And he got up and came over and said hello. It turned out he was nice off the field and I could see why all his teammates through the years, including Cal Ripken Jr., respected him so much. I invited him to be the guest speaker at a Mets luncheon, and he made a great, humorous speech—perhaps he was in such good form because I got him $5,000.

Richie Allen was another guy who got mixed reviews from the media. I went up to him at the batting cage and told him I was doing a postgame interview show and would like to have him on. I didn't want to impose on him. He asked me how long it would take and then told me that he couldn't do it because by the time he got back to the locker room his teammates would have eaten up everything in the postgame spread. And I was thinking: here's the highest-paid player in baseball worrying about missing out on free cold cuts. Richie later did appear on *Kiner's Korner* with me and was a good guest. He was on another postgame show on the West Coast when during the commercial break he asked what he'd be getting for coming on. They told him Green Stamps. He just walked away and the show ended.

Some guys are genuinely nice but think they must play the "star" and show attitude. When I was covering the World Series for CBS radio in the seventies, I went up to Reggie Jackson in the dugout during a rain delay. I asked him if we could talk and was surprised when he said no. I reminded him that he was required to do it, but he turned me down. I walked away. Apparently he was more than willing to do it, but he wanted me to ask him a few more times. Surprised that I had left him sitting there, he called me up and said he would do the interview. Too late.

Jackson was known to talk endlessly to the media to get free publicity. Thomas Boswell of the *Washington Post* wrote a piece on Reggie saying he talked so much that by the time he finished you would disagree with him even if you had at first agreed. The next day he saw Jackson carrying around the sports page, and he got a little worried. Reggie stepped in front of Boswell with a menacing expression on his face and pointed to Boswell's article. Then he said, "You're right." Since Jackson has been in the Hall of Fame I've frequently talked to him. He's a character when he chooses to be onstage, but he's a nice guy when he's being himself.

Albert Belle, the one-time slugger for the Indians, rarely chose to be nice to the media or anyone else. I think he should have been suspended for an entire season for threatening a female reporter, Hannah Storm, when she was in the dugout with him. Nobody cares that he had great stats before he had a career-ending injury. Few people miss him because he was a detriment to the game.

It's now much more demanding to be in the limelight than it was in my day. The pressures are tremendous. For instance, when you arrive in New York, there are 50 guys waiting with tape recorders, each wanting their own stories. I admire players who handle that well because it is an ordeal. When the Mets' Dave Kingman was having trouble with the press when he came to New York in the seventies, he asked me how I handled it when I was a player. I said I couldn't wait to get to New York to talk to the top writers because they were syndicated all over the country. That way people would find out who we were, and our mothers and friends would read about us and know how we were doing. All that meant a great deal to us. I didn't have problems with overly aggressive writers when I played, although I was warned about Dick Young, who eventually became my friend and pushed me for the Hall of Fame. Writers never wanted quotes from me or anyone else. I can't even remember reporters coming into the clubhouse after a game. TV has changed that.

Growing up, I knew ballplayers only for what they did on the field because that was all that was written about them. I didn't care about the off-field stuff. Babe Ruth was my idol, and I had no idea he didn't just go directly home to bed after every game. The media of the forties, fifties, and sixties continued to admire successes on the field and ignore failures off it. The writers protected the players. But since the seventies—perhaps because of Jim Bouton's *Ball Four*, a book I dislike because he copped out on his teammates and revealed what went on behind the scenes in baseball—incidents in which players get in trouble have been well publicized. Since then too many athletes in all sports have made the headlines with indiscreet behavior. Now reporters look for scandals. They justify writing about private lives by saying they affect how the players perform. It's a different psychology.

I think players are less forthcoming to the media now, perhaps because it's very hard to say anything is "off the record" anymore. You can tell a reporter whom you trust something very personal, and he will keep to his promise to not write anything, but he'll give the information to another reporter who will put it in his column. That's done a lot, which is why some players decide it's just easier not to talk to anybody.

The wiser players have become more sensitive to their role as public figures and idols of youngsters throughout America. They have witnessed how disheartened fans become when untarnished stars like Steve Garvey and Kirby Puckett don't hold up to the scrutiny. In the seventies, if you picked a player whom you thought would go on to be a politician, it would have been Garvey, who had a stellar image before he was hit with some paternity suits. His reputation was so squeaky clean—he was dubbed "Mr. Clean"—that the Garvey joke was that he would go out behind the barn to chew gum.

Puckett, a former Twins superstar and a first-ballot Hall of Famer, was the most beloved man in the entire state of Minnesota, someone people named their kids and favorite pets after. But suddenly shocking secrets were revealed about his private life, his seemingly indestructible image was shattered, and his confounded admirers were thinking exactly what Anne Higbe's husband wanted her to believe when she found that incriminating note, that "it must be some other Kirby."

It's encouraging that only a handful of the current players have made the headlines for anything other than their play on the field. Notably, the New York Yankees, since they began their extraordinary run of success in 1996, have been relatively free of bad press. This is most commendable considering the temptation-filled city in which they play and a local media that can be as compassionate as a pack of attack dogs. Prior to the 2003 season, bored Yankees owner George Steinbrenner was so desperate to find any of his players guilty of an indiscretion that he publicly criticized Derek Jeter, perhaps the most dedicated of all current ballplayers, for having been out late at a birthday party. This was a long way from the Bronx Zoo days or when two Yankees hurlers, Fritz Peterson and Mike Kekich, swapped not only wives but entire families, including their dogs.

The great majority of the Yankee players have been first-class citizens, handling themselves in the best way possible off the field. No doubt much of that has to do with Joe Torre, their manager since 1996 and the man who sets the tone. When Torre broke into the majors in 1960, he was a very loose, undisciplined guy. Once when Torre and his manager were having some differences, Joe was asked about their relationship. "He's all right," said Joe. "All he wants is for you to kiss his ring. The trouble is, he carries it in his back pocket." Torre would change his attitude and his whole style of life and become one of the classiest guys in the game. And he did it on purpose. He realized that his way wasn't the way he wanted to go. Now he teaches the right way to his players.

Two players Torre and Steinbrenner tried to help, with at least temporary success, were Dwight Gooden and Darryl Strawberry, who both started out as phenoms for the New York Mets before their careers were derailed by drugs. What happened to them was really disappointing. When I first saw Gooden when he was 19 years old, I was as impressed as anyone. I had been Herb Score's teammate his incredible rookie year, when he was being touted as the next Bob Feller, and I said Gooden was going to be even better. Feller told me, "Give him a chance to screw up his life, then we'll see how good he is." That was prophetic. Gooden was a surefire Hall of Famer until he got trapped in a cocaine addiction. His friend Strawberry, who was an awesome hitter, did the same thing, to an even more frightening degree. Some people can't handle success, so you have to reserve your final judgment on them. The Mets had two of the greatest young players I ever saw, and they both ruined their careers.

Cocaine usage in baseball, which peaked in the early eighties, before the commissioner suspended several high-profile players, still exists, but I believe its use has gone down dramatically. On the other hand, steroids and other performance-enhancing drugs have become a significant part of many major leaguers' lives and is the primary blemish on the image of baseball as a whole. Ballplayers who happen to be idols should hold themselves to a high standard, so I don't understand why they don't mind that everyone who takes a look at their newly bulked physiques and improved power statistics gets very suspicious.

When they are open about taking something, they sound extremely foolish. For instance, reliever Mark Guthrie didn't deny he took the controversial ephedra, an herbal supplement that promotes weight loss but has also been linked to heat stroke, heart attacks, angina, irregular heartbeats, and the death of Orioles pitching prospect Steve Bechler, among other athletes. He said, "I don't care what the doctors are saying now. It increases your workout capabilities and definitely increases your ability to intake oxygen. It also helps me to get ready to play every night. That's why I keep taking it. The stuff is not going to kill you if you take it right. I never take more than two a day. If you overdo it, there are repercussions." Guthrie was being his own doctor, which is what too many naïve players are doing.

I believe that anything that enhances your physical ability should be banned. Also, if anything is detrimental to your health in the long run, it should be banned. As much as I admire the players union, it is definitely remiss in its handling of the drug issue. In 2003, 16 Chicago White Sox players intended to refuse to take the random tests that are stipulated in the collective bargaining agreement. It was their way to force baseball to test all players and bring it all out into the open. But the union talked them out of it. I fear it is letting players hurt themselves by being overprotective of them on health issues. The union is shortsighted because it is more worried about itself than the well-being of its players or the kids who will follow the leads of their idols. I don't see anything wrong with testing.

I should point out that people who believe that there were no drugs in baseball at all in my time are misinformed. There were. In the forties and fifties, we had Benzedrine and Dexedrine. A large percentage of players took them before a game or between games of a doubleheader because they could keep you awake and alert. I admit I took them. It's no excuse, but it wasn't until later that they were considered drugs. Now there is certainly no excuse for players to use them. However, when a team doctor queried major league officials and the union why amphetamines weren't included on their list of substances that should be subjected to drug testing, union counsel Gene Orza responded that the subject was a "dark corner" in the collective-bargaining agreement and should be avoided. Obviously, these substances let tired players play every night, so they fear they won't have the drugs at their disposal, even if they are addictive.

I've been told that steroids give you energy to lift weights for a longer period of time. Some people claim that doesn't really affect anything because hitting depends on hand-eye coordination. But when someone who already has good hand-eye coordination adds bulk, he will hit a lot more home runs. Then it becomes difficult to pitch to him. In earlier days they said *don't bulk up*—when Steve Garvey switched from football to baseball they even told him to de-bulk—but nowadays many players are like Charles Atlas, one-time skinny guys who now look like bodybuilders. I think it's a major issue because it can change a player's life, even end it. Banning those drugs is no different from putting padding on a concrete wall—it can save someone's life. Also, there should be a level playing field. Why should some players use drugs and get an advantage over someone who doesn't want to take a chance using them? The record book is important, so it bothers me to see people breaking records while under the influence of performance-enhancing drugs.

Several players and ex-players have claimed they are one of the 40 percent to 60 percent of all current players using steroids. Unfortunately, they are people whose credibility is suspect—like Ken Caminiti, Jose Canseco, and David Wells. They may be telling the truth, but they are easy to discredit. In fact, when challenged, they each said the percentages they originally stated were too high. But maybe not. Strangely, Major League Baseball was proud rather than embarrassed when testing in 2003 revealed 5 to 7 percent of players test positive for steroids (not including the designer steroid THC). But, like Pete Rose betting on "only" 450 games, what's too high? One game is too high. One player taking steriods is too high. We know it's a widespread problem, but no one is admitting to it. It's common knowledge some guys are using steroids. They aren't fooling a whole lot of people. Will it take somebody with a clean image to say what's going on? Unfortunately, as soon as a whistle-blowing player admits he took some drug himself, there goes his credibility. These things are hard to ferret out. However, there is a possibility that ongoing investigations by law enforcement agencies into doctors, nutrition "gurus," and companies who supply illegal drugs to athletes will implicate major stars, which would cause great embarrassment to major league baseball.

I think the players can stop it easily, but they think they aren't breaking rules and there's no penalty for first time offenders other than having their identities revealed. You don't even get suspended for taking steroids; you get warned. The owners know it's going on to a larger degree than testing has shown, but they're only looking at the bottom line. At some point everyone should start working for the good of the game on the field and the short- and long-term health of the players.

Putting the drug issue aside, I'm impressed that players of today put so much emphasis on conditioning, including during the off-season. Because games are played mostly at night, many spend several hours during the day in the weight room. If lifting hadn't been discouraged during my playing days, I definitely would have done a lot more in order to bulk up and hit more homers.

I also envy today's players because they get to spend their off-days and leisure time playing golf, which also wasn't condoned when I played. No one contends anymore that the golf swing will ruin your baseball swing. In fact, everyone agrees the swings are pretty much the same, and the golf swing can even be therapeutic to the baseball player. Many current players are avid golfers.

During my baseball career, I eventually played golf two or three times a season on off-days, including with my Cubs teammate Hank Sauer, who was a terrific golfer (and, in fact, died on a golf course in California a few years ago). But watching today's players, I wish I could have played more golf during the 10 seasons of my baseball career, and I am still peeved that management forbade it. Considering how the baseball establishment shunned golf for the first 60 years of the 20th century, I think it's ironic that now every year during induction week in Cooperstown, there is a Hall of Famers–only golf tournament. At long last, I get to play with some other players from my era.

Chapter 2
At the **Ballpark**

One of my prized possessions is a peculiar handwritten letter that Ty Cobb sent me in 1952, my last full season with the Pirates. It begins "Dear Kiner." Not "Dear Mr. Kiner," or "Dear Ralph," but "Dear Kiner." Then he sort of apologizes for an article in *Life* magazine in which he stated that only two current players, Phil Rizzuto and Stan Musial, could have played in his era. Apparently, some reporters had asked me to comment on Cobb's assertion, and when he read that I thought he was off by about 398 players, Cobb decided to write me to clear things up. He explained that his ghostwriter with the magazine had slanted his words and that, "having been burned so many times . . . by some obscure critic of baseball," he didn't blame me "one bit" for my reaction. But in his letter, Cobb didn't deny that he believed exactly what was in the article, or say he wanted to add me to his short list of worthy players. Rather, he confirmed that the players of his era were much better and told me to look up the statistics if I didn't believe him. Obviously, the man who had resented playing in Babe Ruth's shadow was still no fan of home-run hitters.

Around that time, Honus Wagner, whose career began before Cobb's, often came out to Forbes Field, just as he did as a star player when it opened in 1909, near Schenley Park, at the intersection of Boquet and Sennott. He'd put on a Pirates uniform and serve as our honorary coach. As he sat around regaling us with great stories of a bygone time, we were in awe because he was an original Hall of Famer, along with Cobb, Babe Ruth, Walter Johnson, and Christy Mathewson. Wagner was considered the greatest shortstop of all time and the greatest player in Pittsburgh's history, so he made us feel special by telling us that the postwar players were better than his contemporaries. Our team was so bad that under Branch Rickey we would become known as the "Rickey-Dinkies," so I was ready for Wagner to say that his present company was excepted from his evaluation. But he generously included us as well. Wagner might be the only old-timer I have spoken to in all the years who has acknowledged that the players who came after him were superior. I suppose that Cobb or another star might worry that if he conceded the current crop of players was better than his own, then everyone would assume *he* wasn't as good as the baseball history books tell us.

On a recent visit to St. Louis, I had dinner with one of Cobb's two favorites, Stan Musial, who is a great guy except that he will pull out his harmonica at the drop of a hat and play "Orange Blossom Special." He is one of the most laid-back and humble people I've ever met and has never been less than gracious when talking about any player from any era. Yet on that night he railed on and on against how many of today's players play the game, as if "fundamentals" had gone the way of the dinosaurs. I understood. If you see players performing beneath the standards of their predecessors, the game loses its appeal. If you go to the circus, you don't want to see aerialists flying off the trapeze; if you go to the ballet, you don't want to see dancers stumbling around like Long John Silver. You expect to see good execution.

As I told Musial, I am disappointed by the way today's players approach the game. But when I broadcast a game or watch it on television, I don't want to see such common things as these:

1. Batters swinging on a 2–0 count with no one on base and the team down by 2 in the ninth inning. If you have 17 in blackjack and the dealer has 16, why would you pick a card instead of letting the dealer have it? Because the same cards will bust both of you, let him have the next one and collect the money. It's the same with a 2–0 count with a 2–0 deficit—why help out the pitcher by swinging?

2. Pitchers throwing a fastball right down the middle on a 0–2 count when the game is on the line. In my day, managers would fine pitchers if they threw a strike on that count.

3. Excellent RBI men bunting for a hit with two outs and a man on second. RBIs are the most important stats in baseball, so if they are something you do well, you should never leave it up to the next batter.

4. Base runners being tagged out at third base as the first or third out in an inning. Rather than kill off an inning, stay on second base, which is also in scoring position. The time to chance a close play at third base is when there is already one out and the manager doesn't want to give up another out to move you along with a sacrifice bunt. Perhaps the worst base-running blunder I've ever seen was when the Mets' Vince Coleman was on at second and tried to steal third with two men out in the ninth inning and the count 3–2 to the potential tying run. It was ball four and Coleman was thrown out at third to end the game. That's not knowing the game or not caring about it, which is why I wouldn't want that guy to play for me.

5. Base runners being tagged out at home as the first out in the inning. Stay on third where you can score in so many ways with fewer than two outs.
6. Base runners sliding into a base headfirst. Pepper Martin, Pete Rose, and Rickey Henderson were famous for their headfirst slides, but those great base runners are the don't-try-this-at-home exceptions and shouldn't be emulated. So many players land on the disabled list when they try to stick their outstretched fingers underneath knees, hard tags, and shin guards and into spiked shoes and bases. We were taught the hook slide, the fadeaway, the straight-in slide, and the pop-up slide where you come up running; and we learned how to slide properly into a catcher to knock him off the plate. We had to practice in sliding pits, which they don't have anymore.
7. Batters sliding into first base. Sliding doesn't get you to first faster than running through the base, and it's dangerous. You never see a sprinter sliding across the finish line, do you?
8. Catchers being out of position and attempting swipe tags instead of blocking the plate.
9. Outfielders throwing to the wrong base or missing cutoff men.
10. Batters not cutting down on their home-run swings with two strikes, especially when all that's needed is a base hit.
11. Players playing the same way regardless of the count, the inning, the number of outs, the score, and who the pitcher is or who the batter and on-deck batters are.

You have to ask the question, "Why do they do it?" And the simple answer is: because they can. It is tolerated by owners and managers. The biggest reason in the past to learn the fundamentals was to keep your job and not be benched or sent to the minors if you didn't comply. That eliminated those who didn't have the desire to grow into a complete player. There's no longer that threat because of expansion. Now the teams need these players at the major league level sooner than we'd like. So players can get away without knowing fundamentals. It's a shame because it doesn't take long to learn the basic fundamentals if the desire is there.

In our conversation, Musial also said, "Ralph, I can't stomach all the home runs that they're hitting today. In our time, they would have been fly balls." I understood Stan's resentment, especially in regard to long-standing home-run records that have been surpassed too easily—because some of them were mine. As Keith Hernandez said, "The powers-that-be want the power game."

To me, baseball is about history, and over the years we have been able to judge the magnitude of players' accomplishments by comparing them to the achievements of players from previous eras. But today's game is so different from when Musial and I played that in most instances it's easier to contrast than compare. The proliferation of home runs that Stan complained about is a case in point. Instead of our witnessing a gradual evolution of increased home-run production, we were jolted by a big bang—in 1995, to be specific, when the new balls were so lively and the other conditions were so right (or wrong) that even the smallest players began to hit opposite-field homers. Suddenly there was a brand-new world, featuring balls flying out of ballparks at startling rates, which excited young fans and angered purists. It was similar to when pole-vaulters switched from bamboo to fiberglass poles and the old records were not just broken but shattered, overnight. Once a sport changes—in style and/or equipment—it's almost futile to compare athletes from the past and present. You almost need separate record books. But that would break the link to the past that is more vital to baseball than to any other sport.

So what can be said about the game in the two eras? Well, to start, I believe that the quality of baseball was at an all-time high when I played after World War II because there was such a concentration of talent on just 16 teams. I think that was the best baseball ever played. However, it's obvious to me that today's players are, in general, bigger, stronger, faster, and more athletic than the postwar players. Moreover, challenging prevailing wisdom, I contend that today's players are the best and most exciting players there have ever been.

But what about the sad lack of fundamentals exhibited by many of today's players that Musial and I commiserated about? I do, I admit, get angry when I see players doing the misdemeanors I listed, but, as I told Musial, I also got angry when players in our day did the same things. We, too, made mistakes and weren't always fundamentally sound, although it's almost heresy for any of us to admit it. And under the same circumstances—in which players are rushed to the majors and some managers don't demand that they do it the right way, or else—we would have been even more lax. What many old-time players get wrong is that they say *all* current players are the same. The good players on the good, well-managed teams like the Yankees and Braves know what they're doing.

I think the longer season makes it harder for today's players to play at a high level all the time. If you play 162 games, there are sure to be days you shouldn't be playing because you don't feel well or are tired out. Only in the postseason, when there is a goal in sight, can you play at your best. It's a hard thing to talk about because no player wants to mention the fact that he isn't going all out all the time. Joe DiMaggio used to tell teammates to play hard every game because the fans watching that day may be seeing the Yankees for their only time the whole year. Despite the more strenuous travel, we had an easier schedule that made it more possible for us to play at our peaks. We played 154 games, and the World Series was our entire postseason. We didn't have two rounds of playoffs or eight additional regular-season games, and we had more days off because we played twin bills every Sunday for one admission price—a grand tradition that has gone by the wayside in order to generate more revenue for the owners. We could start the season at a reasonable time, in mid-April rather than at the end of March, and throw out the first ball rather than the last snowball.

In praising current major leaguers, I am in no way diminishing how good we were, because I have no doubt that our best players would be stars if they played today. I played against four individuals who are still regarded as the greatest players in their franchises' histories: Ted Williams (Red Sox), Stan Musial (Cardinals), Willie Mays (Giants), and Hank Aaron (Braves). I also played against Jackie Robinson, the greatest Brooklyn Dodger. And I played *with* Hank Greenberg, the greatest Tiger ever, and Bob Feller, the greatest pitcher/player in Cleveland Indians history. Of current batters only Barry Bonds ranks with Musial, Greenberg, Williams, and Joe DiMaggio. There have been no better all-around players than DiMaggio and Willie Mays. No player but Mark McGwire has shown the same power as Mickey Mantle, and no one has done it from both sides of the plate. And in my mind, Jackie Robinson remains the best base runner and competitor the game has ever known.

Among pitchers, I have never seen anyone throw harder than Feller—not even Nolan Ryan. And the only pitcher who has had a comparable curve has been Sandy Koufax, who actually began his career in the postwar era, in 1955, my final season and the year Feller won his final game. And as great as Koufax was, I believe the underrated Warren Spahn, who had 13 20-win seasons and 363 victories (a record for left-handers), was even better. People forget that the young Spahn had a fastball and other stuff that was as intimidating as Koufax's.

Were we to play today, we would excel and could challenge the new records if we had all the advantages modern players take for granted, including better equipment and advanced training methods and facilities. I didn't even have access to a batting machine until Hank Greenberg sent me one prior to the 1955 season. We had no weight room because lifting was considered the worst thing you could do. Now players try to put on 40 or 50 pounds of muscle, and to cool down each day they wander over to the state-of-the-art spas in their clubhouses.

We had a whirlpool, but it was just a tin contraption that sat in the trainer's room. When we got it, it was supposedly the greatest thing that ever happened, and everyone raved about its therapeutic benefits and how it would help players shed a few extra pounds. Trouble was, it didn't do a damn thing. It agitated the water; that's it. And sometimes when guys would throw soap in there, the suds would overflow and cover the entire floor, and we couldn't go into the training room.

Not that we'd want to, because the trainers we had back then weren't like today's highly educated specialists who help athletes tone their bodies and work through injuries. If you had a "strawberry," they would pour alcohol all over you and call it a day. That was an unpleasant experience. They were jacks-of-all-trades, not professionals. In the minors, they probably did double duty as the teams' bus drivers. It wasn't much better in the majors. After I left the Pirates, the trainer was Tony Bartirome, who had played first base for us after Branch Rickey signed him out of high school. It turned out he couldn't hit, but he was a fancy fielder, so I guess they figured that he had hands to make a good trainer. While I was in Pittsburgh, we had a trainer named Doc Jorgensen. He had a bad leg and had a tough time walking. One day, a player got hurt at second base, so he grabbed his kit and rushed onto the field as fast as a hobbling man can to see what he could do. Intending to try his hand at a little first aid, he opened up his kit— and it was full of ham sandwiches. We didn't have much confidence in him.

When I toiled in Chicago, an ex-player named Andy Lockshaw was a Cubs trainer. When he'd give you a rubdown, he'd chew tobacco and spit the juice on your body as a lubricant. He was well known for that. Before one game he was tending a player when they got into an argument about hitting. He immediately stopped what he was doing—perhaps he was in midspit—and rushed outside and into the batting cage to demonstrate what he was talking about. The batting-practice pitcher threw him a ball, and he knocked it over the fence on his first swing and walked off, having proved his point.

All these guys followed in the tradition of a character named "Bonecrusher" Reese, who was before my time. He was an actual doctor, but I don't know where he went to school because his method for taking care of sore arms was to have you stretch them by hanging on a door. The only trainer I remember actually helping anybody was Doc Weaver of the Cardinals. He built filter devices to put into the distressed noses of allergy sufferers so we could play with some relief. His invention really helped pitcher John Lanning, who had trouble breathing because his nose was irritated and he was chewing tobacco on the mound.

Back then they would say you were over-the-hill at 34, and it was often true because we didn't know how to take care of ourselves and the trainers were really masseurs and didn't know any more than we did. I never even saw a pitcher icing down his arm after a game, as all pitchers do today. Jim Palmer, the Hall of Famer who rarely went along with conventions, said skeptically, "If icing helps, you should put your head in an ice bucket to make you smarter."

We wouldn't tell the trainer or manager if we were hurting because we feared we wouldn't play again. Even if you had an operation, there was no guarantee it would work, which is why I retired at a fairly young age (rather than have unsure surgeons experiment on my back). Now teams have brilliant trainers, doctors, specialists, and surgeons all around. If a player goes down with a knee injury, he can have arthroscopic surgery and recover in a few days; and they can fix a pitcher's torn ligament with the sophisticated and quite miraculous Tommy John surgery and have him back on the mound in a year or so. So players no longer have to play hurt, and their careers can be prolonged indefinitely. That's a major change from my time.

Other than training and medical improvements, the biggest refinements in the game have had to do with on-field equipment. The most revolutionary change has been the tremendous improvement of the glove. Yet nobody ever talks about this. If players today used the gloves we did, there would be even more scoring and a bunch of hitters would flirt with .400 each year. Fielders can do things now in the field that we never could. They make fewer errors, take away more hits, and make many more fabulous plays.

If you look at old-timers' pancake gloves from before 1930 and dating back to professional baseball's 19th-century origins, you wonder how fielders even used them because they were so flat. Bill Doak, a spitball pitcher who needed a big glove to hide what he was doing, invented the first decent glove. Patented around 1920, his invention had the thumb and index finger joined by strands of material, forming a pocket. The Bill Doak model became the most popular glove through the thirties. In the forties, Harry "the Glove Doctor" Latina, working for Rawlings, designed newer and better gloves, with deeper pockets. I used a Rawlings model, and so did Musial, for whom Latina made a six-fingered glove that Stan could use to play both outfield and first base.

Gloves were better in the forties and fifties, but they weren't great. We still used both hands to make catches, because our bare hand was needed to keep the ball from popping out of the glove. When A's first baseman Vic Power broke in and started catching the ball using only one hand, he was called a "hot dog" and a "show-off," so other players continued to do it the old way. It was hard to break tradition. I'd make catches with two hands except when I was on the run and had no choice. We were told to get under the ball, catch it at the shoulders with both hands, and be ready to throw. The problem is that two-handed catches limit your range and ability to make the fantastic plays that are made today.

I thought I was a better-than-average outfielder with a pretty good arm, very steady. I actually began as a center fielder before I moved to left, which became my permanent position. Late in my career when I was hampered by a groin injury and bad back, I wouldn't have been able to play center.

Playing some outfields was tough nevertheless. Wrigley Field had a gutter down the left- and right-field foul lines, about six inches from the walls, that made footing treacherous. At Wrigley, you'd also have to retrieve the ball in the ivy before they made it a ground-rule double when the ball went in there. Cubs players would plant a ball in the ivy, so if they couldn't find the hit ball, they'd grab that one and throw it back to the infield. Lou Novikoff, who was known as the "Mad Russian" when he played for the Cubs in the early forties, was terrified of sticking his hand into the ivy because he had arachnophobia.

I hated playing the outfield in Crosley Field in Cincinnati because in addition to dealing with the oppressive heat, you'd have to run up an incline that began about 15 feet from the fence. It was the only incline in baseball. You might take the first couple of steps and hit that incline and fall down. The Reds worked hard with an outfielder with two left feet on how to go up the hill without falling down. Finally someone hit the ball over his head, and he went up the hill perfectly . . . and fell coming back down.

There were many great outfielders in my time, although they were handicapped by inferior gloves. Terry Moore of the Cardinals, who ran well and had great range, had the reputation of being a great center fielder. So did Joe DiMaggio because of his gliding stride. His brother Vince, a one-time Pirate, was considered even better, although the oft-told family joke was, "Joe was the best hitter, Dom the best fielder, and Vince the best singer." Jimmy Piersall, who played a very shallow center field for Boston a few years after Dom, was also a marvelous fielder.

The Dodgers' Pete Reiser was a hell of a center fielder and hitter, the Mickey Mantle of his era. He would go after everything and didn't take into account that there was no padding on walls back then. I saw the infamous play when he ran headfirst into the cement wall at Ebbets Field while going after a fly ball. It happened against the Pirates. It was a terrifying collision, and he was carried off the field on a stretcher. We thought he was dead. They actually gave him his last rites. He didn't die, but it affected his career. That was the worst injury I have ever seen on the field, as a player or broadcaster. The old-style ballparks, without padding on the walls and with rocks all over the infield, also limited fielders who, unlike Reiser, weren't willing to risk injury.

Willie Mays excited everyone with his fielding. He was the first of the spectacular center fielders, someone who tried to entertain the fans. When he stood still he made basket catches, and every time he ran after a ball, his cap would fly off. That was by design. He was flashy and had a great arm and made unbelievable throws. When he'd make an impossible catch and throw against the Dodgers, their manager Chuck Dressen would scoff, "I'd like to see him do that again."

When Hank Sauer and I played outfield for the Cubs, the reporters would write how our center fielder Frankie Baumholtz had to track down everything not hit right at us. That was exaggerated, but they said Frankie had a "sunburned tongue"—from letting it hang out like a dog in the hot sun after having to run down everything between us.

Richie Ashburn of the Phillies had great speed, and I can't tell you how many times he caught balls I hit against the batting cage they placed to the left of dead center field in Pittsburgh, 467 feet from home. He had as many putouts as Mays, but he didn't have Mays' arm, although he is still known for throwing out the Dodgers' Cal Abrams at the plate in 1950 on a single by Duke Snider (another fine center fielder) to save the pennant for the Phillies. Ashburn didn't have a good arm, but he was shallow, and third-base coach Wes Stock made a major *fundamental* mistake by waving Abrams home with nobody out.

A number of great outfielders played right field because they had strong arms. Carl "the Reading Rifle" Furillo was the Dodgers' secret weapon. He would position himself in right-center at Ebbets Field in front of a sign at the base of the scoreboard for Abe Stark Clothing. It was rumored that Stark gave him a new suit of clothes to prevent batters from striking the sign and winning suits that were promised in a promotion. You didn't run on Furillo. At Ebbets Field, where the right-field fence was so close, the batter had to think of him as another infielder because he could throw you out at first.

The Braves' Hank Aaron, the Pirates' Roberto Clemente, and the Tigers' Al Kaline came afterward and were extraordinary right fielders with speed and strong and accurate arms. Aaron was always underrated because he didn't play with the showmanship of Clemente or Mays. He and Kaline would do the proper one-bounce throw to the catcher, while Clemente often threw directly into the mitt, too high for the ball to be cut off—two fundamental mistakes on one throw. Clemente, fellow Puerto Rican Vic Power, and Cuban Minnie Minoso (who played left field for the Indians and White Sox) were the first Hispanic players to intentionally exhibit flair in the field—a tradition that continues today.

Although he didn't have any speed, flat-footed Indians right fielder Rocky Colavito had a remarkable arm. When I was the GM for the San Diego Padres in 1956, Hank Greenberg, the Indians' GM, sent Colavito down to our team for some seasoning (we had a working agreement with Cleveland). I was trying to get people in the stands, so between games of a doubleheader, I had Rocky compete in a throwing contest with a few jai alai players. They used a cesta to hurl a pelota, a hard rubber ball that is half the size of a baseball and is harder than a golf ball. Rocky didn't beat them, but he threw a baseball over the center-field fence, which was 421 feet away. Greenberg gave me hell because he thought I was jeopardizing Colavito's throwing arm, but I did get a sellout crowd that day.

As far as infielders, Gil Hodges and Vic Power were considered the best-fielding first basemen. There weren't many second basemen who were known for fielding prior to Bill Mazeroski, although most were pretty steady. Billy Cox was by far the finest-fielding third baseman I saw as a player, and probably the best ever until Brooks Robinson. Luis Aparicio was considered the best at short. He made spectacular plays in the hole and had the greatest arm I ever saw at shortstop with the possible exception of Shawon Dunston. Dunston was the number one draft pick in 1982, ahead of Dwight Gooden. And Cardinals manager Whitey Herzog commented, "He should have been because he had a better arm."

Aparicio, who was from Venezuela, was a rookie in 1956, a year after I retired. He made 35 errors that year, which would be his career high. Even the "steadiest" shortstops in the postwar era would make 30 errors a year, usually through no fault of their own. It didn't help that the infields were in such bad shape in those days. Compare that to the low totals of Ozzie Smith, the first player to make Cooperstown primarily because of his fielding, and current perennial Gold Glove winner Omar Vizquel. In 1990, the Orioles' Cal Ripken Jr. set a record when he made only three errors in 161 games. Mike Bordick set records with 110 consecutive games and 543 straight chances without an error. In today's ballparks, there aren't pebbles all over the infield, and hops are true. It's amazing what a super fielder can do with a great glove and good field conditions.

For my era, Marty Marion was tall and had outstanding range and a good arm. He had the habit of picking up real and imaginary rocks in the infield between pitches and throwing them to the outfield grass. At Sportsman's Park in St. Louis, they weren't imaginary. Marion, who was 6'2", was a predecessor to 6'4" Cal Ripken, who, in turn, was the predecessor to the current wave of tall, power-hitting shortstops led by Alex Rodriguez, Derek Jeter, and Nomar Garciaparra. It's like when 6'9" Magic Johnson played point guard and entirely changed the position. In my time, they always thought a shortstop shouldn't be tall because his main job was defense, and he was needed to scoop up grounders and move lithely around second base. Similarly, they thought catchers should be short so they could both pick up low pitches and give the pitcher a low target. The Indians' Jim Hegan was one of the first tall catchers, and he is still regarded as one of the best catchers of all time. Today, there are many tall catchers. All those myths have been debunked.

Today, the expensive, modern gloves have hinges and fold over and are extremely flexible. They make one-handed catches preferable and allow players to show their athletic skills when running, jumping, and—we were unable to do this—sliding to snare fly balls. Players display more range and acrobatic skills and can make many more circus-style catches. Infielders like Omar Vizquel race into the outfield with their backs to the plate to make catches or reach into the stands and snatch balls away from fans. Middle infielders range onto the outfield grass to stop grounders or leap high to snatch line drives. Catchers, since Johnny Bench in the sixties and seventies, catch entire games with one hand because their mitts are so flexible. (Before that almost all catchers had their fingers broken, and they'd tell the old joke about two catchers shaking hands and it taking them a month to get their hands apart.) Center fielders Andruw Jones of the Braves, Jim Edmonds of the Cardinals, and Torri Hunter of the Twins, whose specialty is leaping over fences to take away home runs, are just three of many highlight-reel outfielders today.

Bats didn't present the same problems as gloves did for players in my day. However, nothing has stayed the same in baseball, so bats have changed, too. Everyone used to swing heavy bats, usually 35-inch bats that weighed 36 or 38 ounces. Many players, including Barry Bonds, now use 31- and 32-ounce bats. They are using a different wood now. It used to be only ash, but following Bonds' example, many players have switched to bats made of the denser maple. These bats, many of which are made in Canada, don't become kindling wood as quickly as the ash bats, but they also have thin handles and break easily. All the bats used today have lots of torque and a springy trampoline effect that propels the ball farther.

People say it's the live balls that are responsible for all the homers. That's why we always see "experts" on television bouncing balls from before 1995 and the present. I'm reminded how back in 1947, when I hit 51 homers, our pitcher Ernie Bonham (who would die during the 1949 season from cancer) would take the trainer's stethoscope and put it on the '47 major league ball and say, "I can hear the rabbit's heartbeat now—he's alive." The spate of home runs since 1995 has not been caused only by the lively ball and the other usual suspects—the smaller ballparks, diluted pitching that has come with expansion, added muscles on batters, and their unwillingness to cut down on their strokes when they have two strikes. No one talks about the newer bats. They should, because they might be the biggest factor of all. When mediocre pitchers throw rabbit balls in small parks to bulked-up batters who wield bats that have a lot of torque, there are going to be a lot of home runs.

Bats are built to be light in order to increase the speed of the swing. It is well known to every ballplayer who majored in physics—didn't we all?—that the distance a ball will travel when hit perfectly on the sweet spot of the bat is determined by the weight of the bat times the speed of the bat squared. Therefore the speed of the swinging bat is the dominant factor. If you don't hit the ball on the sweet spot, it will cause vibrations and diminish the distance the ball will travel. The bat might break due to these vibrations, yet the ball still might go over the fence—which is amazing. There are many broken-bat home runs now, whereas if it happened in my era somebody would inform *Ripley's Believe It or Not!* That's why pitchers throw cutters on the wrists; anything near the sweet spot of the bat can be taken a long way, even if the bat splits in two. On a biting cutter that broke into the handle of his bat, Arizona's Luis Gonzalez actually won the 2001 World Series. His broken-bat RBI single landed safely at the back of the infield, over the drawn-in Yankees middle infielders. Tim McCarver, who was doing color for Fox, actually called that play, saying beforehand that playing "in" was chancy because Yankees closer Mariano Rivera's wicked cut fastball often resulted in a lot of broken-bat pop-ups to the back of the infield.

Louisville Slugger would send me about three dozen bats a year. I could have asked for more, but I didn't break many bats because the ones I used were heavy and had good wood. To harden bats, we used to soak them in linseed oil all winter and then let them dry out. We'd also hone them with soup bones. That would keep the bat from cracking. Today some batters receive a dozen bats a week. No players go through entire years with one or two anymore. Nobody gets attached to bats anymore.

The witty Richie Ashburn, who led off for the Phillies for much of his Hall of Fame career, was asked once if he had a favorite bat. He said, "Whenever I'm hitting well, my favorite bat is the one I'm using." He then was asked how he made sure other players didn't use it. He said, "I watch it closely and protect it. I even take it home at night and sleep with it. As a matter of fact, I've slept with a lot of old bats in my life."

It was during my era that a third piece of vital equipment was introduced that contributes to batters' feeling comfortable at the plate—the batting helmet. There had been sporadic incidents of players wearing protective headgear dating back to the early 1900s, almost always after they had been beaned. But no device caught on because the players thought that wearing protection was unmanly. In the forties, there was a big drive to protect players' heads because a number had their careers shortened by beanballs. The Dodgers came up with a hard plastic liner inside their felt caps. It would break if you were beaned, but that was still better than your head cracking open, so we gladly wore them.

When Branch Rickey came over to the Pirates, Charlie Muse designed a fiberglass batting helmet. He offered me stock if I'd become part of a company that made these new helmets. I sent him to Rickey, who thought they were such a good idea that he invested in the company. Then he made us wear the helmets not only at the plate but also on the base paths and in the field. We were so bad that other teams joked that we had to wear them on defense so we wouldn't get our skulls fractured on fly balls. Most players didn't want to wear them because they provided opposing players with ammunition to make a lot of comments about our sexual identity. We heard the word *sissy* more than enough. By 1958, however, it was mandatory for all major leaguers to wear helmets at the plate. I made about $1,000 from the whole thing; Rickey made a lot more. In 1974, earflaps were added to helmets, further protecting the inventory. It worked out well.

In those days, helmets really were necessary because pitchers threw at batters without restraint. Whether that was good or bad is debatable, but it was certainly a part of baseball. The fear of being hit for the second time took away many players' confidence at the plate and ruined their careers. Most guys never learned the proper way to elude a ball thrown at their heads, but my high school coach taught me how to duck my head behind my body, so I wasn't intimidated—except possibly when Ewell Blackwell was on the mound.

Blackwell was a hard-throwing right-hander for the Reds whose whiplike sidearm delivery made it very difficult for right-handed batters to pick up the ball until it was right on them—so bailing out in terror seemed like our best option. Blackwell was also from California, and we'd hang out together in the off-season, but still he'd throw at me and wasn't averse to hitting me on purpose. I didn't resent him; it was part of the game. I just let our pitchers retaliate. Ben Wade of the Dodgers was another friend of mine who was a headhunter. When I went up to the plate against him it was hard to dig in because I knew he'd knock me down. The Giants' intimidating Sal "the Barber" Maglie threw at everybody, not just the Dodgers.

Allie Reynolds of the Yankees denied charges by Jackie Robinson that he threw at black players. He said, "It didn't make any difference what color they were. I just protected my territory." That was what many pitchers said. Reynolds contended that the only player he threw at deliberately was little Nellie Fox for jiggling around at the plate—a lot of pitchers hated Fox because he hardly ever struck out. The meanest of all pitchers was American Leaguer Early Wynn. When I was his teammate on the Indians in 1955, I actually saw him hit his own son during batting practice. I couldn't believe it. He warned everyone that he'd throw at his own mother if she had a bat in her hands, and no one doubted him.

I didn't get to bat against Bob Gibson because he pitched after I retired, but the Cardinals' frightening right-hander was another guy who would be your best friend yet throw an exploding 95 mph right at your head. He believed the corners belonged to the pitcher and threw inside on one pitch so the batter would be too scared to reach for the next pitch on the outside of the plate. The same was true of the Dodgers' Don Drysdale. Orlando Cepeda said that the best way to approach Drysdale was to hit him before he hit you. Former catcher Fran Healy, one of my Mets broadcasting partners, told on the air how Juan Marichal always invited his friend Roberto Clemente over for dinner when the Pirates came to San Francisco. But one night Clemente failed to appear. The two teams played the next day, and Marichal drilled him with the first pitch. He yelled at Clemente, "If I invite you to dinner, you had better show up!"

Stan Williams, who was a rookie pitcher for the Dodgers their first year in Los Angeles, stood 6'5" and weighed 230 pounds and was one of the most intimidating pitchers of the era. He used to keep a book on batters, with marks by their names. The mark was a skull and crossbones. If a batter hit a homer off Williams, he would get only one mark, but he'd get two marks if he stood at the plate and admired it. When the batter had reached his mark limit, Williams would inform him, "You are going down the next time I face you!"

The knockdown pitch was a very important part of baseball from the thirties into the sixties. It was the dominating pitch, the one used to intimidate batters, and managers did not hesitate to tell their pitchers to throw at you. Leo Durocher and Charley Dressen were among the worst. Durocher was known for yelling from the bench, "Stick it in his ear!" You could hear him all over the ballpark, but umpires let it go because it was part of the game. Can you imagine the repercussions today?

In 1969, I was broadcasting a crucial series between the Mets and Durocher's Cubs. In the bottom of the first, Bill Hands of the Cubs decked the Mets' leadoff hitter, Tommie Agee, with a ball directed at his temple. In the top of the second inning, the Mets' starter, the very tough Jerry Koosman, threw a pitch right at the head of Ron Santo, who fortunately got his hand up in time to block it. After that message pitch, there were no more knockdowns by either side. That's the way it should have been handled and the way it *was* handled prior to this era. But now things have changed. Batters don't fear being hit because few pitchers throw inside. That is another reason there are so many home runs being hit today and so many runs being scored. If you don't think there is a chance a pitch will hit and hurt you, then you aren't going to be intimidated at the plate.

Now a pitcher can't retaliate openly if a teammate is hit, because he will be immediately ejected and possibly suspended. So they have to hold back. If a pitcher knows he will be thrown out if he just looks like he is throwing at a batter, batters can be more aggressive and look outside for the pitch. In my day, a pitcher would never get thrown out for hitting someone, even if the umpire knew it was deliberate. Against pitchers who didn't care if they bounced a ball off your head, we used to tiptoe into the batter's box and pretend that we wouldn't be firmly planted to get more shove-off power. Now that batters know most pitchers won't throw at them, they openly dig in. The elimination of the brushback pitch has changed the game. There are few pitchers who throw inside regularly. Pedro Martinez does; Roger Clemens did.

When a ball occasionally gets away, batters act horrified, as if the pitcher is trying to damage millions of dollars worth of human merchandise. They are shocked if a pitch brushes them back, even if they did some styling after touching that same pitcher for a home run their previous time up. If they're hit, they don't simply take their base but often make a move toward the pitcher. It's as if the batter's manhood is at stake: he wants to show his teammates that the opposition fears him enough to throw at him; and he wants to show them that if a pitcher hits him, he is man enough to charge the mound—even if it was unintentional on the pitcher's part.

In the spring of 2003, Mets star Mike Piazza received a suspension for charging into the Dodgers' clubhouse after Guillermo Mota, perhaps because Mota had thrown at him the previous year, or perhaps because Piazza was often reminded he hadn't retaliated when Roger Clemens beaned him. It reminded me of a famous incident in 1956, when big Joe Adcock chased headhunter Ruben Gomez into the Giants' clubhouse in deep center field at the Polo Grounds. Adcock was so angry because Gomez hit him twice—he was hit on the wrist with the pitch, and when he charged the mound, the scared Gomez threw another ball that struck him on the thigh. Adcock ceased his pursuit only when the terrified Gomez got an ice pick out to defend himself.

Brushback pitches and beanball wars were part of a game that was much rougher in my era. Aggressive base running capped by vicious slides into infielders and catchers were the order of the day. Fielders made hard tags, and fearless receivers protected the plate with stiff legs and hard equipment. Players going up against the league's most aggressive teams—the Brooklyn Dodgers, New York Giants, St. Louis Cardinals, and Chicago Cubs—knew they were in for battles, perhaps even brawls. (If two opposing players still had a quarrel after a rhubarb, they might duke it out before the next game, before the gates opened, while teammates formed a human ring.)

Baseball was like war, where we would do anything to win the ballgame. That included stealing signs. Figuring out the signs the catcher was giving the pitcher was like espionage where you'd try to break the enemy's code. Some people think sign stealing is bad sportsmanship, but it's really what all smart players should try to do. It's simply using your eyes and brain and isn't in the same category as doctoring a baseball or tampering with a bat. It was truly fair and square during my era because every team did it and knew it was going on. (It was a time when groundskeepers with tools and buckets of water fiddled with the mound, infield grass, and dirt around home plate and on the base paths much more than they do today. Bill Veeck was known to put balls in the refrigerator to deaden them. Anything to benefit your team.)

The best teams made sign stealing difficult. The Dodgers had a series of signs that were almost impossible to read. They did it all according to the ball-strike count, so it would change every pitch. All teams changed the signs to deceive you. Also, pitchers would rub down their legs and change the pitch to something else. If you expected a curve and it was a fastball, you'd get your head taken off. So sign stealing was a daring thing to do, and a lot of players refused to take signs from teammates because they might be wrong.

Hank Greenberg, who batted behind me in 1947, taught me how I could signal him what pitch was coming when I was on base and could see the catcher's signs. My legs would be spread, and if my first move was with my right foot, that meant the pitch would be a fastball; if it was with my left foot, it would be a curve. Location didn't mean much. When I got signs at the plate they would be from our third-base coach, Bill Burwell, who was very adept at reading catchers. He would signal with his arms or feet, or maybe with a whistle. Elden Auker, the one-time submarine pitcher who is now in his nineties, sent me this ode to third-base coaches, written by Bob McKenty:

> His loins are girt, his teeth are grit
> His jock itch, he'll conceal
> He knows that if he scratches it
> He'll start a double steal

About two years ago there was a lot of controversy when someone "revealed" Bobby Thomson's historic pennant-winning blast off Dodger reliever Ralph Branca in 1951 may have resulted from his receiving a signal from the center field clubhouse regarding catcher Rube Walker's sign. Some news. We all knew the Giants stole signs in the Polo Grounds long before Thomson's homer. There were offices in dead center field there and someone out there with binoculars was stealing signs. I think he used an electronic buzzing system—one buzz for a fastball, two for a breaking pitch—to relay the sign to the bullpen or dugout. They'd still have to relay the sign to Thomson and other batters, so it wasn't an easy process. Anyway, because we all knew about it, we'd change signs.

Before I played with the Indians, they had a member of the grounds crew sit in bleachers at Municipal Stadium. With powerful binoculars, he'd get the signs off the catcher. He wore white tennis shoes, and if the batter saw one shoe it was a fastball and two shoes it was a curve. It was never too hard to see the fingers of catchers, unless they crouched low and concealed them behind their mitts. We had a catcher named Bill Salkeld, who had a bad knee and couldn't really squat. He'd go into only a half squat, and every-one was stealing his signs. But we knew this so we'd often change the signs.

Sign stealing was a big thing in my day, but it's not done anymore. That's not necessarily because television cameras now pick up everything. It's because most batters don't want to know what's coming. If they did, all they'd have to do is watch the catcher out of the corner of their eyes. In our day, the catchers were stationary. They used to just sit or stand behind home plate, and the pitcher's target was their shoulders and knees. Today they move so much to the right and left that it's obvious what's coming. I can almost call every pitch from the broadcast booth from how they move. A batter's peripheral vision is good enough to see where he is. I don't under-stand why they tip off pitches, but it doesn't seem to be a concern because batters don't pay any attention.

It wasn't imperative that catchers in my era have strong arms because there was very little base stealing. Pitchers usually didn't bother throwing over to first. Pee Wee Reese, Jackie Robinson, Pete Reiser, and Willie Mays were considered threats, but they didn't steal that often. They were more dangerous just running the bases on hit balls. Enos Slaughter was another aggressive ballplayer, someone known to sharpen his spikes in preparation for slides. He was always on my case for some reason. Somewhere along the line, he claimed he could score on a ball hit to me in the outfield from any base. I said the only thing he could do better than me was get divorced. He'd had five or six wives. At the time I hadn't had any.

Instead of the stolen base, managers relied a lot on the bunt and hit-and-run to move along runners. We had players who couldn't bunt and the manager wouldn't ask them to. I practiced bunting and would try to beat one out on occasion in the ninth when I had to get on base to try to bring up the tying run. I don't think I ever was called on to lay down a sacrifice bunt, because my managers didn't want to give up an out when there was a fair chance I'd hit a longball. It was a hitter's game, and managers would often eschew the sacrifice and sit back Earl Weaver–style and wait for three-run homers and big innings—on the Pirates, I was the guy they waited for to deliver.

Managers relied more on the hit-and-run play in my day, although I didn't do it myself. The aggressive managers let their players—the batter and the base runner—put it on themselves. Billy Herman had no peers at pulling it off when he was a player, but he rarely had us do it. He probably thought we didn't have the personnel to be successful. Slow runners often are reluc-tant to take off because if the batter doesn't swing or if he misses the ball, they will probably be thrown out stealing. Yogi Berra was once on first when the coach flashed the hit-and-run sign. The pitcher threw the ball and Yogi didn't move. The batter fouled it off. This happened on the next pitch, too. Yogi was rooted to the base; he never ran. Finally the manager called him over and asked, "Did you see the sign?" "Sure, I saw it," Yogi replied, nodding. "Then why didn't you run?" "Well, I didn't think you meant it."

The hit-and-run is one of the great plays in baseball, which is why most of the National League managers of my day employed it a lot. The New York Yankees under Joe Torre, Mike Scoscia's championship Anaheim Angels of 2002, Tony Pena's Kansas City Royals, and Jack McKeon's championship Florida Marlins of 2003 are good models for current managers who want to keep their players in motion. You want to keep the defense moving around because that increases the chances of the ball going through or being kicked around. You want to put pressure on the defense.

I believe the hit-and-run is a better play to get men into scoring position than the stolen base or sacrifice bunt. I have never been an advocate of the stolen base because if you're going to have a guy thrown out stealing 40 percent of the time (the rate at which good catchers throw out batters today), you will lose the battle. There are choices that are less likely to kill rallies. But if you have guys who can steal at a high percentage rate, it is a bona fide weapon. It sets you up to score. For years stolen bases were a significant part of the game. When Maury Wills, Lou Brock, Ron LeFlore, Rickey Henderson, Tim Raines, or Vince Coleman got on base, it was exciting. Those leadoff hitters would steal from 80 to 100 bases a year—Henderson holds the record with 130—and ignite their teams' offenses by causing havoc on the base paths.

But now there are few players who steal a lot of bases. In fact, the Marlins, with leadoff hitter Juan Pierre swiping 65 bases, were the first World Series winner since the Maury Wells–led Dodgers of 1965 to have led the league in steals. Because of Wills and those other great base stealers of the past, pitchers needed to find a way to hold runners close. First they killed off the steal of home—a specialty of Pete Reiser, Jackie Robinson, and, years later, Rod Carew—by going to the set position instead of using a windup with a man on third. The slide step toward home, a recent innovation, has cut down on steals of second base. However, I'm not sold on it because I think many pitchers lose velocity on their fastballs and aren't able to come over the top to deliver an effective curveball. The arm can't catch up with the body. I think the slide step is a reason for better hitting and more scoring, and when managers realize this they may not let certain pitchers throw it.

Even then, I think the phasing out of the stolen base will continue because managers won't try steals when they know so many of their players can homer now. Players can steal at an acceptable rate of 70 percent, but managers still think the team is better off waiting for a home run. On a homer, a base runner can score just as easily from first base as from second.

Along with fewer stolen bases, sacrifice bunts are done less frequently. Only pitchers in the National League seem to be sacrificing. One reason is that there are few players who can execute a bunt. Because of new defenses, including the rotation play with men on first and second—where the shortstop covers third and the second baseman covers first—and smart pitchers who throw high fastballs at bunters, it has become increasingly difficult to sacrifice successfully. However, the surprise squeeze bunt is still an effective weapon—if you have a daring manager like Atlanta's Bobby Cox and a confident bunter on your team.

The way a team tries to score runs is usually a reflection of the personality of the manager. In my era, managers had much more power in the running of ballclubs, even to the point where they could go to the owners and ask that you be demoted, traded, or have your salary cut. (I was fortunate that my first manager, Frankie Frisch, got me a raise at the end of my rookie season.) So on the field, before free agency gave players control, you played the way they wanted, which in those days was just old-fashioned, hard-nosed country hardball.

It was a simpler game in which managers didn't overburden players with strategy. They didn't even give much thought when assembling a batting order—other than putting fast guys up top, poor-hitting shortstops and slow catchers at the bottom, a slugger in the middle, and a good fastball hitter in front of him because the pitcher wouldn't chance walking him by throwing off-speed pitches. They didn't experiment much on offense or use gimmickry with defenses—although back then, too, managers played the infield in or halfway to cut off important runs at the plate with a man on third and fewer than two outs. Also, they often employed the "Boudreau shift" against Ted Williams, Hank Sauer, me, and other pull hitters. When Lou Boudreau designed the shift, which had three infielders playing on the same side, it was to stop us from hitting home runs by giving us easy singles the other way.

Baseball then was a game bound by tradition, and the managers who had the edge were the ones who also relied on sharp instincts and gut feelings. Leo Durocher was the manager who impressed me most because he was both unpredictable and aggressive. He was a tough manager to play against because he went for the jugular. He'd make players jittery with his bench-jockeying, alternately being vulgar and instructing Sal Maglie and his other pitchers to throw at our heads. I hated his guts. His players, like Eddie Stanky, would slide into our middle infielders with their spikes high, hoping to jar the ball loose. Everyone had their roles—some guys homered, others were adept at the hit-and-run or sacrifice bunt. Stanky made it an art to be hit by the pitch by wearing a very baggy uniform. Everyone hated playing against him, but he would have been a good teammate because he was so aggressive, devious, and overachieving—the perfect Durocher player. Like Durocher, Eddie was a good guy off the field, but something else on it. He had two personalities. He was the nicest gentleman I ever met, but when he played and later managed, it was like death row because he was so serious.

Durocher was one of those battling managers who didn't back down from umpires and, in fact, instigated many memorable heated arguments with the men in blue. He set the stage for the likes of Earl Weaver, Billy Martin, and Lou Piniella, whose best dirt-kicking tantrums were worth the price of admission. I tried to be amiable with umpires because I didn't want any of them bearing a grudge, which was known to happen. The only time I was thrown out of a game was by Jocko Conlan, and afterward I was the one who held a grudge—I wouldn't talk to him for about five years. Conlan, who was a cocky little guy, called me out on a close play at first, and our first-base coach, Bill Posedel, started arguing that I was safe. I came back to the base and stood side by side with Bill as he faced Conlan. Determined to use the shortest route back to his position behind first, Conlan walked between us. There was contact that he initiated, but he claimed I shoved him and ejected me. That infuriated me. I never accused him of lying, but there was a photo the next day in the paper that showed I had my hands in my back pockets.

The other umpire I remember most was Beans Reardon, who was a real character. When Beans received the Bill Klein Award as the major leagues' best umpire, he said, "I'm happy to receive the Bill Klein Award, but in truth Klein hated my guts and I hated his." If you challenged Beans on a called strike, he'd say, "So I missed it, you've got two more." Once I slid into third base at Ebbets Field and Reardon yelled, "Safe!" But at the same time he made the "out" motion with his thumb. I asked, "Beans, am I safe or out?" He said, "I called you safe, but thirty thousand Dodgers fans saw me signal you were out, so you're out!" Where do you go from there? That kind of humor offset any argument. Anyway, I didn't argue with umpires. I left that to my managers.

Charley Dressen of the Dodgers wasn't averse to squabbling with umpires either. I think if you were a manager in New York, that was expected of you. He was Durocher's chief rival from 1951 to 1953, and their battles with each other and the umpires are legendary. We didn't like Dressen either because he was flamboyant and loudmouthed. He was considered a smart manager who knew everything that was going on, and he was known for telling his team when it was losing, "Hold 'em right there, I'll think of something." The Dodgers came within one playoff game of beating the Giants for the pennant in 1951, and they won pennants in '52 and '53, but I don't think Dressen was as good as Durocher. In 1951 he declared the Giants "dead," but his team blew a 13½-game lead down the stretch. He managed strangely in the postseason, and the Dodgers always fell short. In the ninth inning of the famous 1951 playoff game against the Giants, he should have moved first baseman Gil Hodges back to his regular position with a big lead, instead of having him hold on a runner who represented a meaningless run. Then Don Mueller's grounder, which barely eluded Hodges' glove, would have been a double-play ball, Bobby Thomson would never have come up to bat, and the Dodgers would have won the pennant. Dressen was a smart manager, but he bungled it. Nobody brought that up at the time.

My first two managers, Frankie Frisch and Billy Herman, were Hall of Fame players but, unlike Durocher, couldn't get their players to play with the same aggressive style. They were both pretty bad at communicating with players. Frisch was tough to play for because he was very vocal with his criticism. When he didn't like something we did, his favorite expression was: "Get the stomach pump out; I'm gonna puke!" (That line rivaled that of a Washington Senators manager who lined up his players and asked, "Does everyone on this team squat when they pee?") Frisch was never reluctant to express his feelings to players or umpires—in 1941, he was thrown out of a game for coming out on the field to protest bad conditions while carrying an umbrella. Frisch, "the Fordham Flash," was a bad manager on a bad team and was fired before the end of the season. Herman was another terrible manager who didn't last a year with our team. He didn't take what he did as a player, including the hit-and-run, and apply it to his managing, but most of the players on the '47 Pirates probably wouldn't have listened anyway.

Mel Ott was the manager of the Giants when they finished behind the Pirates in 1946. He was the individual Durocher was referring to when he said, "Nice guys finish last." Ott really was a nice guy, but he couldn't swing the bat for his players, and he got fired.

Rogers Hornsby was another Hall of Famer who had little success managing during that era in stints with the Browns under Bill Veeck and Reds under Gabe Paul. He was an unusual guy who would sit for hours in hotel lobbies. He went to the racetrack all the time before Judge Kenesaw Mountain Landis put a stop to that, but he'd still send someone to the track with his bets, even during games. As a manager with the Reds, he'd sign autographs while the game was going on. When the bus was scheduled to leave for the ballpark at about 4:00 for a night game, he'd tell the driver to leave 10 minutes early so it would leave behind players. You wonder why his players didn't like him very much. I got to know him years later when he was a hitting coach on the Mets, and he was very aloof, caustic, and sullen. I was one of the few people he liked.

The Phillies' Ben Chapman was the number one bench-jockey among managers. He really got on our team. He was very abusive and, unlike Durocher, wasn't averse to using racial slurs. He got on Jackie Robinson so viciously that the league had to rein him in.

Billy Southworth, who managed the Boston Braves to the '48 NL pennant, was a very nice, high-class guy. Unfortunately, he never got over his son getting killed when he crashed his bomber on a foggy day during World War II. Pitcher Johnny Sain, who made up a strong one-two punch with Warren Spahn, said the grieving Southworth drank heavily after his son died.

Eddie Dyer, the Cardinals' manager, was laid-back and a good guy. But Phil Cavarretta of the Cubs was another Jekyll-and-Hyde manager, who was a pleasant guy off the field and went nuts on it. He was the player-manager when I was traded to the Cubs in 1953. Phil became the only manager fired during spring training. Cubs owner Phil Wrigley asked him where he thought the team would finish in the standings in the coming year. Phil answered, "Last place," and was gone. Charlie Grimm was the Cubs manager when I broke in, and he then became the manager of the Braves. He was well liked—a funny, happy-go-lucky guy, almost a comedian. The traveling secretary of the Cubs would put on shows for the writers and the public, and they had a great song-and-dance act. You don't see managers like that anymore.

I didn't get to know many American League managers. I did meet Connie Mack, who managed the Philadelphia Athletics for 50 years, always in a suit. Hank Greenberg took me over and introduced me to him in spring training. He was quiet and dignified, ever the gentleman. The reason he wasn't fired in all those years as manager is that he also owned the team.

I did know Casey Stengel. In fact I knew him as a kid, when he lived in the L.A. area. I was playing ball and got introduced to him. He was always a nice guy and very smart. He put on an act for the media—he could actually be as rational as anyone else. Of course, he had tremendous success with the Yankees from 1949 to 1960, leading them to ten pennants and seven world championships. In terms of managing, probably his biggest impact was to reintroduce platooning. John McGraw was the first manager to platoon and, in fact, platooned Stengel. Casey picked up on the idea of alternating players who played the same position—like outfielders Gene Woodling and Hank Bauer—and having left-handed batters play against right-handed pitchers and right-handed batters go against southpaws. Platooning wasn't necessary in the thirties and the early days of baseball because there were so few left-handed batters or pitchers. (Those were the days in which they'd convert left-handed people to using their right hands.) McGraw platooned because of what he witnessed at the plate—in those days nobody kept stats about how well batters did against lefties and righties.

Even with the reintroduction of platooning, few other managers bothered to make lefty-righty switches at the plate or on the mound late in the game. Even Stengel went with the hot bat or pitcher rather than worrying about the percentages. Nobody had lefty relievers who would come in just to face the top left-handed batters on the opposing team in key situations, which almost all teams have today. And only a few teams had managers bring in the same pitcher game after game in late innings to protect a lead and close it out. Those were the days when starters tried to go the distance, when starters made relief appearances, and—at a time when there was no "save" stat—when star relievers were asked to pitch several innings. Middle relievers weren't specialists, but mop-up men.

Paul Richards, who managed the White Sox from 1951 to 1954 and the Orioles till 1961, was probably the most innovative manager at the time. He was known for figuring out ways to score runs in the absence of power. But because his teams always finished behind the Yankees and Indians, I never got to see him in action in a World Series. I do know he was credited with inventing the oversized mitt so his catchers could handle Hoyt Wilhelm's knuckler.

After I became a broadcaster, probably the first manager who had major impact in terms of strategy and philosophy was Gene Mauch. He began managing in the majors in 1960, five years after I retired as a player, but I'd watch him until he retired in 1987. Mauch had one pitcher who was so wild that he couldn't walk a batter intentionally without throwing it away. So Mauch tried to move an infielder behind the catcher. But they wouldn't allow it because the rules allow only one man to be in foul territory. Another time, the Mets' catcher Jerry Grote went into the Phillies' dugout to try to catch a foul ball and Mauch ran over and started chopping on his arms. Because of that incident, they put in the rule that you can't touch a fielder in the dugout.

Mauch's strategy was to score first early in the game. A lot of managers followed Mauch's lead because the first team that scores wins about 70 percent of the time. But the percentage is so high because after scoring one run they score more. Mauch would give up an out with an early sacrifice bunt to get that first run. I don't agree with that. You have to consider who the pitcher is and whether it's going to be a low-scoring game. It's more important to try to get two or three runs in the first inning than to settle for one, because a great pitcher will usually settle down as the game progresses and you will have given up your best opportunity to score a few runs against him. If you can't score more than one run if you bunt, then I don't think you should. The Dodgers of the early sixties were the only team that could get away with it. More than once Maury Wills walked, stole second, moved to third on a sacrifice bunt, and scored on a sacrifice fly; the Dodgers had the great pitchers to make a 1–0 lead stand up.

Other innovative managers came along, such as Sparky Anderson, who did a lot of juggling of his relievers in Cincinnati and Detroit to get desired matchups late in the game. He deservedly got the famous moniker "Captain Hook" and had such success pulling the strings that everybody wanted to know how Sparky did things. Tigers broadcaster Ernie Harwell's great line about him was, "He's written more books than he's ever read." Earl Weaver, Billy Martin, and Jim Leyland were other creative managers. The first time I saw a manager have his first baseman move with the runner off the base was when Leyland was the manager of the Pirates. Bobby Valentine would do that when he managed the Mets.

Tony LaRussa, Bobby Cox, Joe Torre, Dusty Baker, and Mike Scioscia are the current managers who do the best jobs in terms of strategy, because they also let their players play. Too many managers get in the way of their players. Now they present charts that say a batter gets 45 percent of his hits to right field and that kind of nonsense. To me it's a total waste of time. For instance, you don't need a scout or a computer to tell you that every guy who has ever batted in the major leagues has trouble hitting high inside fastballs and low outside curves. Before all the signs and charts and stats came into baseball, it came down to throwing high and up and then low and down. It still works. (I'm reminded of when the Reds' infamous owner Marge Schott wanted to get rid of all her scouts because "all they do is watch ballgames.")

Against the Pirates, NL managers of my day would tell their pitchers, "If the game is on the line, don't let Kiner beat you." It's the same today. When you go in to play the Giants, the manager will say, "Don't let Barry Bonds beat you." That's why he is walked intentionally so often. It isn't science; it's just a matter of common sense. So when computers are brought into play, I have to shake my head. As former Astros manager Larry Dierker said, they're overcomplicating the game to such a degree that it's impossible to play. Davey Johnson, who managed the Mets to a world title in 1986, was a computer wizard. Then he stopped using it. When he was asked why, he said, "Because I kept putting data into the computer and it kept saying, 'Fire the manager!'"

Today's worst managers do too much platooning, too many double switches, and too many righty-lefty matchups late in the game. All those things are so overplayed in baseball, and so many times the best players and pitchers are removed from the game at the wrong times. Managers follow the "book" so they can avoid criticism. If something goes wrong, they say they were going by the percentages, or in the playoffs they say they were doing what they did all year long—although the postseason should be managed differently. They are just copping out. The bad managers in the American League take chances as rarely as race car drivers turn right. No doubt they feel secure having a designated hitter (DH), because it eliminates a lot of decisive decision making involving removing pitchers. The best managers are the ones who aren't so predictable, who diverge from the book at times and trust their instincts—and trust their players. You can put in thousands of computerized facts, but it's like flipping a penny: it can come out heads 99 times in a row, but on the 100th try there is still only a 50-50 chance that it will come up heads again. You have to consider the players and the circumstances. You can't always play the percentages, even if it means you'll be second-guessed.

Too many current managers follow a set pattern: they allow the starter to go five to seven innings; they bring in set-up men who go back and forth to get left-handed and right-handed batters out; and then they call on the closer for the final inning. Even in the National League, where there should be more strategy because there is no DH, they remove pitchers anyway after they've thrown a prescribed number of pitches. They do this to avoid the difficult decision on whether to leave the pitcher in to pitch longer or to pinch hit for him. Back in 1962, Bo Belinsky, who got a lot of publicity after throwing the Angels' first no-hitter, was in Palm Springs, California, with the team at Gene Autry's hotel. At 1:00 A.M. one night, Belinsky was out drinking at the Racquet Club, when somebody asked him how he could drink so much and still have the steam to pitch the eighth and ninth innings. Belinsky replied, "Who says I have to go more than seven innings?" That story would have no punch line today, because starting pitchers on many teams rarely go more than seven frames. Managers now often give their starters a 100- to 110-pitch limit, so the pitchers pace themselves accordingly. I think pitch count doesn't make sense. A pitcher might lose something off the fastball after 100 pitches, but he can adjust or simply pace himself better, because it's ridiculous to take out a solid starter so early in the game and replace him with a middle reliever. What I don't like about this setup is that the middle reliever is often the worst pitcher on the ballclub.

In their championship years under Joe Torre, the Yankees always boasted one or two quality middle relievers, but most teams don't have the luxury of having good middlemen who can keep you in games rather than open the floodgates. The trouble with the worst pitcher isn't that he doesn't have good stuff; it's that he's usually wild and falls behind on counts. If he walks the first batter, that could lead to a big inning. Now all contenders try to acquire better, higher-priced middle relievers to set up the closer. Unlike in the old days, a manager will never think of bringing in another starting pitcher in relief unless it's the postseason.

The pitching in my era, when we had 16 teams, was outstanding. Teams went with four-man rotations, and the good teams had three or four excellent starters. (When I was there, Pittsburgh had only Murry Dickson, whose 20 wins with our last-place club in 1951 were some of the great accomplishments in baseball history.) Since teams have gone to five-man rotations, they have lost overall quality and made it much easier for hitters. I think the four-man rotation is better because you really weaken your pitching going with a fifth pitcher, especially after expansion when there aren't as many good starters available. Today, only the Yankees have been able to afford more than three veteran stars in their rotation at one time, although the Oakland A's have been able to put together a group of standout young starters through the draft. Few other teams go more than two or three deep, leaving two or three weak spots.

Everybody uses the five-man rotation now because they don't want pitchers to wear out their arms. The trainers and doctors have gotten into the game and said pitchers will be better if they get more rest. I don't buy that. If you look at the careers of old-timers who pitched on three days' rest, you'll see that they pitched for a remarkably long time and even relieved between starts. Leo Mazzone, who has coached Greg Maddux, Tom Glavine, John Smoltz, and a number of super pitchers in Atlanta, is one of the few pitching coaches today who advocates a lot of throwing. He believes it strengthens the arm—which I think was proved by many rubber-armed pitchers dating back to the 19th century. Not many pitchers who have been part of five-man rotations have pitched for as many years as the pitchers from the four-man-rotation years.

Babe Ruth and Lou Gehrig didn't face that many left-handed pitchers. Ted Williams and Stan Musial faced a few more, but still not that many. Now there is a much higher percentage of left-handed pitchers. In my time, there weren't enough left-handed batters for managers to need left-handed specialists. Now about half the batters in the majors are left-handed, so lefty starters and relievers are in demand. The left-handed reliever who is brought in late in the game to face Jason Giambi, Barry Bonds, Jim Thome, Todd Helton, Larry Walker, and other dangerous left-handed batters is a staple of contending teams.

An even bigger change is the advent of the lights-out closer. No team reaches the playoffs without a pitcher who can shut down the opponent in the ninth inning. Many closers couldn't be starters because they don't have enough pitches in their repertoire to make it through the order more than once. But for an inning they can throw the ball as hard as they can, mix in a splitter and slider, and set down the side. We had guys who could throw hard for a couple of innings, but managers didn't know what to do with them. The closer role would have been perfect for such pitchers. Usually a closer has hard stuff, although Trevor Hoffman and Keith Foulke have done well with a change-up as their best pitch.

We had flamethrowers in my era, but not as many as today. Now almost everyone throws faster than 90 mph. There are few finesse pitchers anymore.

That's because it's more necessary to strike out hitters today and not allow contact in key situations. Pitchers today have it difficult. They can't knock you down, and in today's game it's too dangerous to pitch outside, which was where they would always throw to us pull hitters in my day, wanting us to hit the ball to the large center fields or to the opposite field. But nobody wants to be a pull hitter anymore because it's now almost as easy to hit homers to center and the opposite field because of the lively ball and smaller parks. I hit three opposite-field homers in my entire career, but now .230 hitters do it routinely. One reason games have slowed down is because homers are so easy to hit that pitchers try to be more careful and throw more pitches. There is no place they can locate the ball and feel safe. This has changed the game. If you can't strike out batters, you may be in trouble.

Pitchers still use the same patterns. They still want to finish off batters with their out-pitches. The pitches themselves aren't much different today. When I came up to the majors almost every good pitcher had a fastball, a curve, and a change-up to use when behind in the count. All the guys on the Indians, Dodgers, and Yankees, who had the best staffs, had those pitches.

The pitchers with the best fastballs I saw were Bob Feller, Warren Spahn, Ewell Blackwell, Don Newcombe, Robin Roberts, and, briefly, Herb Score. They threw fast, and their balls moved in the strike zone or right above it. The Dodgers' Rex Barney threw faster than any of them, but his 100-mph fastball usually went straight down the middle of the plate or sailed high and outside. So he'd either give up hits or walk batters, and his record was mediocre, although he did have one no-hitter. New York sportswriter Bob Cook wrote: "If high and outside were a strike, he'd be in the Hall of Fame." Barney went to a psychiatrist to try to cure himself of his strange wildness, but it didn't work.

Eddie Mathews told me that the hardest pitch for him to hit was the sinker—a two-seam fastball that goes down. You will hear broadcasters say, "He homered off a sinker that didn't sink." But they will rarely hit a homer off a good sinker that goes down sharply. A sinker is a ground-ball pitch because you hit on top of it. To get underneath it, you have to be very good or lucky. It can be tougher to hit than a 98-mph fastball. Bob Lemon was perhaps the best sinkerball pitcher of my era. Orel Hershiser would dominate batters with that pitch years later. Curt Schilling is one of the few pitchers who can throw a sinker with almost the same velocity as a four-seam high fastball.

In the forties and fifties, the curve was a dominant pitch, and Feller was its top practitioner. Because American League umpires wore balloon protectors that made it difficult for them to bend over, the National League was the low-strike league and, thus, had more pitchers willing to throw curve-balls. Before Koufax, the Dodgers' Carl Erskine may have had the best curve in the National League. Harry Brecheen and Max Lanier also had great curves. So did Johnny Sain, who threw it about 95 percent of the time. He got away with it, but some pitchers threw the curve too often. Yogi Berra remembers some pregame meetings with the Yankees, when the manager and coaches would be telling a pitcher that a star on the opposing team had trouble hitting curveballs. Yogi would interrupt and say, "Well, he couldn't hit that other guy's curve, but I know he can hit this guy's curve." It all depended on who was pitching.

For a while we haven't seen many pitchers throw the 12-to-6 curves that Feller and Koufax mastered. Darryl Kile was one of the few who had an effective overhand curve, what we call a drop. But I think they are coming back, as Barry Zito, Roy Halladay, and Josh Beckett all have great curves. The reason for the comeback is that the strike zone has been enlarged to what it used to be, and pitchers now get the curve at the knees called strikes.

Dodgers lefty Johnny Podres, who won the classic seventh game of the 1955 World Series against the Yankees, had a great change of pace. Cardinals reliever Stu Miller, who was one of the only right-handers who was described as "crafty," had a change that was even harder to time. He threw the softest of anybody, but he had a great motion with the shoulder, and you'd think the pitch was coming at you at 90 mph and it would actually cross the plate going 55. He was amazing. Pedro Martinez, Keith Foulke, and Trevor Hoffman throw exceptional changes today. It's an effective pitch, especially when you're behind in the count and the batter is gearing up for the heater.

Many pitchers threw the forkball, the predecessor to the splitter. Relievers Joe Page and Elroy Face, who joined the Pirates during my last year with the team, had the most success with it. Face went an unbelievable 18–1 in relief in 1959. The split-fingered fastball, which Bruce Sutter popularized, is essentially a change-up because the ball is held back in the fingers and doesn't come toward the batter at full speed.

The Phillies' Jim Konstanty, whom I consider the first really great relief pitcher, threw "freak" pitches that may have been the forerunner of the splitter or a variation on the forkball. I couldn't figure out those pitches, and I actually asked people around the league what they were. The ones who ventured a guess said he threw a palm ball. It was a tantalizing pitch that had a lot of motion and changed speeds, and then the bottom just dropped out. He could get that ball over for strikes in 1950, when the "Whiz Kids" won the pennant and he was chosen the league's MVP. (As a starter he lost Game 1 of the World Series, 1–0, to the Yankees on a sacrifice fly by current San Diego Padres broadcaster Jerry Coleman.)

There were a few guys who threw screwballs. Harvey Haddix and Harry Brecheen threw good ones. There were a lot of knuckleballers. I couldn't hit any of them. As Charlie Lau would say, there are two theories on hitting the knuckler but, unfortunately, neither works. I tried everything in the world, including a 42-inch bat. Hoyt Wilhelm had one of the great knuckleballs of all time, which is why he's in the Hall of Fame. (Rick Ferrell deserves to be in the Hall of Fame simply because he caught four knuckleball pitchers on the Washington Senators.)

A lot of guys threw spitters in my era. Lew Burdette, Art Fowler, and ill-fated Dodgers reliever Hugh Casey (who committed suicide when his marriage broke up) threw ones that moved in all directions. Dodgers catcher Mickey Owen would take abuse the rest of his life because of a passed ball in the 1941 World Series that led to a Yankees victory, but it was a Casey spitball that got away. The Dodgers' Preacher Roe threw the best spitters I ever saw before Gaylord Perry surfaced in the sixties. Umpires would keep a close eye on Roe to see if he was loading up, but they couldn't detect anything. That's because his third baseman, Billy Cox, would be the one to doctor the ball.

Of course, no one admitted that they threw spitters until after their careers were over, if then. My original Mets broadcast partner Lindsey Nelson interviewed Schoolboy Rowe at the end of his career. Before they went on, Lindsey asked him what his out-pitch was. Rowe said he usually used a spitter. Then they went on the air and Lindsey asked the same question and added, "I know you threw a mean spitter." And Rowe said, "I never threw a spitter in my life."

The slider came into being in about 1947 or '48, although it wouldn't really be in vogue until the early fifties. It was the pitch you threw when you had to get a strike on a 2–0 or 3–1 count and wanted to throw a breaking ball instead of the predictable fastball. The slider had a smaller break than the curve and could be thrown with better control. It was a hard fastball that would slide over. Today the terminology has changed, and what we used to call a slider is now called a cut fastball. And what they're calling a slider today is actually a nickel curve, a curve that doesn't have a tight spin or go directly down.

Frankie Frisch just hated the slider. Once when he was managing the Cubs, three years after leaving the Pirates, he had former Pirate Bob Muncrief on the mound against us. I came up to the plate my first time up and hit a home run off a slider. When he got back to the dugout, Frisch asked Muncrief what he threw. Muncrief made the mistake of admitting it was a slider. Frisch threatened him, "If you throw that pitch again, I'll fine you $500." The next time up, I hit a fastball out of the ballpark. When Muncrief went back into the dugout he snapped at Frisch, "He hit your pitch farther than he hit mine."

59

The slider is a dangerous pitch when thrown badly. Ted Williams and Joe DiMaggio said it was the toughest pitch for them to hit, but they were talking about a hard one with a dime spin that moves very late and actually slides over parallel to the ground. The slider is a good name for it, but they've changed its name.

I didn't work off the fastball and adjust to the curve, as most batters do. I worked off the slider, which is the in-between pitch, and adjusted to the fastball or curve. Ted Williams was quoted one time saying he worked off the slider, too. In hitting you don't want to be on your front foot, you want to stay back because the longer you can wait for the ball to do something, the better chance you have. The great swings are usually short swings, where the batter waits longer for the movement on the ball before he commits himself.

In my era, we had to figure out hitting by ourselves because we had no coaches or instructors, other than the managers' friends. You learned on your own and from listening to and watching other great hitters—as well as studying pitchers. I was fortunate to have Hank Greenberg, one of the greatest hitters in history, as my mentor in my second season. He taught me that the keys to good hitting were concentration, selectivity, and making contact. The rest was up to me.

I wanted to get into the batter's box, find the position where I wanted to stand, and not move during the whole sequence of pitches. I don't know why batters want to get out of the batter's box to adjust their gloves or scratch their privates. It's like basketball players not wanting to stand in position for both free throws. Why walk away between shots and break your concentration? Ted Williams was the same way. He would keep his back foot where it was. You concentrate on the pitcher, you watch the movement of the ball, you stay in hitting position until the last possible moment, and then you swing. Also, it's important to pay attention to what the umpire is calling strikes and balls. Learning his strike zone is part of the batter's job. I knew umpires who gave the pitcher the benefit of the doubt and those who favored the batter.

Concentration and the ability to stay within your individual pattern of swinging is probably the key to being a great hitter. Most athletes in their individual sports are close to being the same, but what separates them is concentration and staying in that mode—don't get too nervous, don't change what got you there.

Greenberg told me that I must wait for pitches I could handle, even if it meant taking up to two strikes. You have to be patient and be willing to take walks. You can't hit the pitcher's pitch, including the high inside fastball and low outside curve. If you swing at those you make the pitcher happy. If you take those pitches, even if they are both strikes, the pitcher still has to throw another pitch, and that one could be a better pitch to hit or even the one you have waited for. That's basically the philosophy of good hitting: getting a pitch you want to hit by having the willpower to lay off the pitches the pitcher wants you to hit. I led the league in bases on balls. I wasn't upset by it. It's part of the game. At one time in history, walks were counted as hits, and that shouldn't have changed—especially intentional walks.

On-base percentage is very important but was neglected until recently, when the Yankees and the A's under GM Billy Beane began to emphasize its importance in helping teams win. Whole organizations preach it now, but during my time only the truly dedicated hitters understood it as a significant stat. You can't ignore the fact that players who walk score about 45 percent of the time.

Ted Williams, who had an extremely high on-base percentage, was famous for taking pitches in the strike zone if they weren't the types of pitches he was looking to hit. What types of pitches was he looking for? One year at Cooperstown, when Boston owner Tom Yawkey was inducted, Williams, Stan Musial, and I sat around talking about selectivity. Williams asked me if I ever guessed. I said, "I certainly did. I'd figure out what the pitcher was going to throw to me and looked for that pitch until he got two strikes on me. And then I'd become more defensive and look for anything." Then Williams asked the same question of Musial. He said, "No, I never guessed. I'd look for the ball and hit it. If I wanted to hit a ground ball, I'd hit the top of the ball; if I wanted to hit a line drive, I'd hit the middle of the ball; and if I wanted to hit a fly, I'd hit the bottom of the ball." We laughed because hitting is not that easy. But it was easier for Musial—at the end of the year, almost all the dents on his bat were by the label, while most other hitters had dents all over their bats.

Musial wouldn't look for particular pitches; he would protect an area of the plate. For years he was a spray hitter, hitting the outside pitch to left, the inside pitch to right, and down the middle to center. Later in his career he started pulling the ball because I was making more money than he was because I hit more homers. So he hit homers and got more money than I did.

Musial asked Williams if he guessed. Williams said, "I guess I guessed." Like me, Ted figured out what pitchers were throwing and waited. He was the best of what I'd call "controlled hitters"—he wouldn't swing at a ball that he wasn't looking for until he had to.

In being selective at the plate, the count is paramount. Williams was the best example of a batter who was willing to go to two strikes if the 3–0 or 3–1 pitches were not exactly what he wanted. The 3–1 count is better for hitting than 2–0 because there is a demand that the pitcher throw a strike. When he gets 3–0, he may go ahead and walk the batter intentionally. Good pitchers won't throw you a fastball on 2–0 when you're expecting it, but with 3–1 they are more likely to do so. Many times on TV you'll be told 2–0 is a hitter's count; it is, but it's not as strong as 3–1.

Most young hitters don't take the count into consideration. They will work a pitcher into a hitter's count and then, instead of being aggressive, hope to get ball 3 and ball 4 rather than a pitch to hit. That's a philosophy followed by a lot of current players, and it's not a good one. As Greenberg, who had 183 RBIs in 1937, stressed, *you* must drive in runs. That's really an intricate part of being a good team player—driving in the run by any means possible, especially when the runner is on third with fewer than two outs. I think RBIs are the most important thing in hitting, more important than any other stat including on-base percentage.

When young players try to work the count on a pitcher, they still might not understand that they are trying to get counts to be in a good hitting position more than a good walking position. A major reason they don't have high batting averages is that they don't swing on the counts when they get the best pitches to hit. It's not always difficult to figure out what's coming. Today they throw more fastballs on 2–0, but good pitchers usually won't give in to you. If you're a good hitter, they might not throw you a fastball on a 2–0 or 3–1, which are considered fastball counts. So you should be ready in case they try to cross you up with a breaking ball. The slider has become the 2–0 pitch of choice. However, just as it was in my day, if there is a runner on first who steals bases and the pitcher has a slow delivery, you can expect the catcher to call for fastballs.

Hitting 3–0 is nothing new. I hit 3–0 a lot. When you're hitting 3–0, if you don't get the one pitch you want and are looking for—a fastball in your wheelhouse—you have to take it even if it's a strike. It takes a lot of discipline to be a good hitter when you're at 3–0. Greenberg taught me that. It's the same with 3–1. If you have the discipline to hit 3–2, then if the pitch isn't exactly where you want it, you shouldn't swing. That's one of the most important things to hitting.

Like Williams, I wouldn't go the other way against the infielder shift that was invented for him by Indians manager Lou Boudreau. Boudreau also did it against me in an exhibition game, and other managers copied him. I was a right-handed pull hitter, so it was the reverse of the shift that he used against Williams. The reason for the shift was to make us go the other way and keep us from hitting homers. I got a lot of criticism for not hitting grounders through the large opening to the right of second base because I could have picked up a lot of singles. But I was paid to hit balls out of the park, not keep them in. Another reason I didn't do it was because I thought it would screw me up. It was totally foreign to me to hit the ball that way—

it's a different style of hitting. If I had tried to undo what Greenberg had taught me, I might have lost my home-run swing. The shift cost me base hits but not home runs. After I homered when the shift was on, Ernie Bonham would yell to the opposing managers, "You didn't play your infield high enough!"

Musial and Williams moved their hips when they swung, as do most hitters. However, Joe DiMaggio was motionless at the plate. Being motionless makes it very difficult to hit, but he had exceptional weight transfer and hand speed. When people ask me to name the greatest hitter I ever saw, I say DiMaggio. Why? He didn't strike out. The best way to evaluate players is to see how many homers they hit and how often they strike out. In 1941, DiMaggio struck out 13 times all year while hitting 30 homers. That's amazing for a power hitter. (In 1950, Yogi Berra hit 28 homers and struck out only 12 times, which was also amazing.) Today striking out is no big deal. It should be. Many players today average a strikeout a game. That's not acceptable unless you put up production numbers like Mickey Mantle and Reggie Jackson. Players refuse to cut down on their swings with two strikes because they want to homer. It's more important to put the ball in play. Dick Stuart claimed he was the most valuable player on his team. When it was pointed out that he struck out 170 times, he joked he did that so he wouldn't hit into double plays. He actually did it because he was hoping to match the 66 homers he had one season in the minors.

Once you put the ball in play anything can happen. You can get a base hit, or the ball can take a bad hop, or a fielder can make a bad throw. The Angels won in 2002 because they kept the ball in play. They had a lot of clutch two-strike hitters. That's what happened with the Mets in the tenth inning of Game 6 in the 1986 World Series. Down by two with two outs and no one on, they had three singles in a row by Gary Carter, Kevin Mitchell, and Ray Knight. Then, with two strikes, Mookie Wilson made contact and his grounder went through Bill Buckner's legs for the game winner, proving my point.

Putting the ball in play is essential. Young players should take note that Barry Bonds doesn't strike out much, which has led to his being one of the greatest hitters of all time. When I played, striking out was the worst thing that could happen to you at the plate. It was the most embarrassing in Ebbets Field because the roaming Dodgers Sym-phony Band would follow you back to the dugout with a drum pounding and a trombone and trumpet blaring—"the worms go in, the worms go out"—and when you sat down the cymbals would clash loudly. That would teach you to put the damn ball in play.

Today, with a crowded marketplace, every sport is trying to be more enjoyable to draw more people. I think baseball is succeeding. If I were going to invent baseball in order to draw fans, I would take the game today over the game of the past. The game has advanced by intention. The game I played was great but had become somewhat static. We played in black and white, and baseball was ready for color. Unfortunately, we couldn't have advanced too much because there were only 16 teams and 8 in each league, and television wasn't yet a factor. I think we went as far as we could go, and baseball needed new energy. It has found it in the years I have been a broadcaster. It's now a run-producing game with crowd-pleasing home runs and lots of hits. The action on the field is more interesting and entertaining because the players are more athletic and stronger. The fielding is more spectacular, more pitchers throw hard, and the greatest stars perform brilliantly despite the pressures, night after night. The game is also much more scientific than it was in my day, and fans are much more in tune with strategy. Everybody is an analyst—and that's a lot of fun.

Baseball has more appeal than ever, probably because the home run is still the most exciting play in baseball and we have more home-run hitters now than in any era in history. I still love watching baseball—and, despite their griping, so do Stan Musial and all the other old-timers I see each year at Cooperstown at the induction ceremony. And when we have one of those moments when we can't figure out how today's game relates to the game we once played, someone will remind us, "The pitcher still stands 60'6" from the batter, and there are still 27 outs and no time limit." And one of us will say, "That's right. The game hasn't really changed at all. It's just different."

Chapter **3**

From **Integration** to **Internationalization**

I signed with the Pittsburgh Pirates in 1940 after graduating from Alhambra High. My first training camp with the parent club took place the following spring in San Bernardino, which was almost like being at home. But then I was assigned to Albany and had to make my way to its camp in the tiny town of Barnwell, South Carolina, which was nothing like home. I bummed a ride for part of the way with a high school teammate who was driving to a minor league facility in Lake Charles, Louisiana. We drove for two or three hours at a time and then would get out of the car and play a lazy game of catch. Nothing much happened on our journey other than we gave a lift to a hitchhiker. We got to Louisiana and I took the train the rest of the way. When I finally reached South Carolina, I had two realizations: I couldn't understand the people because of their accents, and the hitchhiker had a contagious case of the measles. So there I was away from home for the first time, miserable with fever and red bumps all over my body, and unable to communicate with anybody. It wasn't a great introduction to life as a professional ballplayer.

I finally got out of my sickbed, joined my new team, and learned the ways of the Deep South. In those days, most people were unaware of the types of individuals who lived in other sections of the country because we never traveled and had no television to be our window to the world. Before I started to play pro ball, I had never even been east of New Mexico, and I was only there till I was four, which was when my father died and my mother moved us to California. All of a sudden I was playing and living with guys from the Midwest, East, and South. They had different views and attitudes, especially the Southerners who were biased against "colored" (which was the most common "acceptable" word used by players in those days) and ethnic people.

During that eye-opening spring, I played in ballparks in Southern towns in which African-American fans had to sit in their own sections of the bleachers. Everywhere, there were separate water fountains, bathrooms, and entrances for African Americans, and restaurants, hotels, and other places of business that prohibited them from entering at all. And years before Rosa Parks, it was the law that only whites could sit in the front of the bus. Schools were seg-regated, there was no dating between the races, and African Americans and whites did not play sports together. This was a whole new education for me.

At the time professional sports were segregated, with the exception of boxing. In baseball we had the major and minor leagues where white players—and the rare light-skinned Hispanics or Native Americans (such as Allie Reynolds)—played; and the National and American Negro Leagues, which had African Americans and some dark-skinned Hispanic players. As a youngster I figured African Americans wanted to have their own league, and it took a few years before I was aware that the Negro Leagues were formed because African Americans had been banned from the major leagues since the late 1800s. That made no sense to me because where I grew up, directly east of Los Angeles proper, there was no segregation. Although there weren't many African Americans in my area or in my schools, there were a few, and it was common for African Americans to play on mostly white teams. Nobody would say you couldn't play with an African-American person. It wasn't an issue.

In the thirties, the entire L.A. area was a hotbed for both hardball and soft-ball—for both sexes—and wherever I played, it was likely to be in a mixed game. Memorably, when I was about 13 or 14, I played a game or two of fast-pitch softball at Brookside Park in Pasadena against teams that included the most touted young African-American athlete around. His name was Jackie Robinson.

Jackie was in his late teens, and by that time I had read numerous articles about his achievements. In high school and then at Pasadena Junior College he was an unbelievable football player, great basketball player, and fantastic track star. He played baseball on occasion, as an infielder, but it was his worst sport! He received the most attention for his football exploits. Pasadena played its games at the Rose Bowl, and he'd make headlines by scoring four or five touchdowns every Saturday. So I knew who he was. Later Jackie went on to star in all four sports at UCLA, becoming an All-American in football and basketball and breaking his brother Mac's national long-jump record. Again, you didn't hear much about baseball. Interestingly, another football star on the Bruins was Kenny Washington. In 1946, Washington would be one of the four African Americans to integrate professional football, one year before Robinson would do the same in baseball.

I never played hardball against Robinson. But while in high school I played against many other African-American people. Did they impress me? Not par-ticularly. But what did I know? The ones I remember most were players from the Negro Leagues who would come out for the winter and play against white semipro teams from the area. They'd play in such venues as Wrigley Field and White Sox Park, near the Coliseum, and draw up to ten thousand fans, many coming from South Central L.A. It would be unusual not to have between one and five thousand people for Saturday and Sunday games at fields throughout the area. According to an account written by Wally Berger, who set a then–major league rookie record by hitting 38 homers for the Boston Braves in 1930, a 1934 game he played in between the barnstorming Dizzy Dean All-Stars and a Negro League team at Wrigley Field drew eighteen thousand fans. That is not surprising considering that Dean, the major leagues' best and most colorful pitcher, went up against his Negro Leagues counterpart, Leroy "Satchel" Paige, who was a living legend and at his peak.

I don't remember being aware of that particular game, but many of the players Berger mentioned, including Paige, were again in the lineup when my semipro team played a Negro League All-Star team at Wrigley Field five years later. I didn't know much about African-American baseball, but still I had heard of several players on the field that day. Biz Mackey was the first catcher I ever saw who threw from his knees, anticipating what Benito Santiago would do in the majors 45 years later. Goose Tatum played first base. Most people remember him as a remarkable basketball player and showman with the Harlem Globetrotters, but he also was a flashy baseball player. At short-stop they had Willie Wells, the future Hall of Famer. Their most imposing hitter was Mule Suttles, who was called the "Black Babe Ruth" even before Josh Gibson was. He was a Bunyanesque figure who stood 6'6", was a rock-solid 240 pounds, and swung a 50-ounce piece of lumber. The word was that he hit a ball in Cuba that traveled 600 feet, and I didn't doubt it.

At 17, I was the fresh-faced kid on a team with a few minor leaguers and many men who played ball only on weekends because they had to make a living. We had a few hitters with power, but I was the one who managed to homer off Paige! Wrigley Field was a bandbox and I got lucky—he struck me out the next time up—but it was a such a thrill because everyone knew about Satchel Paige, the slim and sly pitcher who took delight in throwing beebees anywhere he wanted. Of the pitchers, the great Paige was the leading man, but I also batted against Chet Brewer and "Bullet" Joe Rogan, who had a helluva fastball.

The crowd, as it was for most games, was mixed. We had no African-American players and they had no white players, so probably the white fans rooted for us and the African-American fans rooted for them, but it was friendly and everyone mingled. Honestly, I don't remember who won, but I can say without equivocation that the African-American players were much more entertaining than we were. Before the game, they played pepper and were fast and loose with their hands, like the Globetrotters during "Sweet Georgia Brown." You couldn't take your eyes off them. Fans loved coming to see them, and such games were a good way for them to pick up some extra money and exposure. (Paige toured for years with and without All-Star teams in the United States, Mexico, Central and South America, and the Caribbean, sometimes pitching 30 days in succession and 200 games per year. It's estimated that 10 million people saw him pitch—that's a lot of tickets for someone who got a slice of the gate.)

How good were the players on Paige's team? I had never seen a major league game, so at the time I wasn't qualified to judge if any could have succeeded in the majors if organized ball had no "color line." But once African-American players started having success in the majors in the late forties, I realized that some of the stars I played against in Wrigley Field could have made it.

It was hard for any outsider to evaluate African-American stars for several reasons. Their clowning around—one team was even called the Clowns—made it hard to fully appreciate their skills or exciting style of play. Because the Negro Leagues scheduled far fewer than 154 games during a season, their statistics—which were incomplete and often seemed to be guess-work—defied comparison with the records of major leaguers. Moreover, the Negro Leagues were so disorganized that it was hard to keep track of teams, much less the players, from one year to the next. That most of the owners of Negro League teams were involved with the numbers racket or other unsavory practices also cast a shadow on the game and its players.

Finally, there were too few games played between African-American and white professional teams for anyone to resolve whether they belonged on the same field. Curiosity about the quality of Negro Leagues players was aroused in the midthirties when it was reported that Paige's All-Stars more than held their own against Dizzy Dean's All-Stars in a barnstorming series. After Paige outdueled Dean 1–0 in a 13-inning contest at Hollywood Park—which Bill Veeck said was the best game he ever saw—Dean shook his weary head and said, "You're a better pitcher than I ever hope to be, Satch." He told reporters, "My fastball looks like a change of pace alongside that pistol bullet old Satch shoots up to the plate. If Satch and I were pitching on the same team, we'd clinch the pennant by the Fourth of July and go fishing until World Series time." This prompted the far-from-humble Paige to tell the scribes, "That Diz is about as smart a fellow as I ever looked around for."

There was even more speculation that African Americans were better than anyone thought in 1946, when a new edition of Paige's All-Stars played a hotly contested, sold-out, 14-game series against Bob Feller's All-Stars, and it was reported in many places that Paige and Feller broke even when they went head-to-head. Feller, however, still insists he won many more games than Paige and has the box scores to prove it. After the tour, Feller told *The Sporting News* that he didn't think any Negro Leagues player other than Paige—if he were younger—could make the majors. He made a point of adding, "Not even Jackie Robinson." Feller labeled Robinson, "Good field, no hit." So here was the rare major leaguer who played against African-American players, and even he underestimated them.

I was on Feller's All-Stars after the 1947 season, when they played several more games with the Paige All-Stars. Because they were exhibition games, I didn't keep track of which pitcher or which team got more victories. But I do know that while Feller wanted to beat Paige badly, overall the African-American players wanted to win more than we did because they were trying to make a big impression on anyone who doubted they were as good as white major leaguers.

By that time Jackie Robinson had proved himself in the big leagues by having an outstanding rookie season, but the other Negro Leagues veterans who had debuted, including Larry Doby on the Indians, had rough sailing. So the jury was still out on whether African Americans in general would succeed in the majors. I admit I didn't disagree with Feller as much as I should have. I believed that the Negro Leagues had some other talented players who possibly could play in the major leagues, but I didn't see many other than Robinson retaining their star status. I thought most would turn out to be of minor league caliber. That's how we thought of Japanese players for decades, until we opened the doors to them and found out they really could play.

I think integration of baseball would have been much more difficult before World War II than after. The war changed things. African-American people, including Jackie Robinson and world heavyweight boxing champion Joe Louis—the rare African-American man who was idolized by many whites in America—enlisted in the service to do their patriotic duty. African-American troops courageously went to battle with white soldiers to fight a mutual enemy. At home and abroad, African-American and white servicemen played music and various sports together. Color didn't matter. Soldiers returned to civilian life with the belief that the equality that was experienced in the service should carry over into all aspects of American life, including its pastime. Resistance to the idea that African-American men should play in the majors was no longer nearly universal among white Americans.

When Phillies owner Bill Cox was kicked out of baseball for gambling in the early forties, Bill Veeck, the owner of the minor league Milwaukee Brewers, attempted to purchase the team. He said he wanted to stock the Phillies with Negro Leagues players, which may be why the deal never went through. Some baseball historians claim that Veeck was just bluffing, but he always said he was serious about shaking up the status quo for the betterment of the game and the country itself. Baseball wasn't ready to embrace such a radical idea, and probably America wasn't either, but certainly the ahead-of-his-time, one-legged maverick served notice that big changes weren't that far away.

Meanwhile, the National Association for the Advancement of Colored People (NAACP) and the country's African-American newspapers put increasing pressure on the major leagues to address the race issue. To deflect criticism, owners had to display a pretense of compliance. With deceit that bordered on genius, several teams, including the Pirates, held much-publicized tryouts for Negro Leagues stars, without having any intention of signing them. The most famous phony audition was given by the Red Sox after Isadore Muchnick, a powerful member of the city council, threatened to introduce a bill to ban Sunday baseball in the city unless Boston signed an African-American player. So to appease him, the Sox, in consultation with African-American sportswriter Wendell Smith of the *Pittsburgh Courier*, held a tryout in April 1945 for Jackie Robinson of the Kansas City Monarchs, Marvin Williams of the Philadelphia Stars, and Sam Jethroe of the Cleveland Buckeyes. It is not clear if anyone in the Red Sox front office actually showed up for the charade. Afterward all three players were given "application forms," but they never heard anything more from the club. Rather than the Red Sox being the first team to integrate, they would be the last, in 1959. They even spurned the opportunity to sign a rising young star of the Birmingham Brown Barons—so Ted Williams didn't get to play alongside Willie Mays.

Soon after that sorry episode, Smith was talking to Dodgers owner Branch Rickey about Rickey's stated desire to recruit African-American players for the Brooklyn Brown Dodgers of a new African-American league he was creating. The league was a ruse conceived by Rickey to keep secret his plan to integrate the Brooklyn Dodgers. Rickey was looking for an individual of character and talent to break the color line, so he asked Smith if any of the three players who tried out in Boston were ready for the major leagues. Smith suggested Jackie Robinson. So Rickey set his sights on Robinson, even having him followed to make sure he had the right stuff to handle being the majors' first African-American player of the 20th century. Satisfied, Rickey made the monumental decision to sign him to a contract with the Dodgers' Triple A team, the Montreal Royals. That was the beginning of the "Great Experiment."

When Robinson signed, I didn't have a major reaction. I'm sure I was aware it was a big deal, but I didn't think in political or sociological terms then and never put it into proper focus. Most players were that way. Perhaps I should have thought about it at least in regard to my own career because if the major leagues opened its doors to Robinson and other Negro Leagues players, that meant there would be even more competition for jobs. But I had been in the minors in 1941, 1942, and part of 1943, and my feeling was that I was becoming good enough to make the majors no matter what the competition. If I couldn't make the grade, I'd just go back to California and find another way to make a living.

As Rickey surmised, Montreal was the perfect home city for Robinson because African-American and white people mixed there, even intermarried. However, Jackie endured hostile treatment from bigoted fans on the road, particularly in Syracuse and Baltimore, and experienced head-hunting pitchers, spikes-raised sliders, and vicious hecklers on opposing teams. That he was able to struggle through the season while turning the other cheek—as Rickey asked him to do for the first two years—and still lead the International League in hitting indicated that he was prepared to take the next giant step.

The first time I ever played hardball against Jackie Robinson was when the Pirates met the Dodgers in Atlanta during the exhibition season in 1947. By that time everyone expected Robinson was going to be with the parent club when it arrived in Brooklyn to begin the season, so he was drawing tremendous crowds in the South. That day there were about twenty-five thousand strong to watch him, which was a record at Ponce de Leon Ballpark. There was only a small section of seats set aside for the African Americans, so the overflow had to sit on an embankment behind the outfield fence. Obviously baseball was changing much faster than the South was. I had experienced culture shock when I first arrived there in 1941, but I knew it had to be almost intolerable for an African-American man from California to deal with the antiquated customs. It must have been particularly appalling to Robinson, who had barely escaped a court-martial at his base in Texas during the war for defying Jim Crow statutes.

When it was announced that the Dodgers had purchased Robinson's contract just prior to the 1947 season, I was too busy worrying about improving on my own rookie season to think much about him. I knew what was happening was historic and inevitable, but I didn't know what more to make of it. I wasn't sure if Robinson would turn out to be a good major league player—I still thought of him more as a star in other sports—and even if he did, I couldn't picture a parade of other Negro Leaguers marching into the majors on his heels.

It's a ticklish point, but the general view of white players in professional baseball after the war, primarily in the major leagues, was that African-American players weren't as good as they turned out to be. We didn't talk about it among ourselves, but I think most of us didn't believe they were equal to us as players or that so many would become superstars. There was a myth that they were primarily entertainers and that if they played for all the marbles, they wouldn't be nearly as competitive as we were. That was really a mistaken impression. I can't fathom why I didn't equate talent with being competitive.

On April 15, 1947, Jackie Robinson made history when he played in his first major league game against the Boston Braves at Ebbets Field. Looking back, he must have seemed an odd choice to integrate the major leagues because he was far from being the best player in the Negro Leagues. I don't think anyone in that league or ours had any idea that when put to the test he had the ability to become such a tremendous all-around player. He proved Feller wrong by being an excellent hitter as well as fielder, and no one ever ran the bases better. In fact, it struck me that Robinson was the greatest athlete ever to play baseball, including Jim Thorpe. Even more important, no one would ever be a better competitor. A fire raged inside him constantly, and that was so clear to everyone that it wasn't necessary for him to say that famous line, "Above anything else, I hate to lose." He was that special on the diamond. Additionally, he was well educated and very intellectual and, having been commissioned a second lieutenant in the army, would become a leader on and off the field.

Perhaps another outstanding Negro Leagues player could have assumed the role of first African American in the majors. One immediately thinks of Larry Doby, who broke the color barrier in the American League with Cleveland only two months after Robinson did and endured much of the same treatment. But consider that the first player in the eye of the storm was burdened with the knowledge that if he didn't succeed as a rookie, the integration of the majors by Negro Leagues players would likely be aborted. Doby would become an All-Star, but he had a very rocky rookie season, as did pitcher Dan Bankhead of the Dodgers and second baseman Hank Thompson of the St. Louis Browns. Of the four African-American men who played in the majors in 1947, only Robinson excelled. So unquestionably, he was the best choice for the risky historic role, and nobody has ever said different. What Jackie Robinson did changed more than sports, it changed society as a whole. It was a major step in the integration of America that had to happen, so I wasn't surprised by its impact or that Robinson justifiably became a hero and symbol of social change.

Robinson had a terribly difficult season, although he hit over .300 and was voted the National League's first ever Rookie of the Year. The entire citizenry of the borough of Brooklyn rallied around him, but before the season some Dodgers, led by Dixie Walker of Georgia ("the People's Cherce"), circulated a petition stating they would not play with an African-American teammate. The Dodgers' tough-as-nails manager Leo Durocher stood by Robinson, telling his players, "I don't care if the guy is yellow or black or if he has stripes like a f***** zebra. I'm the manager of this team and I say he plays." He quelled the rebellion, yet tension remained until the malcontents were traded during and after the season (mostly to the Pirates). What eventually won over most of the players is that Robinson proved to be the team's best player and was leading them to a National League pennant—and that meant more money in their pockets.

Robinson couldn't stay at many of the same hotels or eat at all the same restaurants as his teammates while the Dodgers were on the road. At times he went off by himself to an African-American hotel or stayed in private homes of prominent African-American citizens. I didn't know a lot of what he endured until long after I'd retired, but I read about the hotels. It didn't shock me so much because it reminded me of my own minor league experience when we'd stay at boarding houses and eat at the table with the families who owned them. It wasn't prejudice in my case, just a lack of money. But Robinson had to be frustrated. When you're young you never think of the future, just the present.

Throughout the year, Robinson received hate mail and was harassed by fans everywhere he played. Fans in Cincinnati threatened to kill both him and his chief supporter on the team, shortstop Pee Wee Reese—the classy Dodger captain's response was to demonstratively put a supportive arm around Robinson's shoulders while out on the infield. Opposing teams let fly with every racial epithet imaginable, and numerous pitches came close to Robinson's skull. To keep him out of harm's way, he was moved from second to first base, an unfamiliar position, yet that didn't prevent a number of baserunners from stepping on his heel or running their spiked shoes up his leg as they ran past the bag. Robinson was not the kind of guy who normally turned the other cheek, and I'm sure he did it with reservations, but by following Branch Rickey's edict, he showed how intelligent he was.

Some teams didn't want to play against Robinson and were vocal in their protests. As I found out years later, the St. Louis Cardinals were forced to play because National League President Ford Frick threatened to ban for life those players who refused to take the field. I'm sure that woke them up. Still, Robinson was spiked a few times by Cardinals players. One spiking by Enos Slaughter at first base was particularly vicious. Slaughter would always deny it was racially motivated, and in his defense, he was so mean and aggressive that he might have spiked anybody. He didn't spike Robinson again, but I'm sure Robinson remained a prime target of his very loud, obnoxious heckling.

In Philadelphia, it was the manager, Ben Chapman, who led the heckling against Robinson. Jackie was called names and told to go back to the jungles or cotton fields, and it got so ugly during a three-game series that he seriously considered taking a bat and charging into the Phillies' dugout, and to hell with his career. Chapman, who also was said to be a vocal anti-Semite, evidently went so far over the line in his attacks on Robinson that the league ordered him to make a public apology. The following year, he was fired and never managed in the big leagues again.

Robinson had some problems when he came to Pittsburgh, too. I'm sure the hecklers in the stands gave him trouble. Pittsburgh was really tough on players, even worse than Philadelphia was. On Opening Day in 1946, they booed our best player, Bob Elliott, who was converting from the outfield to third base, when he booted a ball in infield practice! I'm sure there were also hecklers in our dugout because it was the custom to get on the other teams' players by pointing out their weak points. There were guys who harassed Robinson—particularly the Southerners (maybe even the same players the Dodgers traded to us)—but I'm sure he was treated far worse by some of the other teams because there weren't any incidents that stand out years later.

His first game in Pittsburgh in May drew a small crowd. This wasn't surprising in that his momentous first game in the majors drew only about twenty-six thousand fans, even though it was at Ebbets Field. Attendance for the Dodgers at home and on the road would increase dramatically as the year progressed and Robinson turned into a bigger story than anticipated. No vote was taken by our players about whether to play or not. We considered it just another game. In fact, I can't remember there being much publicity surrounding the game or extra media presence, other than Wendell Smith, Sam Lacy, and the other members of the African-American press who followed Robinson during his rookie season. I met Smith, who was a very nice man, and we talked baseball but not about Robinson. He didn't want to stir up any controversy because there was enough of that already.

I also introduced myself to Robinson before the game. I told him I'd grown up in Alhambra and had played softball against him. He didn't know me from a hole in the ground and didn't say much. That was his way, unfortunately. Regrettably, we didn't talk much during our careers, other than occasional hellos on the bases and some minor interplay when we were both on the National League All-Star team in 1949. However, we would have conversations years later, and I got to like Jackie—what struck me most about him was his true sense of decency and honesty. When he started out in the majors he was more concerned with being treated with respect than making friends, which is a reason esteemed sportswriter Jimmy Cannon contended, "Jackie Robinson is the loneliest man I have ever seen in sports." At the time, he kept his distance from me, but he was appreciative when Hank Greenberg talked to him under different circumstances.

What happened was they collided on a play at first base. Later, when they were together at first, Greenberg made sure Robinson hadn't been hurt. Knowing Robinson had been the lightning rod for wretched behavior from opposing players, Hank made a point of giving him words of encouragement. I watched them closely as they spoke quietly and later learned Hank told him, "I know what you're going through. I went through it as a Jewish ballplayer. Just hang in there and you're going to be all right." Afterward Jackie said that Hank was the first opposing player to offer support and acknowledged it meant a great deal to him. Hank even asked him out to dinner in that conversation. Robinson turned him down because he didn't want Hank to be put on the spot, but they remained friends.

To digress: Hank understood what Robinson was going through because before there were African Americans in baseball, Jews were the players who were most singled out for slurs and hate mail. The Yankees went so far as to bring up farmhands for the specific purpose of shouting anti-Semitic insults at the Tigers' great Jewish hitter during games. Prejudice didn't occur only on the ballfield, as Greenberg learned in the America of the thirties and forties. At Hank's memorial service in 1986, his dear friend actor Walter Matthau recalled the time Hank and some fellow soldiers were seated in a nightclub during the war. A loud patron who had had one too many drinks stood up and shouted threateningly: "Anybody here named Ginsberg, Rosenberg, or Goldberg?" No one moved. Finally, after a dramatic pause, Henry Louis Greenberg, all 6'4" and 220 pounds of him, arose from his chair. "I'm Greenberg," he said. "Will I do?" The man's sneer disappeared when he looked at his prospective opponent, and as he slumped into his chair he said softly, "No. I'm looking for a Ginsberg, Rosenberg, or Goldberg." Hank Greenberg faced prejudice head-on and never backed down, which is what he knew Robinson was doing in 1947. (Sid Gordon was another Jewish friend Robinson had—they were together after the season on a barnstorming tour organized by Dodgers coach Charley Dressen. Similarly, Larry Doby, who was spurned by several Indians teammates upon his arrival, was befriended by the Indians' Jewish rookie third baseman, Al Rosen, and their shortstop-manager, Lou Boudreau, whose mother was Jewish.)

Robinson was a topic of conversation among players throughout his first year. Some guys predicted he wouldn't make it and others said he'd do just fine—the same as it was with any new player. The veterans would say, "He has a lot to learn," as they did with all rookies. We would mostly talk about his running, because he was truly dazzling on the bases, like nobody else in the majors. He was the first of the many Negro Leaguers who would bring an exciting run-through-the-base style of baseball to the National League, making it much more aggressive than the station-to-station American League. He stole a lot of bases for that era, including home (19 times during his career). Even when he didn't take off he'd unnerve the pitcher just by dancing around on the base paths, eyeing the next base like some starved animal waiting for campers to look away from the food they are cooking. From his track days, he had an explosive first step and a big finish. Undoubtedly, he was the most intimidating and disruptive runner in the game. Joe Garagiola, who caught for the Cardinals, recalls that prior to playing the Dodgers the whole team discussed different strategies for when Robinson was on first, second, or third base. But they didn't do a very good job, did they? There's nothing you can do to foil someone with that talent.

By the end of his rookie year, Robinson was established as a bona fide major leaguer. He had survived his baptism by fire and fulfilled his part of the bargain with Rickey to keep his views to himself and be passive to even the most virulent abuse. In his second year, his personality changed. Robinson started to be Robinson. He was more outspoken, expressing strong feelings and ideas, and more than willing to fight back. I wouldn't say he was more defiant—he was just more human, getting mad when anyone would get mad. If he was knocked down, he no longer dusted himself off and smiled. More likely, he yelled at the pitcher and then bunted and tried to spike the pitcher when he covered first, which was a common practice then. With his new attitude, Robinson became an even better player. He would bat above .300 five more times—including a league-leading .342 in his MVP 1949 season—and lead the Dodgers to four more pennants before retiring after the 1956 season.

It's no coincidence that Larry Doby also improved after the pressure-packed 1947 season in which he went along with Indians owner Bill Veeck's order to ignore racial taunts and even bad calls from umpires. Now he was free to just play baseball. Doby would win two home-run titles, drive in more than 100 runs five times, appear in six consecutive All-Star Games (the same as Robinson), and be a major force on Cleveland teams that won the World Series in 1948 and 111 games and the American League pennant in 1954. Eventually he'd join Robinson in the Hall of Fame.

The second African-American American Leaguer, Hank Thompson, didn't play in 1948, but he resurfaced with the National League's New York Giants in 1949—at the same time they made the significant move of bringing in Negro League star Monte Irvin. Thompson became a footnote in history as the only player to be the first African American on two different teams. Thompson would play eight years for the Giants as an outfielder-infielder. Although not nearly as talented as Irvin, he was a very tough, solid player. His only drawbacks were his difficulties off the field. He spent some time in jail and had a drinking problem that shortened his career. Dan Bankhead, the National League's second African-American player and the majors' first African-American pitcher, was the only one of the four African Americans who debuted in '47 who didn't eventually have success. He was easy to hit—I homered the first time I faced him—which is why he didn't stick around too long. I believe Rickey brought up Bankhead just so Robinson would have a roommate.

Once Robinson proved African Americans could play in the majors and, if Dodgers, be taken to heart by all of Brooklyn, Rickey apparently came up with a plan to bring up one star African-American player each year. Realizing African Americans in other organizations were flaming out because they couldn't deal with playing in the South, he placed his players on teams well above the Mason-Dixon Line. Following Robinson, Roy Campanella came up to the Dodgers in 1948 and was an instant star and crowd favorite. When

Robinson was scowling, Campy was smiling because he loved baseball and didn't worry about politics.

Campanella was a great hitter and outstanding catcher. I still remember how tricky he was behind the plate. He'd always be chatting to try to distract me and I'd hear him pounding his mitt low and outside to get me to think they would pitch me low and away. So I'd lean over the plate and the pitch would come in high and inside. He was a starting catcher when he was just 16 with the Baltimore Elite Giants in the Negro Leagues, so he had accumulated a lot of experience, savvy, and ability as he matured. He called a great game and did a tremendous job of handling Brooklyn's great pitching staff. Those guys completely trusted him. For years, other major league baseball teams wouldn't consider African-American players who were receivers because they didn't consider them smart enough to handle the position. Campanella, who would be a three-time NL MVP and Hall of Famer, was visible proof that they were wrong, but they remained blinded by their prejudice. There were a lot of catchers in the majors who routinely called lousy games—but not Campanella.

Don Newcombe came up to the Dodgers in 1949. He claims to this day that he would have been there earlier than even Robinson if he had been willing to turn the other cheek. In the minors, he didn't refrain from throwing at white players who harassed him when they came up to the plate, and that scared off Rickey. He was a big, tough, angry right-hander who could throw a ball through a brick wall and had no problem knocking you on your ass. He wanted you to know he was in charge, and you weren't likely to tell him otherwise. The first time I faced him, I knew he was going to be good. He quickly became the ace of an outstanding staff, and he and Campanella constituted the most formidable battery in the big leagues. He had 17 victories and was 1949's NL Rookie of the Year, and he, Robinson, and Campanella—and Larry Doby in the American League—became the first African Americans to play in an All-Star Game, which was a big deal. Although it didn't get nearly as much attention—or any attention at all back then—when Newcombe pitched to the Giants' Hank Thompson, it marked the first time an African-American pitcher ever faced an African-American hitter in the major leagues.

Newcombe would lose a couple of prime years to the service, but he'd still have three 20-win seasons. In 1956, he followed a 20–5 campaign by going 27–7 and became the first pitcher to win the Cy Young and MVP Awards in the same season. Despite some hard-luck losses in big games, Newcombe was the only truly great African-American pitcher in the major leagues until Bob Gibson in the sixties. So when I recently looked in a baseball record book, I couldn't believe he wasn't in Cooperstown. I made sure to put his name down when I filled out my ballot in the 2003 election, when Hall of Famers voted for the first time.

The African-American player who was next in line to join the Dodgers was Sam Jethroe, who had been one of the three players at that infamous Red Sox tryout. After he had several sensational years in the Negro Leagues, Rickey signed him and sent him to Montreal, as he had done with Robinson. After banging out more than 200 hits and scoring an out-of-this-world 154 runs, he was primed to play in Brooklyn. But the Dodgers had Duke Snider ensconced in center; and Rickey suddenly was preoccupied by a front-office power struggle that resulted in Walter O'Malley's taking control of the team and the handsomely paid-off Rickey moving on to take over, unfortunately, the operation of the Pirates. Because the Dodgers no longer had plans for Jethroe, he signed with the Boston Braves, becoming their first African-American player and getting the chance to be a pioneer after all. In 1950, the slap-hitting, switch-hitting "Jet" led the league in steals and earned Rookie of the Year honors. But after one excellent and one mediocre season, his brief major league career came to a mysterious halt. As Jethroe looked for a job in the minors, the Braves brought up Billy Bruton, who also was African American, stole a lot of bases, batted leadoff, and played center field (a bit more skillfully than his predecessor).

Even with Rickey out of the picture, the Dodgers continued to snap up Negro Leagues players and send them to their minor league affiliates. In 1950, they signed pitcher Joe Black and utility infielder Junior Gilliam, who would turn out to be NL Rookies of the Year in 1952 and 1953, respectively. One of the many quiet African-American players of the era who never acknowledged they were playing an important role, Gilliam would be an invaluable Dodger well into the sixties. Black's star burned out quickly. In 1952 he became the first standout reliever among African-American pitchers (along with Paige, who was having an outstanding year in the Browns bullpen). He won 15 games and saved 15 more, and then became the first African-American pitcher to win a World Series game, which he did as a starter in Game 1 versus the Yankees. When I faced him that year, I thought he was untouchable. Joe was a very intelligent guy—he would later become the vice-president of Greyhound—and had great wit. At the end of the season, he bought whiskey for the beat writers who covered the Dodgers. He passed out a bottle of Scotch to each one and thanked them for writing nice things about him. They looked at the label and saw that it was called "Black and White" scotch. That had a touch of irony. He wanted to remind them that he was an African-American man breaking into the white man's world.

Branch Rickey must be acclaimed for breaking the color barrier. But there is controversy over whether he did it for ethical or economical reasons. Don Newcombe always has insisted that Rickey did it from the heart. Jackie Robinson obviously believed that, too. If I didn't get to know Rickey so well,

I would agree. I wasn't privy to what Rickey was thinking when he owned the Dodgers, but after he came to the Pirates and I had years of personal dealings with him, I could say that he wouldn't do anything for purely altruistic reasons. In all his deals as our general manager he got money on the side. He was a brilliant man and did well for himself. He probably had a moral commitment to integrate baseball, but I think that he did it before anyone else primarily because he was under the impression that African-American players would attract many African-American fans to major league games—which, unfortunately, never proved true. He didn't even bother giving financial compensation to the Negro League teams he raided for players.

I think it's telling that when Rickey came to the Pirates in 1950, he was in no hurry to bring in any African-American players to integrate or upgrade our team. Nobody ever mentions this when assessing baseball's "Great Emancipator." I never had an African-American teammate until I was traded to Chicago. The first African-American Pirate, a little round guy named Curt Roberts, wasn't called up until 1954, which was already Rickey's fourth year with the team and by which time most other clubs had African-American players on their rosters. Rickey's only possible defense is a sorry one: he might have been too penurious to pay a star African-American player.

I had more faith in Bill Veeck, who had become the owner of the Cleveland Indians in 1946. He was always on the side of the underdog and the downtrodden, so I believe his contributions to desegregating baseball were based on his personal convictions rather than economic concerns. He was antiestablishment—he had a hard time getting into the Hall of Fame because of that—and relished being the rebel in the baseball arena, taking comfort that he was on high moral ground. He and his new farm director, Hank Greenberg, my former teammate and great friend, were truly the odd couple. Hank was very straitlaced and wanted to play by the rules. But Veeck enjoyed making a mockery of some rules, as when he plotted to put an outfield fence on rollers and move it in and out depending on which team was at the plate. Even more memorable was when, as the owner of the St. Louis Browns in 1951, he had newly signed midget Eddie Gaedel and his tiny bat jump out of a cake and make a beeline to the plate to pinch hit against the Tigers—the greatest promotional stunt in baseball history. He claimed he didn't want to break the rules but "to test their elasticity." Veeck and Greenberg balanced each other out and made a great combination. They were both adamant about integration and signed a number of talented African-American players. Unlike Rickey, Veeck gave Negro Leagues teams compensation.

Abe Saperstein, who owned the Chicago American Giants as well as the Harlem Globetrotters, supposedly convinced Bill Veeck to sign Satchel Paige during the 1948 season. I'm sure Veeck didn't need much persuading because even though Paige was at least 42, making him the oldest rookie ever, he still could pitch and draw huge crowds—which is exactly what he did. The American League's first African-American pitcher won six of seven decisions and had an impressive 2.48 ERA in helping the Indians win the pennant, and then he became the first African-American pitcher in a World Series. Nobody in the majors had ever seen a pitcher with so many quirky windups and such a mystifying array of high fastballs, crackling sliders, screwballs, sinkers, bloopers, and change-ups. He even named a few of his favorite pitches: the bee ball, jump ball, trouble ball, two-hump blooper, and Long Tom. AL President Will Harridge actually dreamed up a new rule to outlaw his "hesitation pitch."

Paige would be released after Veeck sold the team in 1949, but Veeck would sign him again in 1951, when he was the owner of the Browns. And when Veeck ran the Miami Marlins of the International League in the mid-fifties, they were reunited once more. Paige swore he finally learned how to throw a hard curveball at the age of 54! Paige would pitch for years after that, explaining philosophically, "Age is a question of mind over matter—if you don't mind, it don't matter."

Luke Easter was already in his midthirties when Veeck brought him to Cleveland in 1949. Unlike the other pioneers, he came not from the Negro Leagues but from the San Diego Padres of the Pacific Coast League. In the spring, I had taken a look at him at Greenberg's request, and he was hitting balls well out of the huge park down there. I was thinking, that's not bad for someone who had played only softball until three years before. Greenberg signed him after he had become a local hero by going on a tape-measure home-run spree. At 6'4" and 240 pounds, he had prodigious power from the left side, like an early version of Willie McCovey, and hit the longest drive in the history of Municipal Stadium. After his release from the Indians in 1954, he would continue to boom mammoth home runs for Charleston, Buffalo, and Toronto for almost another decade, as his legend grew.

Cuban Minnie Minoso was a colorful black Hispanic player, whom Veeck signed out of the Negro Leagues. He had been given a phony tryout by the Cardinals in 1947, and after that he was wary of major league teams that professed interest in him. But he trusted Veeck. He became Veeck's favorite player, and wherever Veeck went, he tried to acquire Minoso. Veeck loved sitting in the stands with the fans and watching him play. He was a flamboyant offensive player who smoked the ball and could run the bases—he led the league three times each in steals and triples—and he had a flair in the outfield. He also set the record for being hit by pitches, which verified that his style wasn't appreciated by the opposition. Minoso was another tough competitor who, according to a teammate, would be so distraught

That's me, at age two or three, and again at age four. These are both at my childhood home in Santa Rita, New Mexico, shortly before my mother moved us to California. I wouldn't wind up traveling east of New Mexico until I reported to my first Pirates farm club in South Carolina.

A fresh-faced 18-year-old in the Pirates farm system. A few years—and a lot of home runs—later, I'm loading some lumber into my Cadillac convertible. Inset photo courtesy of the National Baseball Hall of Fame.

With Hank Greenberg (left) in 1947, the year he came over to Pittsburgh and helped turn me into one of the game's best power hitters. Photo courtesy of AP/Wide World Photos.

Here I'm clowning around with Bing Crosby, a minority owner of the Pirates who eventually became a close friend and neighbor.

Congratulations are in order in 1947, as two Cardinals and three Pirates combined for nine home runs in one game. From left are St. Louis' Whitey Kurowski (two home runs); Pittsburgh's Hank Greenberg (two); me (two); Billy Cox (two); and the Cardinals' Terry Moore (one). Photo courtesy of AP/Wide World Photos.

Posing with one of the most accomplished players the game has ever seen, and a real character to boot: the great Honus Wagner.

Partly because of my friendship with Bing Crosby and partly because of my own relatively modest celebrity status, I was lucky enough to meet some of the big stars of the day. Here I'm escorting 17-year-old Elizabeth Taylor to a movie premiere. Photo courtesy of AP/Wide World Photos.

Truly one of the highlights of my career: tying up the 1950 All-Star Game with a ninth-inning home run at Comiskey Park in Chicago. That's Stan Musial congratulating me at home plate. Photo courtesy of AP/Wide World Photos.

Again at the 1950 All-Star Game in Chicago, talking shop with probably the greatest hitter of all time: Ted Williams. I was honored when Ted included me on his own list of the 20 best hitters of all time. Photo courtesy of AP/Wide World Photos.

I met Janet Leigh at the ballpark while she was filming Angels in the Outfield *in 1951, and we dated for about three weeks.*

My wedding to tennis star Nancy Chaffee, with dear friend and best man Hank Greenberg. Photo courtesy of AP/Wide World Photos.

after going 0-for-4 that he'd climb into the shower with his uniform on to wash away bad spirits.

When Minoso was dealt to the White Sox in 1951, he became their first black player and the first black major leaguer in the Second City. It was there that he blossomed into a star and became as popular on Chicago's south side as Ernie Banks would be on the north side with the Cubs. (Though Minoso wasn't a dominant player, many baseball fans think he deserves Hall of Fame consideration because of his many All-Star selections and impressive statistics, especially when his Negro Leagues career is factored in.)

After Veeck's departure, Greenberg became general manager of the Indians and continued to sign African-American players. A rookie in 1950, Sam Jones would become the period's best African-American starting pitcher other than Newcombe. The right hander was called, alternately, "Red," "Sad Sam," and "Toothpick," because he always had one in his mouth while he pitched. He had really good stuff, including a hard round-house curve that made right-handed batters bail out, yet he won 20 games only once and barely had a winning record (102–101). Perhaps his trouble was that he rarely played with a team more than two consecutive years. He pretty much personified the term "journeyman," in that he played with six teams (one team twice) in his 12 major league seasons. In fact, in November 1954 I was traded by the Cubs to the Indians for Jones, another player, and $60,000. The next year he would lose 20 games but would no-hit my other former team, Pittsburgh. He was almost taken out in the ninth inning because he walked the first three batters in the close game. But then he came back and struck out the side for one of the most dramatic endings in baseball history. Harry Creighton was doing live beer commercials during the game, and I think that must have really distracted him because after Jones got the last out, Harry ran down to the field and put the mike under Jones and asked as his first question, "Sam, how's the family?"

One star of the Negro Leagues got away from both Rickey (who tried to sign him in 1946, but couldn't get him out of his contract) and Veeck (who turned him down in 1947 as part of a package with Larry Doby rather than pay an extra $1,000). Monte Irvin ended up signing with the New York Giants in 1949. Already 30, he admitted he was past his prime, when he had hit over .400 three times in the Negro National League. Still he had a number of good years with the Giants to solidify his Hall of Fame credentials. He was an outstanding hitter who drove in a lot of runs. And he was a very high-class individual who was a clubhouse leader on Leo Durocher's pennant-winning team in 1951 and the world champion team in '54. I have been told that he was pretty much the older brother to a lot of African-American players who came to the majors and couldn't connect with Robinson. I'm sure he was a good influence on Willie Mays.

Baseball players have a grapevine, word gets around somehow, and we all heard about a phenom from the Negro Leagues who was hitting close to .500 at Minneapolis. I had heard he was amazing, and I was looking forward to seeing him play. However, when Willie Mays came up to the Giants he couldn't buy a hit. His confidence waned, but Durocher, who protected him like he was an orphaned cub, refused to take him out of the lineup and continued to encourage him. Finally Willie homered off Warren Spahn, and from then on he started wowing everyone. You can tell if a guy is different right away, and that's how it was with Mays, even in batting practice. He crushed the ball and it sounded different coming off his bat. Everything he did at the plate, in the field, and on the base paths was electric. It was always like he was on center stage, and he wouldn't have had it any other way.

I didn't think of Mays as a pioneer because there had been African Americans on the Giants before him. He certainly had impact, but it was mostly on his team, as it came from far behind the Dodgers in mid-August to win the National League pennant in that memorable playoff. Mays also drew fans, but it was because he was such an exciting talent, not because he was African American. Jackie Robinson's impact was far more global in that he changed both sports and society. As Mays himself acknowledged, he was a product of those groundbreaking African Americans who came before him and made it possible for him to even have a career in the majors. "Every time I look at my pocketbook," he would say later, "I see Jackie Robinson." He added, "And don't forget Larry Doby."

An incredible talent and a good guy, Mays was at the forefront of the second phase of talented African-American players who were entering the majors after the locked doors had already been opened. Those players included future Hall of Famers Ernie Banks, Hank Aaron (Mays' lone equal and eventually the last major leaguer who had been in the Negro Leagues), Roberto Clemente (the first Hispanic superstar), and Frank Robinson. The Puerto Rican Clemente spent much time as the only black and only Spanish-speaking player on the Pirates, but of these remarkable players, only Banks should be considered a pioneer because he, along with Gene Baker, broke the color barrier on a major league team.

I was traded to the Chicago Cubs in 1953, the same year that Banks, who played shortstop then, and Baker, a second baseman, were rookies. They were the first blacks I played with in the major leagues. I wasn't there when they broke in with the team, but I was told that Banks came up in training camp and promptly got hit right in the head by his new teammate Don Elston, who threw hard. I don't know if it was intentional. Banks didn't seem to have trouble adjusting to playing with white teammates and dealing with life in the big leagues, but I wouldn't know because he didn't talk very much at all. I'm not sure he even recognized his pioneer role because he never opened up about such things. Banks was a good hitter, even at the beginning of his career, and I liked watching him. He would lightly rap his fingers on the bat and look like he was playing the flute. Although he looked too thin to generate much power, he was known for his quick wrists and would eventually slam 511 homers. I should (modestly) mention that he has publicly stated that I helped him with his hitting when we were teammates.

The National League was quicker to bring in African-American players than the American League. Every team was integrated by 1954, except for the Phillies, who added an African-American player in 1957. The American League was taking its sweet time and losing out on the best African-American players. The New York Yankees received much criticism in the press for taking so much longer than the other two New York teams. In 1953 and 1954, everyone expected them to bring up Vic Power, a promising Puerto Rican prospect who had two tremendous minor league seasons at Kansas City. Power would later complain, "They were waiting for my skin to change color, but I knew it wasn't going to happen." He would become as good a first baseman as any who ever played, but the Yankees got rid of him, partly because he was the original "hot dog" and caught the ball with one hand, and partly because they didn't like that he charged white pitchers who threw at him, openly dated white women, and was outspoken. So Power was traded to the Athletics and became the first Puerto Rican to play in the American League and first, ahead of Clemente, to play in an All-Star Game. The Yankees continued to wait for "the right black."

In 1955, my final year in the big leagues, catcher Elston Howard, who had been Power's make-no-waves roommate at Kansas City, made history as the first African-American New York Yankee. This was eight years after the Dodgers and six years after the Giants had their first African-American players. In those days, almost all the African Americans who teams signed were fast, so when Yankees manager Casey Stengel heard that Howard was coming to New York, he indelicately remarked, "They finally got me a Negro, and he can't run." Howard wasn't fast, but he would be a huge contributor to the Yankees, even capturing an AL MVP Award in 1963.

In the American League, integration wasn't complete until the Tigers brought up Ozzie Virgil in 1958 and the Red Sox brought up Pumpsie Green in 1959. Green's historic moment came 12 years after Jackie Robinson joined the Dodgers and a year before the long-sputtering Negro Leagues, depleted of its best players, shut down for good—a sad but necessary casualty of social progress. Before the likable infielder was signed out of the Pacific Coast League, reporters asked Boston owner Tom Yawkey the reason he was taking so long to integrate his ballclub. His answer was, "I'm not prejudiced against blacks. I have hundreds of them working on my plantation in South Carolina."

Elsewhere I have written about the tremendous camaraderie there was on major league teams during the decade after World War II. Integration caused some friction on some teams to be sure—including that between African Americans and light-skinned Hispanics—but for the most part, the bond among the 25 members of a team remained strong. In truth, even while ballplayers in those days were close, they rarely spoke of personal problems to each other. So the fact that African-American players didn't open up to whites about what they were going through wasn't surprising, especially because so many of them—including Mays, Aaron (who became increasingly outspoken after he retired as a player), Banks, Campanella, Gilliam, and Howard—avoided talking about anything controversial, and some of the black Hispanic players didn't speak much English.

In my last year in baseball, Al Rosen and I would go out with Larry Doby in Chicago and New York. He seemed like a laid-back individual who enjoyed being on his own and not at all angry about anything he had experienced. We didn't know that he harbored resentment toward white players who hadn't made an effort to befriend him when he broke into the majors. Or that he felt that he was still the victim of prejudice in and out of baseball. We didn't know these things until years later. We were aware that Doby and other African-American players were still forbidden from staying in the same hotels as their white teammates in towns like Washington, Baltimore, St. Louis, and Kansas City, and that Jim Crow laws continued to be observed in Florida, where many teams had spring training. But I think most of us who had African-American teammates assumed they didn't have many problems in the years after Robinson and Doby broke the color barrier. Roberto Clemente and Frank Robinson seemed to walk around with chips on their shoulders, but even they didn't voice displeasure about discrimination.

Only years later did some African-American players contend that in the fifties they were still experiencing many of the indignities that Robinson and Doby had back in 1947. They thought white players would think they were complaining if they brought up anything negative, so they said nothing. We didn't know that African-American players believed that if they weren't good enough to be starters, they'd be cut rather than given an opportunity to beat out white players for the spots on the bench. Likewise, we weren't aware that there was resentment over the fact that few African-American pitchers were brought to the majors and those that were weren't considered smart enough to call their own games. Years after he became the American League's first top-notch African-American starting pitcher, Mudcat Grant (who was no militant when he played for me in San Diego before joining

Cleveland in 1958), confessed this was his main gripe with baseball in the fifties.

Significantly, African-American players said nothing to us of their bitterness toward the baseball establishment for not protesting that they had to stay in African-American hotels, private homes, and even funeral parlors. Finally in the early sixties, outspoken African-American stars on the St. Louis Cardinals—Bill White, Bob Gibson, Curt Flood, and Lou Brock—took on a pioneer role when they demanded that they be given the same accommodations as the team's white players during spring training. The Cardinals management gave in, and soon other teams followed suit. Hotels had no choice but to comply, or they lost a great deal of revenue. This was a major step in breaking down barriers between white and African-American players and achieving the equality among all players that was Jackie Robinson's goal when he put himself on the line.

⚾ ⚾ ⚾

In 1997, to mark the 50th anniversary of Jackie Robinson's breaking the major leagues' color barrier, Major League Baseball honored him by retiring his No. 42 on every team. Baseball today is still a reflection of his remarkable legacy—although a shocking number of current players don't know who he is, including the African-American stars who are the most indebted to him. By the time of his death in 1972, most of his major objectives were on the way to fruition. Today players assume that their teammates will be of all races and nationalities, and neither skin color nor language separates them. On the field and in the clubhouses, prejudice has been replaced by player harmony. All players are, in regard to race, treated the same by fans, management, and the baseball establishment.

To understand how far the fans have come in accepting African-American players since the late forties, consider that back then only African Americans laid claim to Roy Campanella, although he was half Italian. Now the Yankees' handsome and vastly talented shortstop Derek Jeter, whose father is African American and mother is white, is probably the game's most popular player among all fans and is surely the number one heartthrob of female fans of all races. And as the Yankees' captain and leader, he is a unifying force among all his teammates. Incidentally, Jeter, a student of baseball history, acknowledges his deep admiration for not only Jackie Robinson but also his wife, Rachel Robinson.

At the time Jackie Robinson retired after the 1956 season and left baseball, I don't know what he thought in terms of African-American people continuing to work on the management side of the game after they stopped playing. When I retired a year earlier, with the full integration of 16 teams still four years off, I realized that an increasing number of African Americans would play major league baseball as time passed and the game would continue to improve. But integration was still a new concept and most of the African-American men who broke through were still playing, so I never even considered what would happen if African-American players who retired wanted to remain in the game. As it turned out, breaking the color line as players was only the first struggle for African Americans (and other minorities) in baseball.

Frank Robinson didn't become the first African-American manager until Cleveland gave him the opportunity in 1975—a major event for African Americans in sports. Two years later Robinson also became the first African-American manager fired, but he would serve his second tour of duty as a major league manager with the Giants in the early eighties. Otherwise, African Americans were routinely passed over for managerial positions. Major league owners denied race was a factor, but in a truly embarrassing moment on national television in 1987, the Dodgers' longtime executive Al Campanis let it slip to *Nightline* host Ted Koppel that the feeling in baseball was that African-American people didn't have "some of the necessities to be, let's say a field manager or perhaps a general manager." Koppel kept trying to get him off the hook, but it kept getting worse. I don't know if Campanis was on medication, because all of a sudden he was saying African Americans can't swim and all of that.

It was strange because I'd known Campanis for years and knew he wasn't a prejudiced man. He had even roomed with Jackie Robinson. What he said caused a furor, akin to what would happen to politician Trent Lott years later, and Campanis was fired. I was surprised Dodgers owner Peter O'Malley (Walter's son) didn't stick up for him, because the success of the Dodgers had a lot to do with Campanis' bringing in African-American players when he was the right-hand man in Brooklyn. There is so much exposure if you're on television, and anything you say can be held against you. I think that before you go on the air, they ought to read you your rights.

Today, because of the success of Don Baylor, Dusty Baker, Frank Robinson, and Felipe Alou, a Dominican, minority managers are becoming more common. However, there continues to be controversy over whether some candidates without managerial experience are bypassed for whites with similar credentials. The same holds true for front-office positions. Bob Watson had the distinction of being the first African-American general manager in Major League Baseball, when he took that position with the Houston Astros in 1993. He later spent a few years as the Yankees' GM before working as Commissioner Bud Selig's vice president of field operations (the man who levies fines and suspensions). Because

Major League Baseball has been under attack for its minority hiring practices, when the commissioner's office took over the financially troubled Montreal Expos in 2002, Selig assigned the GM position to Omar Minaya, who became the first Hispanic to hold such a position. (Frank Robinson became the manager.)

Arturo Moreno became baseball's first Hispanic owner when he purchased the Anaheim Angels in 2003, leading many to think that an African-American owner can't be too far away—though I'd think nobody with a sound mind would want to get into that kind of situation in today's climate. I don't know how quickly there will be progress in regard to managerial and front-office positions, because there aren't many talented people in the business making the decisions. Now it's a corporate game run by outsiders who don't know baseball. So it's very hard for anyone, including members of minorities, to work their way up through the ranks.

But largely unnoticed is an even bigger minority crisis on the field. I was surprised to read recently in the *New York Post* that on Opening Day in 2003, there were only 79 African Americans of the 750 players on the 30 teams. The 10.5 percentage of American-born blacks ranked as the second lowest percentage since 1968, after 2002's 10 percent. According to the article, which was headlined, "Losing the Race: Decline in Black Players Presents a Major Problem," seven teams had only one African-American player, seven teams had but two, six had three, and ten teams had four, the most. The 2002 ALCS had only two African Americans on the field: Derek Jeter of the Yankees and Garret Anderson of the Angels. In the article, South Carolina–born Willie Randolph, a former All-Star who is now the Yankees' bench coach, lamented, "It's almost like a dying breed."

The decline in the number of African-American players is seen as a result of the influx of Latin-American and other foreign players into the majors; young African Americans gravitating toward other sports, particularly basketball and football; and the lack of facilities and youth baseball programs in urban areas. That all makes sense, but there is a worrisome set of statistics that seems to show that most people in Major League Baseball are indifferent to losing African-American players. Consider that the percentage of whites in the majors today (about 60 percent) is down less than 10 percent compared to what it was 10 years ago. Meanwhile, Latin-American players are at an all-time high of 28 percent, which is more than a 50 percent gain over the previous 10 years. Clearly, Latin-American players have displaced mostly African-American players.

From those figures, one might jump to the conclusion that Major League Baseball is trying to phase out African-American players. But the fact is that many of the Latin-American players who are picking up jobs are themselves black—the reason the general public may not have noticed a decline in the number of African-American players. What is happening is really about economics, as is everything else in baseball today. The owners are always looking for ways to save money, and signing Latin-American players is a way to do just that.

This is how it works. Players from the United States and Canada are subject to the amateur draft—the higher a player is drafted, the more the club will have to pay. But south of the border, all players are free agents. Therefore, teams can sign a hungry 16-year-old who already can field like Omar Vizquel and may learn to hit like Miguel Tejada for as little as $500. Many of these kids don't go to school and have to work for a living, so they are eager to sign for almost nothing. The object for scouts is to sign as many players as possible for as little money as possible and then assign the kids to their clubs' baseball academies. Only about three in a hundred will make it to the big leagues, but it's worth the small investment. This adheres to the old Branch Rickey theory when he built huge farm systems for the Cardinals and the Dodgers.

What is going on with Latin-American prospects reminds me of the old days when scouts tried to sign as many young players as they could. Of course, the richer teams, like the Yankees, could afford to sign the most players. Then they'd tell you to travel at your own expense to a team's camp, and when you got there, they'd inform you and all the other young men trying out that they didn't have to pay your salary until the season started—*if* you made the club. If the player developed, fine, he'd be paid; but if he got released, he'd hitchhike home without a cent in his pocket. So owners have a history of exploiting hopeful players.

Willie Randolph suggested that even as teams pursue Latin-American players, they "would do well to tap into the rich talent base in the inner cities." As he pointed out, a lot of potential major leaguers are not even seen today because scouts are fearful of going to the inner city to watch them play. So is there a solution? Randolph said that if teams can establish academies outside America, then they should be able to do it here as well. A voice of sympathy in the commissioner's office, Jimmie Lee Solomon, suggested that academies be placed in all major league cities. He now is trying to get a baseball academy that will serve inner-city Los Angeles. I think it's a good idea. But the problem with that is that these players will be subject to the draft and the best will cost a lot of money to sign, so unless a player is too good to resist, owners will still prefer the less-expensive Latin-American players. Obviously, in addition to the plan for academies, foreign players should be made part of the main amateur or a supplemental draft and be paid accordingly.

Since 1960, baseball has expanded from 16 to 30 teams—during a stretch of time in which football, basketball, and other sports have competed successfully for the American athletes baseball used to have to itself. Baseball could still find players, mostly white, on college teams, but otherwise it saw its talent pool dwindling. Consequently, the major leagues have had to combat dilution by finding new sources of talent. Baseball was saved once owners started scanning the globe for players. If today you removed foreigners from major league rosters, the caliber of baseball would drop precipitously. Instead, the new talent base continues to help the game improve. The downside? As long as baseball can continue to mine the world for its future stars, it needn't pay attention to the decline in African-American players reaching the majors. Integration has given way to internationalization.

Kids in America have so many other things to do, and they have money, so they aren't compelled to do the hard work necessary to develop into baseball players. If they don't have money, they play basketball. They think that has a better chance of helping them escape the ghetto than baseball does. But there are kids elsewhere who play baseball as much as I did. One can expect more major leaguers to come out of the Dominican Republic, Puerto Rico, and other Caribbean islands, as well as Mexico, Venezuela, Korea, Japan, and even Australia. Eventually, perhaps, baseball will recruit from China and Europe. And it's likely that a few more Cuban ballplayers will defect, find political asylum in America, and ply their trade with the Yankees or some other team.

During the fifties, before Castro came to power, Cuba was a major source of talent for the major leagues, particularly the Washington Senators. Minnie Minoso, who starred for the Indians and White Sox, was the biggest star to come from Cuba prior to Tony Oliva (who debuted for the Twins in the early sixties), but he reached the majors via the Negro Leagues. The Senators had a scout named Joe Cambria who, beginning in the late forties, signed light-skinned Cuban players directly for their farm system, offering them about $350 a month. They picked up a few excellent pitchers, including Connie Marrero, Pedro Ramos, and Camilo Pascual, who had a devastating curve and would become a 20-game winner. The Pirates also had a scout who went into all the Spanish-speaking countries in search of talent. He was a pretty well-known guy named Howie Haak, and he spoke Spanish. Branch Rickey used him in Brooklyn.

The Dodgers preceded the Yankees in making ties to other Latin-American countries. They were already scouting in Mexico when I became the general manager of the San Diego Padres after my retirement as a player. I was also trying to find Mexican players for the Padres in order to draw fans from the border towns of Mexico. We did sign one Mexican star, and I had visions of the entire Mexican population coming through our turnstiles. I wondered where I could seat them all. But he never did anything and no Mexican fans showed up at all. Nobody tapped into the Mexican market after that, but then suddenly in 1981, the Dodgers got a big boost in attendance when Fernando Valenzuela, who was born in Navajoa, Mexico, had a sensational rookie season. He had a bizarre left-handed delivery, an unhittable screwball, and a lot of charisma. By that time, it wasn't necessary to try to convince those baseball fans living in Mexico to migrate up north to see the games because the Mexican population had exploded in the Los Angeles area. Valenzuela attracted Mexican Americans and other immigrants from Latin America to games in Los Angeles.

Similarly, when Japanese import Hideo Nomo had a terrific rookie season with the Dodgers in 1995—displaying an equally weird windup and an unhittable split-fingered fastball—he drew so many Asians to the park that vendors started hawking sushi.

Nomo was the first player to make the jump to the majors directly from a top-level Japanese professional team. But there had been one Japanese player who had played in the majors earlier. Masanori Murakami had been a relief pitcher for the San Francisco Giants in 1964 and 1965, before he was pressured into returning to Japan. He was just an average pitcher who was more of a curiosity than a legitimate media item. I think the Giants wanted to find out if he would attract a lot of the city's Asian population to the ballpark. He wasn't a good enough player to do that.

Ichiro Suzuki has been able to attract thousands of Asian fans to games in Seattle since he broke into the majors in 2001, and was the American League's Rookie of the Year and MVP. I'm reminded that I once turned down going on tour in Japan, and I regret it. At the time, Japanese players were thought of in the same way African Americans had been, which was that nobody thought they had the ability to play in the majors. Maybe people think nobody can do anything as well as they can. We were told two players had major league talent—Sadaharu Oh, who hit a world-record 868 homers, and his Yomiuri Giants teammate Shigeo Nagashima—but not any of the others. I'm sure they were wrong. As we can see now, there are outstanding Japanese players. Suzuki has been as great a player here as he was in Japan. He has opened a lot of eyes.

I am sure American teams will continue to court Japanese players, which is great for the players over there because Japanese teams are now paying more to hold on to them. (The Japanese teams limit the number of American players they can have on their rosters, so Americans won't be going over to compensate for the star players they lose to us.) It will be interesting to watch the development of Hideki Matsui of the Yankees, who was an All-Star and a solid RBI man in 2003, his rookie season. He was known as "Godzilla" when he starred for the Yomiuri Giants and was considered by many to be the best Japanese player after Suzuki, who is a hit machine, exceptionally fast, and a Gold Glove outfielder with an amazing arm. Will Matsui hit 40 homers in the majors as well? We haven't seen a power hitter come out of Japan yet, but we have seen American players who have struggled in the majors, like Tuffy Rhodes (whose major league highlight was hitting three homers off of Doc Gooden), go to Japan and hit more than 50 homers. (Tuffy could have broken the season record over there, but they wouldn't pitch to him at the end of the year.) So Matsui has joined Suzuki and the long list of pioneers in the major leagues who must prove themselves under pressure.

The major leagues now have African-American and Hispanic managers, and I think they are even ready for a Japanese manager. Everything is dependent on what you get back. If a Japanese manager would come over here and attract Japanese fans to come to the ballpark, then they'd hire him in a second. The bottom line today is making money, and it overrides any social statements.

It's interesting to consider that in 1947 there would have been no serious talk about a Japanese manager in the major leagues. In fact, it would have been impossible for a Japanese player to break into the major leagues then because of the hangover from Pearl Harbor and the war itself. In the late forties, Japanese Americans Wat Misaka and Wally Yonamine played with the New York Knicks and San Francisco 49ers, respectively, but in baseball the resentment would have been too strong, especially if the player was from Japan. I'm sure even bigoted Americans of the time would have preferred seeing a black American play in the major leagues to seeing a Japanese player.

Now it's a moot point. African Americans and Japanese ballplayers playing together in major league ballparks is not unusual anymore. Since I first arrived in Barnwell, South Carolina, with a lousy case of measles and a lot of ignorance about America, professional baseball sure has come a long way.

Chapter **4**

Labor **Unrest**

When I arrived in Pittsburgh for the first time, it was pitch black. That would have been just fine if it weren't 10:00 in the morning. Coming from sunny California, I found the darkness that was caused by the pollution from the coal to be downright eerie. If that wasn't depressing enough, I then saw the vast dimensions of Forbes Field and wondered if I would ever hit a home run there.

My rookie year was a difficult period of adjustment. I lived in a blue-collar eastern city that was much different from where I'd grown up, my teammates were hardened veterans, and at times I felt I was out of my league trying to play in the majors. With all that on my mind, the last thing I needed was to step into a political firestorm in the Pirates clubhouse.

When the war ended and the soldiers returned to civilian jobs, there was heightened union activity throughout the country, including organizing and strikes for better wages and working conditions. Robert F. Murphy, an attorney and labor organizer from Boston, came into the picture and wanted to organize professional baseball players. Contending they were among the most exploited and oppressed employees in the nation, Murphy registered the American Baseball Guild in Massachusetts as a labor organization. If ratified by the players and recognized by the owners, it would become the first union in baseball since the Fraternity of Professional Baseball Players of America was formed in 1912. Murphy chose the name of his operation carefully, avoiding the word *union* because many people associated it with communism. *Guild* was acceptable because it was used in the movie industry and elsewhere.

Murphy stated that the intention of the Guild was to get a "square deal" for players. That would include a minimum salary, a fair contract (which, I assume, would be based on performance and time in the big leagues), a substantial amount of money if traded, and 50 percent of the money received by the team if sold. That he didn't ask for an end to the reserve clause, which bound players to the organizations that first signed them, was a calculated decision. He hoped to make Major League Baseball less fearful of the Guild than it was of the new Mexican League that, also in 1946, was trying to coax major leaguers to cross the border for much higher salaries.

Murphy knew that three decades earlier Major League Baseball's National Commission had recognized the Fraternity of Professional Ballplayers of America—and scared owners doubled salaries—only because it was one way to prevent a new competitor, the Federal League, from stealing away all its star players. Murphy believed Commissioner Happy Chandler and the owners would quickly recognize the Guild as a way to strengthen ties with players and make sure they stayed put. At the same time, he probably wanted the Mexican League to succeed, to provide competitive bidding and push up salary offers made to major leaguers.

The Mexican League was the brainchild of Jorge Pasquel and his less flamboyant brother Alfonso. They wanted their new league to be on the level of the major leagues and figured the quickest way to do that was to put major leaguers on the field. So they offered major leaguers substantial sums to sign. (I didn't receive an offer during the off-season because I wasn't a major leaguer yet.) Stan Musial, the National League's best player, was making less than $15,000, and the Pasquels tried to get him to come to the Mexican League by offering him a guaranteed long-term contract for much more. Surely when he found several signed checks worth $10,000 each on his bed, he was tempted to head south, but he stayed put in St. Louis.

His Cardinals teammate Max Lanier did jump for a considerable amount. Other players who left for more money included Danny Gardella, Sal Maglie, Vern Stephens, and Mickey Owen. More might have gone, but they didn't trust that they would really get money. The majority didn't go because they felt loyalty to the major leagues and their teams. Or perhaps they were secure with what they had—even though they made little money, it was more than the salary of the average working man. Some who might have been tempted to test the waters of the Rio Grande backed away when those players who had left returned quickly from the floundering league and found themselves blacklisted.

Chandler stated that all players who had walked out on their contracts would be banned for five years from the major leagues. (After Gardella took baseball to court, Chandler relented and let players come back ahead of schedule.) At the time, Chandler and the owners made it seem like the Pasquels and the major leaguers who accepted their money were committing a criminal act. All I knew was that my new team got its name in the 1890s because they "pirated" players from other teams—they had been the Innocents!

While the baseball establishment worried about the Mexican League, Murphy began his work. He needed a test team to organize, and when each club came into Boston to play the Braves or Red Sox during the '46 season he talked to them about his plans. He also had visited several teams during spring training in Florida. When we went to Boston for the first time, we had meetings with him at our hotel. Because we had trained in California, we had not met him before. He was young, in his midthirties, and a baseball fan; and rather than being a slick eastern lawyer in an expensive suit, he was a forthright guy who was serious about his work and didn't seem to care about making money. He made a favorable impression on many of our players, and they were happy when he picked the Pirates to be his test team. He thought his test team might have to threaten to strike to settle grievances and knew it would be best to do that in a union town.

With the threat of a strike as his leverage, Murphy tried several times to get the Pirates' management, led by our owner Bill Benswanger (the son-in-law of the deceased longtime owner Barney Dreyfuss), to allow the Pirates players to vote on whether they wanted to be represented by the Guild. But Benswanger steadfastly refused. I wasn't surprised. Although I thought Benswanger was a nice, quiet man, he was a hard-liner when it came to players challenging the autocracy of owners. In 1943, since I figured I was going into the service, I thought I had nothing to lose by writing him a letter and asking for a raise to $400 a month for the upcoming year in Toronto. I still have his reply, in which he wrote that my letter:

> . . . reveals the attitude of a Communist. Making "demands," as you call it, has as much justification as if you wanted to be Admiral of a fleet. . . . Whatever your demands are . . . they will be ignored. . . . There is no assurance from your record that you are a good Class A player, to say nothing of AA or the majors. Therefore, we feel the offer was a liberal one and I doubt if it would be renewed. However, that is up to you. If you wish to toss away the opportunity which you seem to feel you can fill so well, that's your funeral. . . .

He went on to threaten to place me on the ineligible list. That's how owners treated players who expressed any dissatisfaction in those days.

Murphy believed that the National Labor Relations Board would eventually rule that the players could choose the Guild as their bargaining agent and that various owners were guilty of unfair labor practices. But the pro-union players on the Pirates didn't want to wait any longer after Benswanger's refusal to allow them to vote for the Guild. So they pushed Murphy to take the next step, which was to call for a player vote on a real strike. Murphy sensed that if he didn't agree, he would lose the backing of the players.

Murphy explained to us that we would in effect hold a strike vote for better working conditions. What we would ask for was minor—better bullpens, better clubhouses, better drinking fountains, et cetera—but if granted, the impact would be huge. It would have been the first step for the Guild to represent *all* major leaguers and bargain with the baseball establishment on more important issues like minimum salaries and a pension plan (though we didn't discuss that with Murphy). The strike vote was scheduled for June 7. Because what we were doing was so important, the players agreed that we would need a two-thirds majority to walk out on a home game versus the Giants.

Not surprisingly, there was a lot of heated politicking done by players for and against the strike. By then I was good friends with the two highly intelligent veteran players who led the opposing factions, catcher Al Lopez and pitcher Rip Sewell, but neither tried to sway me toward his side. In fact, Al, who was the elder statesman on the team and the main proponent of a strike, said, "If you're smart, Ralph, you'll stay out of it." He didn't think it was smart for a rookie to stand up against half of his new team. I took his advice and didn't participate, but I couldn't help watching what was going on.

We had a couple of militant players, but most of the guys weren't that political. Most had gone to high school only and didn't understand all the issues. The ones from the South or off the farm didn't trust unions, but it was easy for Murphy and Lopez to sell some of them on the idea that they would be in a better position to make more money if the Guild's demands were met. Other players were aware that unions had been successful in helping workers. Right there in Pittsburgh, since well before the war, unions had helped the steel- and coalworkers get benefits they never would have had otherwise. Now the Congress of Industrial Organizations (CIO) was strongly behind the Guild if it should initiate a players strike. Strikes weren't foreign or frightening to the players—in fact, during the season, there was a nationwide strike that shut down the railroads and stranded us at stations. Some players were adamant about striking. They felt something major had to happen because times were different after the war, but the owners still treated the players like chattel.

As the vote approached, things got divisive and ugly. There was one incident when a couple of our players who didn't want to strike were attacked in a parking lot. Our second baseman Jimmy Brown, who was at the tail end of his career, got beat up and cut up, and he had his car damaged. He claimed he had no idea who did it. The case was never solved, but everyone knew that the unions played that way in the forties.

The papers covered what happened to Brown, and everything else in regard to the strike. It made the front-page headlines. So the people of Pittsburgh knew that a strike was a possibility. Unlike what happens today when anyone breathes that players may strike, the local papers, including the *Pittsburgh Post-Gazette*, and the Pirates fans didn't have a hostile reaction toward the team. As Murphy hoped, if we elected not to play the Giants, those many fans who were in unions would understand. They knew that we didn't make much money. At the time, only the highest-paid players were making more than steelworkers; others were struggling to get by.

What Murphy was offering us was so intriguing because we all wanted to make more money and some of us *needed* to. I happened to be one of the better-paid players, and my salary was only $5,000. Many players throughout the league who had been around longer were making much less. At that time you couldn't even supplement your income by playing winter ball in Latin America, so you had to find winter jobs.

Some of my teammates were afraid Murphy's plan would cost them their spots in the major leagues. Consequently, they sided with Sewell, Lopez's chief adversary. Rip was a smart, well-spoken college graduate, so the players respected him. He earned his place in baseball annals by throwing a blooper ball, which he called his "eephus" pitch. A pitch with high arc, it came about after a hunting companion with miserable aim shot buckshot into Sewell's big toe and he had to alter his delivery to accommodate a damaged digit that stuck up in the air. His novelty pitch revived his career. In fact, he would pitch in the '46 All-Star Game only a few weeks after our strike vote. In that game he'd yield one of the most famous homers ever to Ted Williams—later he claimed Williams was the only batter ever to go deep on his "eephus" pitch.

Sewell could be a lot of fun, and I enjoyed going out on the town with him in later years when I roomed with him. But he was very serious about the strike issue. As the mouthpiece for the establishment, he made this widely quoted statement: "First the players wanted a hamburger, and the owners gave them a hamburger. Then the players wanted filet mignon, and they gave them filet mignon. Then they wanted the whole damn cow, and now that they got the cow they want a pasture to put him in. You can't satisfy them." I have read quotes and articles dating back to the late 1800s in which reporters and owners railed about how greedy players were for wanting to organize, but this time it was a *player* speaking. For leading the fight for the owners and arguing against the Guild, Sewell hoped Benswanger would have an obligation to keep him in the organization after his career ended. But it wouldn't happen because by the time he retired, after the 1949 season, Pittsburgh had new ownership. (At least Sewell remained on the team following the '46 season, while Lopez was dispatched to Cleveland.)

Sewell told us not to strike and risk our jobs. And on June 7, prior to our vote, he escorted Bill Benswanger into the clubhouse. Meanwhile our owner made sure Murphy was barred from the clubhouse that day. Benswanger obviously was not sympathetic to players who wanted to strike.

He appealed to us not to do it, saying that if we walked out, he would field a team of semipro players. The use of non–major leaguers in a game happened once before, in 1912, when Ty Cobb's teammates struck after American League president Ban Johnson suspended the temperamental Tiger for charging into the stands during a fan riot (the real reason for their boycott) to punch out a handicapped heckler. The Athletics beat the pickup team 24–2.

Our vote was closer than that. It was something like 21–16 or 20–15 in favor of the strike. However, it wasn't the two-thirds majority that was needed to stop play. If it hadn't been for Benswanger's last-minute plea, I'm sure it would have been a larger margin, though I don't know if it would have been enough. A lot of players were visibly demoralized, but we all suited up and filed out of the clubhouse. We played the game rather than make history.

Obviously Murphy had suffered a major setback. But he moved forward and arranged for the Pirates players to vote in August on whether they wanted Guild representation. At that point, it was painfully obvious to Chandler and some of the more practical owners that something had to be done quickly to subdue player discontent, because Murphy was still trying to get better working conditions for the players and the Mexican League was still offering the players better money. Also, court battles were being waged against owners who had ignored the Veterans Act and illegally demoted an estimated 140 major leaguers and 900 minor leaguers during the year. The baseball establishment wanted desperately to find a way to make all its legal and image problems disappear while both maintaining the reserve clause that was the bedrock of its monopoly and dissuading the players from unionizing.

So the commissioner formed an executive committee. It included owners Larry MacPhail of the Yankees, Tom Yawkey of the Red Sox, Phil Wrigley of the Cubs, Sam Breadon of the Cardinals, and the presidents of the American and National Leagues, Will Harridge and Ford Frick. Braves owner Lou Perini also had input. The MacPhail-led committee met with player representatives from each league to address player concerns. Three players in particular worked with the committee: Johnny Murphy, a relief pitcher for the Yankees; Dodgers outfielder Dixie Walker; and Marty Marion, the All-Star shortstop of the Cardinals. Murphy and Walker probably became the AL and NL representatives because they played in New York, where the majority of the meetings took place. A smart college man, Walker was enlightened about labor, but in 1947, he would demonstrate he was behind the times on racial issues when he became ringleader of the Dodgers who were opposed to playing with Jackie Robinson. (For that action, Branch Rickey traded him to the Pirates.)

Together the owners and players established a minimum wage of $5,500; limited pay cuts on salary renewals to 25 percent; extended the 10-day severance notification time to 30 days; and gave players $25 expense money during spring training—which we named "Murphy money" after Johnny, not Robert, Murphy. But the biggest development was the creation of baseball's first pension plan.

The pension plan, which would need renewal in five years, would begin officially on April 1, 1947, but the players (and coaches) and owners put in the initial money in 1946. The owners agreed to put in about $1 million, and players and coaches put in $300 apiece, regardless of their salaries. In following years, a percentage of All-Star and World Series proceeds would go into the fund and we would give a portion of our paychecks, amounting to only about $2 a day. At the age of 50, 5-year veterans would get $50 a month and 10-year veterans $100 a month. A lot of players didn't participate. They either couldn't afford to pay the money or didn't think they'd benefit from the plan and didn't want to waste their money. There was no resentment toward them for not being a part of the plan. It made no difference to us because they had no effect on whether the plan got off the ground. Many got left holding the bag, because when the plan did take hold, they were left out and couldn't change their minds. Those of us who did contribute to the fund knew we were doing something for our future, but nobody forecast that the pension plan would become such an important part of baseball and develop as it would, even leading to the players union. In my mind, there was no question about putting the money in, but I was making almost twice as much as some guys. If a player's yearly salary was $3,000 in 1946, that meant he had to contribute 10 percent, which was a huge amount. Maybe the owners had the lowest-paid players contribute as much as the highest-paid in the hope that many of them would object and the plan would fall through.

After the July meetings, the players thought that they had made big inroads bargaining for themselves. So it was no surprise that when the Pirates finally voted in August on whether to accept Robert Murphy's American Baseball Guild as the team's bargaining agent, most of the team didn't bother to show up and those that did voted no. After that, Murphy fell by the wayside. With the Guild out of the way, the MacPhail committee immediately trimmed the minimum wage to $5,000. And MacPhail himself tried to increase the schedule from 154 to 168 games to make the players play more for the extra money they were getting—and, perhaps, to punish them. Fortunately, the other owners rejected his idea because of baseball tradition.

Robert Murphy's attempt to unionize baseball and the formation of the Mexican League both turned out to be ill-fated ventures. However, they awakened the players to the idea of bigger salaries and made them realize that their complaints about baseball's paternalistic and autocratic management were legitimate and worth pursuing. It was obvious that there needed to be a continual battle for players to get more of the action.

Despite the concessions granted by the baseball establishment, life remained tough for players in the late forties and early fifties. They had the chance to make a living playing ball, but even with the minimum wage, veteran players still didn't receive fair salaries. And even with the pension plan in place, players had no security. If you were injured or released, you had no recourse but to enter civilian life for the first time as an adult and try to find a full-time job. Considering that players were forced to take off-season jobs, it's a fair assumption that few had any savings to speak of. Ballplayers played for the love of the game, but money was always a concern.

When we were on the road, we used to get about $6 a day meal money, the same amount the Pirates paid for our rooms on a special rate. Many players would pocket their meal money or just buy hamburgers. Hamburgers were 25 cents, so you'd save $5.75 a day. Or you'd eat at a friend's house. That's how bad it was in those days, money-wise. Some clubs allowed you to sign your checks at the hotel and the team would pay the bill. We were told not to take advantage of the team's generosity like Vince DiMaggio did before I got there. When the Pirates were staying at a hotel in Cincinnati, Vince cavalierly signed a $25 check for dinner, which was a lot in those days. He was sent to the minor leagues right after that. He ate himself out of the league.

Other than the pension money that players would receive 20 or 30 years down the road—*if* they played a minimum of five years (at a time when *four* years was the average!)—there were no benefits. Even at my peak, if I got hurt, that was it—I would receive no financial compensation from baseball. I would have to get an insurance policy elsewhere, and that wasn't easy. I didn't know any players who had insurance. Some guys would work in the insurance business in the off-season, but I don't think they had much luck selling policies to other players. (Now insurance against injury is a big deal for teams. For instance, when the Dodgers gave Kevin Brown a long contract, they got him a ton of insurance—in true Hollywood style, they insured his arm for more than the $1 million policy 20th Century Fox once took out on Betty Grable's legs!)

Baseball was hardest on the married players. They knew it was even worse for their wives. They had to move from one place to another and worry about schools, temporary homes, finances, and whether their husbands were about to lose their jobs and not bring home any more paychecks. Anxiety came with the instability because there was no way to know if the player's career would be over in one or two years or whether it would keep going.

Unfortunately, your whole future was determined not by how talented you were but by whether your manager, owner, and, a few years later, general manager liked you. The manager was the one who doled out salaries. He'd go to the owner and say who should be on the team and what they should be paid. And then they'd talk it over. You were at their mercy. They could shorten or end your career. They could bench you, deal you, or demote you to the minor leagues and make sure you were never heard from again—in fact, there were many buried or banished players in the minors who had major league talent but never got to show it. The reserve clause was a lifetime contract, unless they decided to release you or trade your contract to another owner with the same powers. The deck was stacked against you.

In those days we all knew owners made a lot of money because, unlike today, they didn't bother to hide that fact. Unfortunately, most of the teams were cheap. Most followed the tradition of Charles Comiskey, who was a former player yet paid his players on the White Sox practically nothing. That was one of the reasons his team was willing to fix the World Series in 1919. Branch Rickey was so stingy that in 1952 he paid the entire Pirates infield the minimum. When he arrived in Pittsburgh, he said, "Boys, there are going to be changes. Garagiola, change uniforms with Kiner; Westlake, change uniforms with . . ."

There were very few owners who were benevolent. Bill Veeck of the Indians, Browns, and White Sox; Phil Wrigley of the Cubs, who was one of the richest men in the world; Horace Stoneham of the Giants; and Tom Yawkey of the Red Sox had reputations for having good relations with their players. The Red Sox were considered a luxury team because Yawkey's salaries were so generous. The Yankees were more businesslike under Dan Topping, a multimillionaire, and Del Webb, who started out as a carpenter and made a lot of money building in Las Vegas.

In those days, players on all teams, with the possible exception of the Red Sox, were invariably disappointed when they received new contracts prior to a season. Our idea of a fair raise was much different from the ideas of general managers and owners. If we went to them armed with our best stats to argue for more money, they would counter that we stood a *good* chance to play in the World Series in the fall so we should pencil in a winner's share in addition to their salary offers. One might think it ludicrous that intelligent players who weren't on the Yankees or other top teams would swallow the bait and forget their salary demands. But as management knew, if you appealed to their pride, ballplayers immediately pictured a victory parade in October. In a flash, we forgot whose uniforms we wore. In most cases you had no chance because only a couple of teams dominated the World Series.

No matter who you were, you were told no one could negotiate your contract but you. My mother couldn't come in and say, "My son deserves a raise." When you went in to discuss your contract with a manager, general manager, or owner, you had to do it alone, without an agent, an attorney, or a parent. Players kept figures to themselves, but they told other players how they were treated during negotiations. At one time or another, every player confided that the owner or general manager told them, "If you don't want to accept our offer, we'll send you to the minors." Those were the words that would get every player to sign in a hurry. A team like the Dodgers had about 500 players under contract, so major leaguers understood there was a huge supply of players who could be brought up to take their places.

One of the reasons it was difficult to negotiate contracts was because you could never find out who was making what, other than players in transition who were probably making the minimum—especially when the person who ran the club was someone as penurious as Charles Comiskey of the White Sox, Clark Griffith of the Senators, or Branch Rickey, who moved from the Cardinals to the Dodgers to the Pirates. We never knew what other players were getting, and that was a big advantage the owners had over the players. Reporters would speculate. When I became the highest-paid player in the National League, making $90,000 in 1952, the papers published the amount. Stan Musial went to Cardinals owner Augie Busch and said, "I'm a better player than Kiner, so I want $91,000." Busch did better than that and gave him $100,000, and he became the highest-paid player. That's why owners didn't want their players to know anyone else's salary.

Players on the Dodgers who wanted to negotiate a new contract often took less than they had wanted after being told erroneous salaries of their teammates. (They were also given a demonstration in which a pie represented the Dodgers' entire payroll, and the individual slices, big and small, represented the salaries of the other 24 players, showing the player that almost nothing was left for him.) When players would ask a raise from Buzzy Bavasi, who became the Dodgers' GM in the early fifties, he pulled out a phony contract of a star player, like Duke Snider, Jackie Robinson, or Roy Campanella. He would hold up the contract, but not show it to the player because, supposedly, that would be an invasion of his teammate's privacy. At that moment, a secretary would inform Bavasi that he had an urgent phone call and he'd leave the room. While he was gone, the curious player would sneak a look at the fake contract on Bavasi's desk and see that Duke Snider was making peanuts. So he'd think he was getting a good deal in comparison and sign Bavasi's contract. Bavasi would tell this story as if he were proud of it. I think it was a despicable practice, another way players were exploited. It was lying and cheating, and he did it for years. GMs on other teams would do the same thing.

There's a great story about Bavasi's predecessor at the negotiation table, Branch Rickey, whom sportswriter Dick Young called "El Cheapo." He was trying to get Preacher Roe to sign a contract that was for less than he deserved. Roe was stubborn, so Rickey decided to make an offer that appealed to his heart rather than his wallet. It was well known that Roe hunted birds in the winter, so Rickey sent him two beautiful bird dogs. Preacher was so touched by Rickey's present that he signed the contract. The minute he dropped it in the mailbox, the dogs took off for parts unknown and he never saw them again. I doubt if that story is true, but it's the one that everybody told.

Before Rickey became the vice president and general manager of the Pirates in November 1950, I negotiated my salaries with Roy Hamey. When John Galbreath and Frank McKinney bought the Pirates in 1946, they hired him to be their GM. He had been in the Yankees organization, running their Kansas City team for years. He was fair and honest. Typically, he'd send a contract that you either accepted and mailed back or said wasn't good enough. After I hit 51 home runs in 1947, Hamey even came out to California to see me. We went out to dinner and it was amiable. So, it was never as tough for me as it was for the other guys because I was the team's lone asset, the reason we were attracting as many fans as the Dodgers.

Galbreath, who bought out McKinney in 1950, also was friendly to me. He asked me to visit his home in Columbus, and we went duck hunting on his preserve. More important, he also came up with a contract that helped me offset the tremendous taxes I was paying. People assume that when I was making $90,000 it was tax-free, but the truth was that I was paying out an astronomical 91 percent in taxes! Even with write-offs such as entertainment, I was only able to get it down to 50 percent. So Galbreath put me into real estate, and I took my profits out of that instead of a straight salary. It was never publicized, but I was probably the first player to do that. It was also unusual that I got a two-year deal. Rickey was not happy with my arrangement when he came to Pittsburgh.

Most players in baseball, even stars on other teams, did not have it so good. Exploitation was still rampant, and there was speculation it would get worse because the pension plan was in danger of being shut down after a five-year test run. It was up to the players to get the owners to renew or renegotiate it instead and have it become permanent. That's when Allie Reynolds, the star pitcher for the Yankees, and I got heavily involved as the American League and National League representatives. We were the player reps for our teams, but I don't know how either of us got the jobs as chief negotiators. We didn't step forward, but all the other reps stepped back and we got left out there. One reason they wanted us is that we didn't worry that we were putting our careers in jeopardy when doing battle with the owners. Also, because we were stars, the media was more inclined to write about us and bring attention to our fight. *The Sporting News* made us their cover boys for one issue.

At our own expense, Allie and I flew to Atlanta, where baseball's winter meetings were being held. We were too naïve to be scared, but we did realize we were walking a plank with no help in sight. Nobody had voted for what we were supposed to accomplish, so we had no list of demands and we weren't reporting back to anyone. We weren't even certain that any teams were on our side. Who knew what the players on the Phillies or Browns wanted? We didn't. We knew some players wanted petty things like sunscreens over bullpens, and some high-salaried players tended to be self-satisfied and took the attitude of, "I got mine, you get yours." Some players were happy with what they had, not knowing they could have a lot more. Others were afraid to rock the boat—the general feeling was that they would ship you out if you were disruptive.

We had to deal with the owners' executive committee. Its chief negotiator was Walter O'Malley, the Dodgers' majority owner. O'Malley was imposing because he ran baseball more than did the commissioner, Ford Frick (who got the job after Happy Chandler was booted out because he made the original deal favoring the players on the pension plan). If you wanted to make a movie about a boisterous, extroverted, Irish-looking guy you could cast O'Malley. I was thinking I would have liked him if he weren't my opposition at labor talks. In fact, after I became the GM of the San Diego Padres in the Pacific Coast League, I met him at several parties and enjoyed his company. He loved to drink and socialize. I know some ballplayers didn't like him, including Jackie Robinson, but I think he was a ballplayer's owner. Of course, he was frugal, just like most of the other owners, including Bill Veeck. And that's what made him a tough negotiator. When we first proposed renewing the pension plan, he scoffed, "If you think the plan is so important, you take the plan and you run it." My eyes opened wide and I said, "OK." He realized he'd said the wrong thing and backed off, because the owners wanted to control the whole thing.

We had packed our suits and ties for our four or five days in Georgia, but we were such bad businessmen that we didn't even carry briefcases for show. It was obvious that we needed legal help in the negotiations, so Allie contacted the attorney J. Norman Lewis in New York and told me Lewis wanted to represent us. I told him it was OK with me. We walked in with Lewis, and O'Malley said we couldn't have him. We said, "You have attorneys representing you, why can't we?" And he said, "It isn't going to be that way." So we walked out, which was the closest we got to being militant. There was something un-American about not being allowed to have our lawyer there while a lawyer sat with the owners. We were angry and felt our competitive juices flowing.

So now we were at an impasse and were afraid of losing the pension plan entirely. That was a real possibility. We were helped by the media; they played both sides as they always do, and of course there were some writers who accused us of being greedy. But the fact that the players were so underpaid pushed several influential newspapers toward our side, as did O'Malley's refusal to let us have a lawyer. The wave of bad publicity and rumblings among players convinced O'Malley that he had to have good-faith negotiations with us *and* our lawyer. For our part, Allie had to argue that the hiring of Lewis was not the first step in the formation of a union. We also made sure the owners didn't feel they had lost control or they wouldn't have accepted changes.

The owners appointed a committee of Hank Greenberg, the GM of the Indians; John Galbreath, the owner of the Pirates; and an attorney to work with me, Reynolds, and Lewis. My friendship with Hank was a major factor in getting us through some very productive labor negotiations and getting the historic deal done. Hank had gone from being a player to the owners' side, but he remained his own man and refused to be part of the negotiating committee unless the owners gave him full authority to say yes or no.

Allie thought the most urgent request by the players was an increase in the minimum salary. With a minimum salary of $5,000, many players couldn't make a decent living, particularly because they had to set up a second home in a major city and pay that city's high prices. Allie wanted at least $8,000. We knew the owners wouldn't go for such a big increase. Even Veeck was strongly against that. He said salaries cost owners 50 percent of their operating costs and an increase in the minimum could have a snowballing effect. We also asked that American players be allowed to play in the winter leagues to supplement their incomes. Allie asked for a central bureau of player relations and for an individual to represent the players in the commissioner's office.

In regard to the pension, we wanted to raise monthly checks from $50 to $100 for 5-year vets and from $100 to $150 for 10-year vets. We also tried to get a locked-in percentage of monies from television into the pension plan. I was living in Palm Springs, and there were a lot of Hollywood people who talked about television expanding, so I figured that if it ever happened, there would be a hell of a lot of money generated, and I wanted the players to have a percentage. We asked for 66 percent of the revenues from television and radio broadcasts of the World Series and All-Star Games because that was the percentage of the radio rights the players received before television.

When Greenberg and Galbreath took back our requests to the owners, they had to put up a fight. They did it successfully because Hank convinced them that our terms were reasonable. The raise in the amount of monthly checks to retired players was increased to the numbers we wanted. However, there were compromises on the other major issues. The raise in the minimum from $5,000 to $8,000 was rejected, but if a player stayed with his team for a month he'd get $6,000. We got 60 percent of the revenue for TV and radio broadcasts, and that was watered down a bit because in addition to that percentage coming from the World Series and All-Star Games, the owners made sure to include the unprofitable *Game of the Week* in the deal as "shared TV monies." Still, that was a big concession from owners who wanted to give us nothing and probably could have gotten away with it.

Much of the dealing toward the end took place over the phone, and that's how Allie and I learned the deal had been accepted. I don't think we even signed anything. It was Hank saying, as he always had, "We are going to give you this and . . ." We felt such elation because we had bluffed our way through the early part of negotiations. We were almost beggars, without trying to make it look like that. The only threat we could muster was to strike during the World Series, but we were so poorly organized that it's doubtful we could have pulled that off. We got what we wanted, but we didn't jump up and down or celebrate. I don't think we even went out to dinner! We were just thankful that it was over with and took a train back home. It was a tremendous step to secure a very strong pension plan. The players were very happy with what we had accomplished under fire.

I continued to be the National League player rep. I found it easier to help the other players than myself, particularly in negotiating with Branch Rickey. When Rickey came to the Pirates in November 1950, I knew I was going to be traded because I was making a lot of money and we were a lousy ballclub. He didn't take into account that I was the reason we drew tremendous crowds. No one knew Tony Bartirome or Bobby Del Greco. After we lost 112 games in 1952 to set a new record for futility, Rickey told me, "We can finish last without you," and offered me a contract with the maximum 25 percent cut. He said we'd have a hard time making money because we were so bad—but he ignored the fact that he signed a bunch of players who couldn't play. I held out, and we wired back and forth. Finally, I said that if I were traded, I wanted $5,000 of the cut back. So he agreed, and I signed the contract.

While Rickey tried to swing a trade for me, he worried that the fans would have a negative reaction. So he fed the papers a lot of lies. The Pirates fans would read, "Ralph Kiner demanded that the fences be shortened and insisted that he didn't have to travel with the other players." But I kept copies of my wires and there were no demands at all on my part. I sent them to John Galbreath because I wanted him to know the truth.

I was traded to the Cubs in June. The Cubs were supposed to pay me the $5,000, but I didn't get the money. Warren Giles, the president of the

National League, called me in and said I had signed an illegal contract with Rickey. He said that if a player knew he'd make some extra money if he got traded, he might influence games by playing in a way that would get him traded. So I lost out on the money.

I was traded once more, to the Indians, after the 1954 season, the year the Major League Baseball Players Association (MLBPA) was formed, with my new teammate Bob Feller as its first president. Because I was sent to an American League team, I lost my position as the NL representative. The Phillies' Robin Roberts took my place. Years later, it was Roberts who brought in Marvin Miller to become the first full-time executive director of the Players Association. Baseball would never be the same.

⚾ ⚾ ⚾

As the National League representative I tried to get players more money and more security during a time when there was no union and the owners held all the power. I never even thought about the possibility of free agency; binding salary arbitration (which has been as responsible as free agency for the huge increase in salaries); long-term contracts; multimillion-dollar yearly salaries; players having the right to have agents bargain for them; and players arguably having more power than owners. All those miraculous things that are present in today's baseball are the result of Marvin Miller.

When the players and owners decided that there would be a permanent director of the Players Association in 1966, the owners wanted the position to go to Judge Robert Cannon, who had been handling the duties since J. Norman Lewis had been ousted by the players in 1959. That's because Cannon had been surprisingly conservative and pro-owner, which made sense because he had set his sights on being commissioner. The players were relieved when the disappointing Cannon dropped out because he was from the Midwest and didn't want to set up his office in New York. That's when Robin Roberts, Bob Friend, Jim Bunning—all pitchers—and other activist players settled on the Brooklyn-born Miller, who was voted in decisively, 489–136. Many dissenting votes came from the ranks of conservative managers, coaches, and trainers. The owners, who had approved of a permanent position because they expected Cannon to step in, were totally unprepared to deal with Miller, whose loyalty was 100 percent with the players and who was immediately adversarial toward the owners.

In 1968, Miller was responsible for the first Basic Agreement between owners and players—the minimum wage instantly jumped to $10,000—and won recognition by club owners that the MLBPA was the sole bargaining agent for all players. Not only did baseball have a certifiable union, but Miller turned it into the best-run and most powerful union in the land. He did this by using the legal tactics employed for decades by labor organizations such as his former employer, the Pittsburgh-based United Steelworkers of America. He never lost a confrontation with management. They never had a chance because he knew all the union rules and regulations. When baseball's brass was obstinate, he had no problem calling for a walkout, as when the players stayed home 51 days in 1981, before the owners met their demands.

When Roberts brought in Miller and put him on the ballot, he said to Miller, "Promise me one thing."

"What's that?"

"Promise me you won't strike."

"I won't strike."

When the players did strike, Robin called him up. Miller picked up the phone and said, "I have been expecting your call." That's when the union became more militant in negotiating. When Miller got his powerful position in the union, he didn't know if the players would back him. With ballplayers you're never sure which way they will go. Only once did he worry that he might fail them. That was when the owners threatened to retaliate against the union by making *all* players free agents after a single year. The owners didn't do it because they believed the richest team would then sign all the best players. Miller later confessed that act would have broken the union and changed the direction baseball was going.

There were other major figures who helped bring about the upheaval in player-owner relations. For instance, in 1966, while Miller was touring spring training camps, Dodgers pitchers Sandy Koufax and Don Drysdale did the unthinkable when they hired an agent and jointly held out for large salary increases. I thought it was a bold, brilliant move doing it together because it gave them more leverage. There was no rule that prohibited players from having an agent—it was illegal only in the minds of the owners. That set the precedent, and in the 1970 Basic Agreement, it was stated that all players had the right to representation. During my career none of the players thought of hiring an agent. In fact, the word *agent* was used only in Hollywood. (Businesspeople, not agents, got players the few endorsement deals that were available but never discussed contracts with the teams. Bob Prince, the announcer for the Pirates, got me a few endorsements for a few hundred dollars each, but he did it as a friend and didn't take out a percentage.)

In 1970, St. Louis Cardinals outfielder Curt Flood refused to be part of a multiplayer trade with the Philadelphia Phillies, and in 1972 he gallantly went down fighting—and pretty much finished off his career—in a ground-breaking trial that challenged the legality of the reserve clause. Bill Veeck even testified on his behalf. I didn't think he was foolish. A lot of guys said they didn't want to play in Philly, but he was the only one independent enough to sit out the season. It was late in his career, so he felt he could risk losing his job for a principle. He lost his case, but it paved the way for free agency and made him into a hero.

In 1975, pitchers Andy Messersmith of the Dodgers and Dave McNally of the Montreal Expos played one year without contracts and were declared free agents, effectively bringing an end to the reserve clause that had been the owners' chief weapon against players for 95 years. Arbitrator Peter Seitz, who had been hired by the owners, made the historic decision to free the two pitchers. Not surprisingly, the owners immediately fired Seitz. (They should have known Seitz would be impartial because in 1974, he ruled A's pitcher Jim "Catfish" Hunter was a free agent because his irrepressible owner Charles Finley had failed to deliver on an insurance policy that was stipulated in the contract.) At the time, I wondered why the owners would ever agree to arbitration. But they had no choice. Union laws state that when you come to an impasse, you must present your case to an impartial arbiter. So the antitrust laws didn't protect the owners.

The owners had always argued that the reserve clause kept competitive balance by not allowing ballplayers to go to the highest bidder, the best cities, or teams that always won. But in truth there never had been competitive balance. Paul Richards, the ambidextrous innovator from Waxahachie, Texas, who held numerous management positions from the late thirties to the early eighties, once worried that free agency would "be the end of baseball as we know it." There's no question he was right. But that's good. My immediate reaction to free agency was that it was the greatest thing that ever happened to a ballplayer. He was now protected; he was no longer cattle. I realized free agency would change the game, but not to the extent it did. Free agency, high salaries, long-term contracts, and binding arbitration changed the whole picture. It's like everything else in our lives—things change and, though there is sacrifice, it's usually for the better. The question is whether the reserve clause is better for the game itself. I think it has been because the game has prospered. It is certainly better for the players, because they can make tons of money and move around among teams.

Marvin Miller reigned from 1966 to 1982, when his able assistant Donald Fehr took over. During that time, the minimum salary rose from $7,000 (or $6,000 if the player was no longer on the roster June 1) to $32,500; and the average salary shot up from $19,000 to $185,651. Players no longer were treated like indentured servants. I now vote for Marvin Miller to be in the Hall of Fame. The person who first championed him for induction was the ultra-conservative New York reporter Dick Young, who was antiunion. He recognized that Miller brought about the biggest change in baseball history. Miller changed all of sports and he has a good chance to eventually get in. It would be a shame if he were kept out because he wasn't on the side of the owners. The Hall of Fame should be independent.

Today, the minimum salary is $300,000, the average salary is $2.3 million, and baseball's priciest player, Texas Rangers shortstop Alex Rodriguez, earns more than $20 million a year playing on a cellar-dwelling club—which, as Branch Rickey surely would point out, could finish last without him. Players make great money beginning in their rookie season and can make a bundle when they become free agents after six years. And the overall attendance is strong and television revenues are sky-high. So it would seem like everyone would be content. But there continues to be trouble in paradise. Each time the Basic Agreement must be renegotiated, the collective bargaining between baseball and Fehr's union is contentious at best.

As they go at each other, they each try to win the public relations game, putting up their best fronts for reporters and fans. The majority of the sports-writers side with management, just as it was when Marvin Miller headed the union. Most writers who side with the players are powerful and independent and won't be fired for speaking their minds. Usually the editorial policy of the paper determines which way the reporters cover the story.

Fans today, who are more vocal and cynical than ever before, don't have sympathy for either side. They have an unflattering image of players and owners who are squabbling over a limited amount of money that is generated by fans—and yet those fans are not taken into consideration. While they debate ways for each side to do better financially, there is never discussion about lowering ticket prices. I don't see that happening too often, although when Arturo Moreno purchased the Angels in 2003 the first thing he did was lower ticket prices across the board. It seems that it's up to the individual owners. They can be creative in making games affordable to fans or come up with promotions—fireworks on Independence Day, bobble-head giveaways, Cuban night, Greenlanders day, anything but another Disco Demolition night—that give fans more for the buck.

It's hard for fans to understand why players making millions of dollars are not satisfied. But when you have fought for something for more than 100 years and someone else wants to take it back, it's human to do anything to keep it. I don't think the players are overly greedy. They want what they are entitled to, which is self-determination and a fair share of the money. If an owner offers a player a high salary to sign, it's not the player's job to make sure the owner can afford that sum. That's why Pete Rose said, "If they want to pay me this kind of money, I'm certainly going to take it." It makes sense.

When the 1994 season was aborted and the World Series was canceled, the fans found it distasteful. Strikes make fans antagonistic. They feel it's their game and the World Series belongs to them, and in a way they are right. I don't think the owners and players figured the impact on the fans would be as strong or as lasting as it was. But people are creatures of habit, and when something stops being available, they change what they do and move on to something else—and there are a lot of other sports to choose from. Then it's hard to get them back. Fortunately, the Mark McGwire– Sammy Sosa assault on the home-run record in 1998 stimulated fans who had turned away from the game to care about it again. But those fans who have returned can be fickle.

Both sides learned their lessons from the '94 strike. I'm sure the last-minute collective-bargaining agreement in 2002 came about because everyone understood they couldn't afford to shut down baseball again. They knew that they'd probably have an even more difficult time winning back the fans than they had after 1994, and that in the long run it would hurt both the players and owners.

A basic goal of the union—which for obvious reasons causes owners to circle the wagons—is to increase player salaries to the maximum. That is why it is so vigilant about owners being competitive for free agents. For example, in 2003, when competition for top free agents was lukewarm and salary offers were low, the union brought charges of collusion against the owners. In past years, arbitrators had agreed with the union that the owners had conspired to give free agents a collective cold shoulder, and had made them pay a great deal of money in compensation. It's difficult to prove collusion, especially when a free agent signs for more than $10 million a year. But there's no way all the owners at the same time, on their own, would exhibit fiscal prudence.

While players should feel justified in taking whatever money is offered to them, there's got to be an understanding sometime soon that all the money owners are giving them might kill the game. There has to be restraint; it has to slow down, because some franchises can't make money.

Long-term contracts, which the union loves because they are pro-player, often hurt teams that can't afford bad investments. Many players who were stars elsewhere come to their new teams with lucrative multiyear deals and don't perform well at all. For instance, when superstar second baseman Roberto Alomar went to the Mets in 2002, he almost played himself out of the Hall of Fame before the Mets were able to unload him during the 2003 season. In 2002 another Mets acquisition, Jeremy Burnitz, had what may have been the worst year I've ever seen a position player have, and because of his multiyear eight-figure contract, he got a substantial raise for 2003. What kind of sense does that make? Because drafting players and bringing up minor leaguers is not enough for a team to become competitive with the Yankees and other good major-market teams, owners have no choice but to offer multiyear contracts and hope the acquired players come through and

111

their teams improve. But if a player flounders, then the team is locked into his contract for years and can't afford to get anyone better.

As a player I couldn't say, "I'll take $70,000 for hitting 20 homers and another $1,000 for every homer I hit above that." The owners would say, "There's no way in the world we can do that because we want to protect you." "You want to protect me?" "Yes. What if the manager won't play you so that the ballclub won't have to pay you that kind of money?" Well, today, baseball is such a big business and the stakes are so high that there is no manager who wouldn't play me just to keep the owner from paying out money for reaching targets. They want to pay you to perform. That's why I think it's unfortunate that today's players can't get contracts based on performance. You can get a contract based on games played or games pitched or innings, but not on homers or strikeouts. Think about it: if all contracts were based on accomplishments, which everything in life usually is—in golf you have to play well to win money; a salesperson gets commissions on sales—then we wouldn't have the problem we have today of long-term guaranteed contracts harming teams. Performance contracts could eliminate long-term contracts and be beneficial to both owners and players.

The players union has been against a salary cap, which the small-market owners insist would bring more competitive balance to baseball. It has consented to the so-called luxury tax, which taxes the rich teams whose payroll goes over a certain figure. That hasn't seemed to work because only a few teams even approach that budget—which the union wanted to be high— and the Yankees, the franchise others are trying to catch up to, continue to spend money on free agents other teams can't afford without worrying about the penalty. The other problem is that financially strapped owners who receive money from the tax often pocket it to offset their losses rather than use it to develop or acquire players to upgrade their teams.

If the luxury tax isn't the equalizer, is there any way to rid baseball of the revenue disparity that, with few exceptions, allows only big-city teams to play in the postseason? I think it's logical that television monies should be split to keep the weakest links from being out of business. In football the television money is split, but it's all from national broadcasts. Baseball doesn't operate like that because the big money is local, in New York City, Boston, Chicago, Los Angeles, and so on. So for this to work, unfortunately, it's up to the major-market owners with the lucrative media deals to be generous for the greater good of the game. But owners who make big money in TV aren't eager to give a big share of their profits to small-market owners, even if they need those partner teams to compete against.

It is through their own mismanagement that most teams don't make profits. Yet they tend to blame the union for forcing them to spend money unwisely. Should we believe them when 90 percent of the owners claim they are losing money? If that were the case, then why would John Henry sell his rights to the Marlins and then pay $750 million for the Red Sox? Wouldn't he prefer getting out of baseball entirely to buying another team that despite selling out 99 percent of its tickets and having a great TV deal was *supposedly* losing money? If these owners are so shrewd, I doubt they would want to buy teams that their owners say are losing money unless that isn't the truth.

In 2003, *Forbes* printed a list of the 30 baseball teams and their sales values. The Yankees were by far the most valuable team in baseball, worth more than twice as much as 26 of the other 29 clubs. The Yankees' estimated worth was $849 million—$351 million more than the next most valuable team, the New York Mets ($498 million). The Red Sox were third at $488 million, followed by the Los Angeles Dodgers at $449 million, and the Atlanta Braves at $423 million. According to *Forbes*, the most profitable team in baseball in 2002 was the Seattle Mariners, which made $23.3 million. They were followed by the Yankees at $16.1 million, the San Francisco Giants at $13.9 million, the Baltimore Orioles at $12.4 million, the Chicago Cubs at $11.9 million, and the Mets at $11.6 million. So even as almost every owner claims to be losing money, every team's value is going up.

One reason some owners claim losses is to get public funding for new ballparks. If there is resistance, they say they will have no choice but to move away, as when George Steinbrenner said that if New York City didn't build him a new Yankee Stadium, he would move the team to New Jersey. The owners are using suspicious numbers and threats to go elsewhere because they want to get the best deal possible—isn't that the American way?—which is to spend everyone else's money but their own. In a perfect world, stadiums would be paid for by team profits. The next best thing would be private funding. A reasonable compromise on financing for a needed stadium that benefits the community as well as the organization is a combination of profits and private and public money, as was done in San Francisco. Better that than to lose a team to another city.

Baseball is a business, and it's run for the benefit of the owners rather than the employees or stockholders. However, while bosses in business try to get people to buy their stocks by reporting profits and losses, baseball owners don't have to report to anyone. So they run their business the way they want and keep their books locked away. I used to say that baseball's financial problems won't be solved until the owners agree to show their balance sheets. Until then, I said, the players will assume they are crying wolf when they bemoan their losses. But Enron and WorldCom changed everything. Now everyone sees how books don't necessarily reflect the truth because everyone has *two* sets of books. They have lost trust in the people who run businesses and make enormous profits even while their corporations go under and the stockholders lose everything.

The union has always asked the owners to open their books to prove they are losing money, but now we know savvy bookkeepers can make it seem as if there is a deficit even if the club is making money. It depends on what they write down for assets and liabilities. It doesn't mean a thing to open the books because you'll find out only what they want you to find out, just as it is when the Chinese government allows tourists to visit only certain places. After Enron, we suspect the books they'd open wouldn't show that the liabilities have been passed on to a subsidiary or that the assets from television deals weren't written down as part of the club's profits.

It's hard for me to believe teams are losing actual cash in operations because there is one big factor no one ever mentions. As a player rep I knew that one of the great things about owning a baseball team is that you have tremendous *depreciation* of your assets—the assets being the players. (The baseball union is the strongest, most effective union in America because it deals only in baseball players' talents, which are extremely hard to put a value on.)

In my day, the depreciation of a player took place over a four-year period. That amount of time was based on owning a racehorse, where you would depreciate the cost of the horse, including breeding, for four years and then start again. I'm sure depreciation is determined a bit differently today, but let's say Barry Bonds is given a $60 million four-year deal. That would mean $15 million came off each year, so his value would decrease to $45 million to $30 million to $15 million to $0 after four years. His value on the books would be zero. Then you can get rid of Bonds and take capital gains on that "property"—that's because when you sell a player, all the depreciation has lowered your capital investment. Or, you can negotiate a new deal and start the depreciation process again. Depreciation also applies to purchases and sales of teams. So why doesn't anyone talk about it?

The richest teams come up with the best ways to hide their values because they have the most to lose—or gain. One way rich teams with television interests shrewdly hide their worths is by transferring only a minimum amount of what they are receiving for TV rights to the accounts of their ballclubs. They don't put the large assets on the books of the teams because they can put it in the networks' books instead. Consequently, it doesn't show up in the team's records as income. That just shows you can carry things in your books in any fashion you want. An outsider can never get a true picture.

The owners' questionable practices keep me on the side of the players union. However, I have a couple of gripes with Donald Fehr's organization as well. In a previous chapter, I objected to the union stance against regular drug testing. I said that the union should take into account that the players' health is being placed in jeopardy in the name of privacy; that the players who take even over-the-counter performance-enhancing drugs set a horrible example for young fans; and that the players who take drugs and supplements have an unfair advantage over those who don't.

My view of the drug issue is the same as any outsider's. But my other problem with the union regards something I was very much part of during my playing days. I am not satisfied with the handling of the pension fund by the current players. Unfortunately, only active players can be part of the union, which means that we old-time players who set up the pension fund no longer can participate in how it is handled.

My onetime teammate Gene Woodling, who was very active in labor relations in my day, said years later:

> When I was the player rep, I should have insisted that the players and owners put everything in writing. But I just didn't think that ballplayers would be the ones to give retired players a hard time. We hadn't trusted the owners or general managers, who were the biggest liars imaginable, but we trusted ballplayers. That turned out to be a mistake because the new players who came in didn't care about the men who played before them. If things had been in writing, it would have tied their hands and retired players or their widows would get what they are entitled to. Sadly, once a player got out of the game, he became an outcast and a pain to those greedy new players who cared only about their own pensions. He found he wouldn't be able to get necessary and accurate information about entitlements from the new people in charge and that he had lost his voice in how the pension plan should be run.

I owe a lot to Woodling because I used his model bat to hit all my home runs in 1947, so I can buy everything he said. Despite increased revenues coming in, the players in power did not go back and pick up the old-time players who were out of the game.

Back in the eighties, Early Wynn was very adamant that we get more money because of all the money that was rolling into the pension fund. There was a surplus, so Early thought that if he appealed to the owners, they could force the players to give money to the original players in the pension plan, who weren't getting a lot of money because there wasn't much money to be invested back then. Robin Roberts and I agreed, and we flew at our own expense to New York to talk to people in the commissioner's office. When Early didn't show up, we pleaded the case for the old-timers. What Early didn't know is that somewhere down the line, the owners gave the players a percentage of money from television revenues to run

115

their own pension plan. Under Marvin Miller, the players did pick up the old-timers at one time, but the new players said to hell with them.

Because the players union gives money only to players who played after 1947 and were part of the pension plan, the Baseball Assistance Team was established. B.A.T., a nonprofit organization, provides money to former players and widows who need it. They have taken in a lot of money and taken care of a lot of people. They pick up a lot of those old players and pay their bills. The union isn't obligated to do it, but it should. In addition to helping with bills, it should establish a home for old-time ballplayers, just like the motion picture home for former actors. They could spend time there and talk baseball.

But players needn't wait for the union to take action. For tax purposes, ballplayers give a lot of money to their favorite charities. That's commendable, but today's players could be big contributors to B.A.T., giving money back to the players who fought for the pension plan and all the benefits the players have gotten. Why not put the money back from where it came? It's not that other charities aren't worthy, but this cause is close to home. It would benefit all players and their families who need money. A lot of ballplayers, including those who played after 1947, never made the money today's players do and were unable to accumulate enough money to pay for their retirement years and sicknesses. They should be helped, whether it's done through the players union or through individuals.

The players shouldn't do this great deed in order to improve their images. But it certainly would help. We'd no longer say that the current members of the players union forgot about the old players who paved the way.

Chapter **5**

Yankee **Dynasties**

I f the Oakland Raiders, or Quantrill's Raiders for that matter, had bullied their way into the American League in 2003, not even they would have been as pitiless as the New York Yankees were at the beginning of the season. With heartless precision, they ran roughshod over 20 of their first 24 opponents to serve notice that the pieces were in place for an easy run to their eighth consecutive postseason and possible fifth world title under manager Joe Torre. It was a surprise to no one because as usual they were the odds-on favorites to win it all. We all could have come up with the headline that ran in one New York newspaper:

There's The Yankees, and Then There's Everyone Else

It was no different in my day. The New York Yankees, the richest team in sports, dominated postwar baseball—and in effect extended the era all the way to 1964—strictly because they continued to win. In 18 years, they overpowered so-called contenders to the tune of 15 American League pennants, taking a break only for the Cleveland Indians in 1948 and 1954 and the Chicago White Sox in 1959. And they captured 10 World Series, including every year from 1949 to 1953—one of two times they won five straight pennants. They never went two consecutive years without a pennant or three without a world title. With no playoff system in place then, champions had to defeat only one team in the postseason rather than the three they must beat today, but there is no disputing that the Yankees were one of the great dynasties in sports history.

They were so omnipotent that fans of the other 15 teams despised them enough to call them the "Evil Empire" and equated being a Yankees fan with rooting for US Steel. As humorist James Thurber once observed: "The majority of American males put themselves to sleep by striking out the batting order of the New York Yankees."

I'm sure it was a challenge not to have a depressed, defeatist attitude when you were an American Leaguer and the Yankees were running pennants up flagpoles so often that they might have given somebody the idea for instant replay. At least in the National League, usually two or three teams—typically the Dodgers, the Giants, and, later, the Braves—were in the mix and had a genuine chance to win the pennant each year. They had to beat only each other to reach the World Series, but the bad teams for whom I played, the Pirates (1946 to mid-1953) and Cubs (mid-1953 through 1954), had no patsies and needed to leapfrog over all seven other teams for the opportunity to face the Yankees, which—and you can look it up—we never did.

Rusty Staub, who played on no world champion teams and only one pennant winner—the 1973 New York Mets—during a 23-year, 2,716-hit career, got it right when he said, "If you can't be optimistic in the spring, when the hell can you be?" Ballplayers are by nature really positive before the season—often foolishly so. They look at the standings and see that *all* the teams are tied for first, and they buy into their management's claim that their ballclub should be a contender. Even on the lowly Pirates and Cubs, we played the "what-if" game and everything seemed possible in March. All through camp, we heard everyone raving about our rookies, and we watched our veteran hitters stinging the ball like never before and our suddenly healthy pitchers really zipping the ball. So we thought, *Hey, we finally have a damn good team that is going to surprise a lot of people.* We didn't resent the Yankees (or Dodgers or Giants), but welcomed the challenge of competing on their level.

However, about a week into the new season, reality set in, the phenoms turned out to be busts, and it was evident that the only pitchers our hitters had any luck against were our own, and vice versa. And we looked at the standings and we were anchored to the bottom. It fell apart quickly. As the players on bad teams woke up to the fact that the good teams in the league were a whole lot better, they became increasingly jaded. Come October, they were back home and working a second job to make ends meet, the World Series was on their radios or black-and-white televisions, and, more likely than not, the Yankees were beating up on the Dodgers. At spring training, with 154 games to play, it would have been unhealthy for us to concede that the Yankees were going to celebrate another world championship. But when checking our bank accounts six months later, we wondered how management had been able to talk us out of asking for legitimate raises. I never resented that I wasn't on the Yankees rather than on perennial losers, but at such frustrating moments I recalled that I could have been.

When I was 13 or 14, I was approached to play on an amateur team sponsored by the New York Yankees called the Yankee Juniors. Having grown up a Babe Ruth fan, I thought it was the greatest thing that ever happened to me. I even had the thrill of wearing a uniform with George Selkirk's name on it. In the four years I was with the Yankee Juniors, I pictured myself being on the real Yankees. That wasn't far-fetched because there was an unwritten rule that the Yankees had first rights to sign players on that team once they came of age. After my high school graduation, the Yankees offered me a contract and, to please my mother, a scholarship to USC if I agreed to the deal. My intention had been to sign with them, but then Pittsburgh scout Hollis Thurston told me I'd reach the majors much sooner if I signed with the Pirates, a team that needed help as soon as possible and didn't have many surefire prospects in the minor leagues. He won me over when he pointed out that if I signed with the Yankees, I'd be sent to D ball and I'd be stuck in the minors for five or six years. So we broke the "rule."

A major reason the Yankees were consistently strong was that most young players *did* sign with them when given a choice of teams. The Yankees offered paltry deals yet were so renowned that they were able to fill the rosters of all the teams in their vast farm system. Owners and fans of opposing organizations resented that the Yankees had the resources to hire a large group of talented scouts to scour the country and snatch up an inordinate number of prospects. The parent club was so strong that the organization could be patient for their minor leaguers to develop, allowing them one year at each classification. By the time they reached the majors, they were already seasoned pros. Indeed, it was probably true that some Yankees minor league teams were stronger than a few major league clubs.

In the late forties, some of the key Yankees were aging and there was the very real danger of a long period of decline. But in addition to trading for Allie Reynolds, Eddie Lopat, and Gene Woodling, they brought up a whole slew of young players, including Yogi Berra, Vic Raschi, Whitey Ford, Mickey Mantle, Hank Bauer, Billy Martin (whom Casey Stengel managed at Oakland in the Pacific Coast League), and Gil McDougald. And suddenly they were loaded with talent. Undeniably, teams like the Yankees and the Tigers, as well as the Cardinals and Dodgers (the two teams for whom Branch Rickey established huge farm systems full of underpaid players— called "chain gangs"), had a huge advantage because they were able to stockpile players in the minors.

The outspoken Bill Veeck, who owned the Indians from 1946 to 1949 and then bought the St. Louis Browns, thought that an effective way to achieve competitive balance in baseball was to strip the Yankees and other rich teams of their power to control the destinies of so many prospects. He suggested that all minor leaguers be declared unrestricted free agents after only one year—rather than after being optioned three times—and be offered in a draft to teams in higher classifications, including the majors. He was advancing a concept voiced in the twenties by Judge Kenesaw Mountain Landis, baseball's first commissioner. (Landis wanted to do away with the "gentleman's agreements" by which major league owners sold players to minor league owners with the understanding that if the players developed they could be bought back at the same price.) Without the reserve clause in the minors, poor organizations could upgrade themselves by drafting talented minor leaguers who would otherwise be buried in another team's farm system in perpetuity.

It vexed Veeck that the Yankees could afford a huge farm system while small-market organizations like the Browns could not. In order to close that financial gap, he proposed that visiting teams get 50 percent of gate receipts. He argued that the Browns deserved to split the money with the Yankees when they came to Yankee Stadium because as great as the Yankees were, they couldn't play that day if the Browns didn't show up. He was being sarcastic, knowing he wouldn't get what he wanted. But to me his thinking was very logical because it would have helped financially strapped visiting teams operate. In fact, when I was the GM of the Padres in the Pacific Coast League beginning in the midfifties, we had a 60-40 split of gate receipts that worked quite well. Going one step further, Veeck wanted teams to stop televising home games so fans would have to pay their way into the park. The Browns made most of their money on the road, so their share of road game receipts was a major concern.

Veeck reflected a great deal about the impact of television, especially how the new medium helped the Yankees more than any other team. Because they played in New York they could make lucrative local media deals; and because they were the sport's most famous team and biggest attraction, they were scheduled far more than other teams on Saturday's *Game of the Week*, at about $25,000 a pop. He asked how the Browns or the Senators under tightfisted Clark and then Calvin Griffith hoped to compete when the Yankees started the season already $1.5 million ahead of them in operating money. That was a huge sum in those low-salary days and made it possible for only them to trade for star veterans like Johnny Sain, Johnny Mize, and Enos Slaughter to help in pennant drives.

In conjunction with advocating sweeping changes in the procurement of players and the sharing of gate receipts, Veeck asked the league to mandate that teams split television fees. Of course, Yankees GM George Weiss had no intention of being that generous, and he voiced the loudest objection. Of these and his other suggestions for establishing parity, Veeck wrote in his autobiography *Veeck as in Wreck*: "Now this may not sound quite so inflammatory as, say, *The Communist Manifesto*, but to the Yankees it was revolutionary, un-American and just about what you would expect from that fellow Veeck." Weiss led a successful campaign to—at least temporarily—discount Veeck's ideas, prompting Veeck to accuse the Yankees of "trying to keep the league from being competitive."

Despite the Yankees doing everything in their power to eliminate pennant races—although, as Veeck pointed out, rivalries would have increased their attendance, too—occasionally another American League team would be more than competitive. In 1946, my rookie season and the year when players came back from the war, the Boston Red Sox easily won the American League pennant. The Yankees, the top team before the war, could do no better than third place, a whopping 17 games behind the Sox. The Yankees seemed to be on their way out—*before* savvy trades and the influx of minor leaguers reversed things—and if any team seemed on the verge of beginning a dynasty, it was Boston. They had a strong offense led by Ted Williams, Bobby Doerr, Johnny Pesky, and Dom DiMaggio (who was also, arguably, a better defensive center fielder than his older brother Joe). And they had two young 20-game winners, Tex Hughson and Boo Ferris, plus two other solid starters in Mickey Harris and Joe Dobson. But somebody on the Yankees must have been assigned to jab a bunch of sharp pins into a voodoo doll—perhaps another reason the Yankees won all the time—because the next year there was a mysterious wave of arm injuries and only Dobson continued to be effective.

In 1948, Boston's big bats carried them through the season but were stymied by Indians rookie Gene Bearden's nasty knuckler in a one-game playoff, and their season was suddenly, and shockingly, over. However, it looked like they'd get over the bitter taste of defeat in 1949, when they seemed to be the best team in the league again. Left-hander Mel Parnell and Ellis Kinder (who would later move to the pen) each won more than 20 games, Williams took the Triple Crown, and shortstop Vern Stephens (who had moved Pesky to second base in 1948) matched him with an eye-opening 159 RBIs. But for the second straight year—or third time in four years if you count their seventh-game defeat by the Cardinals in the '46 Series—their season ended with heartbreak. They had the pennant for the taking, but the Yankees beat them the final two games of the season to capture the flag. Casey Stengel, the new Yankees manager, humbly remarked, "I couldn't have done it without my players."

For many, that first Stengel year, not 1947, was when the Yankees dynasty truly began. The '49 pennant race was the postwar Red Sox's last gasp. The voodoo continued its cruel work in 1950, when Williams was knocked out of the lineup for half a season when he busted his elbow catching my long drive against the wall in the All-Star Game at Comiskey Park. He came back in 1951 but would miss almost the entire 1952 and 1953 seasons because he was called back to active duty during the Korean War (almost losing his life when he was forced to crash-land his plane). Had a Yankee called the draft board? While he was away, Doerr developed a bad back and DiMaggio a bad eye, and both retired to avoid being traded as part of new Sox manager Lou Boudreau's youth movement. Pesky was dealt to Detroit.

After Williams returned, the Red Sox always managed to put enough good hitters around him to give the team a formidable batting order. But despite

Parnell, Boston's starting pitching—a problem since owner Harry Frazee sold lefty ace (and part-time slugging outfielder) Babe Ruth to the Yankees in 1920, supposedly to finance the Broadway musical *No, No, Nanette*—never was comparable to the Yankees' rotation. Their consistently mediocre pitching accounts for why they wouldn't win another pennant until 1967. (By then, the Yankees were no longer a contender, Williams had been retired for seven years, and another fixture in Fenway's left field, Carl Yastrzemski, became the first Red Sox player since Williams in '49 to win the Triple Crown.)

Cleveland was the only American League team to have the pitching to compete with the Yankees. In 1948, the Indians, owned by Bill Veeck, got excellent offensive production from infielders Eddie Robinson, Joe Gordon, shortstop-manager Lou Boudreau, and Ken Keltner and second-year outfielder Larry Doby. But the main reason they nosed out the Red Sox and Yankees and won the World Series over the Boston Braves was their starting pitchers: Bob Lemon, Bob Feller, one-year wonder Gene Bearden, and late-season acquisition Satchel Paige.

Lemon and Feller were still part of Cleveland's rotation in 1954, along with another future Hall of Famer, Early Wynn, and tough Mike Garcia, when the Indians set a then–American League record with 111 victories. The Yankees won 103 games that season but still finished 8 games behind in the pennant race. I think the 1954 Cleveland Indians were a great team, as good as any Yankees team of the period. Lemon and Wynn tied for the league lead with 23 victories, and Garcia, Feller, Art Houtteman, and even Hal Newhouser, who had won two MVP Awards during WWII, had exceptional win-loss percentages. Don Mossi and Ray Narleski were the best righty-lefty bullpen combo in baseball. (Lemon quipped, "The two most important things in life are good friends and a strong bullpen.") In addition, second baseman Bobby Avila led the American League in hitting and Larry Doby led in both homers and runs batted in. And third baseman Al Rosen followed up his 1953 MVP season with another good year despite seeing his stats slip after he got hurt playing first at the request of GM Hank Greenberg. Hank and manager Al Lopez, two longtime friends of mine, thought the Indians' only weakness was not having another power-hitting outfielder. So they sent surplus pitcher Sam Jones and cash to the Cubs for me. I was expected to be the missing puzzle piece.

I was thrilled to finally be on a contender. I came to camp and, for the first time in my major league career, my team had justification for its winning attitude. The writers asked the players if they could repeat, and they confidently answered yes. It was business as usual, and our order of business was to win more games than any other team, not to set our sights on the Yankees. We were the team to beat, not them. All the key players were back on offense, I was now there to provide more pop, and the best staff I ever saw in baseball was improved, if anything, with the addition of Herb Score. Herb was the rare phenom who lived up to his billing. He had the best fast-ball since Feller in his prime and set a rookie record for strikeouts. We were all sure he'd join Feller in the Hall of Fame one day, not knowing he'd lose effectiveness after being struck in the eye by a line drive in 1957 (while playing the Yankees, naturally).

Though my back limited my production, and Avila, Doby, and Rosen (who had a major rift with Greenberg over his salary) had significantly worse stats than they had in 1954, we were in first place on Labor Day and ready to make our move. Unfortunately, our move had a downward tra-jectory. After leaving Yankee Stadium with a small lead, we played lousy ball the rest of the way and the Yankees went 17–6 to beat us by three games. I hate to admit it, but we may have faltered because we were a little intimidated by the Yankees in a tight race. In 1954, the Yankees didn't threaten in September; this time they were right there the whole way. We were better, but they were the best clutch team in baseball. They were used to the media exposure so they performed better in the spotlight. Moreover, the New York media boosted their confidence by saying they were better players than they really were. They exuded confidence that they were going to prevail—they had a New York City swagger—and that might have made us feel a bit shaky. That was unfortunate because if we had won the pennant again that season, the 1954–55 Indians might be remembered as the greatest team of the fifties.

The Milwaukee Braves probably felt the same way after they blew a 3–1 lead to the Yankees in the 1958 World Series after having beaten them the year before. They had a great team with Hank Aaron, Eddie Mathews, Joe Adcock, Warren Spahn, Bob Buhl, and onetime Yankees farmhand Lew Burdette, who had three complete-game victories in the '57 Series. If they had won back-to-back World Series from the Yankees, then the Yankees' star would have been diminished and the Braves would at least be remem-bered as the best team of the late fifties. Similarly, Brooklyn would be regarded as the best team of the midfifties if they had followed up their 1955 World Series victory by beating the Yankees again in 1956. But the Yankees didn't let that happen either, just as they refused to let the Indians beat them out in two consecutive pennant races—which is why baseball in the fifties was the Yankees and everybody else.

In 1956, the Indians again finished second behind the Yankees, this time 9 games back. Al Lopez then moved over to the White Sox and continued his string of finishing second to the Yankees in 1957 and 1958. Finally, in 1959, the White Sox stopped being the bridesmaid. A scrappy White Sox team, which had been purchased by Bill Veeck during the off-season, won the pennant by five games over an entertaining, revamped, racially mixed Cleveland Indians team, which included Minnie Minoso, Rocky Colavito, Vic Power, Mudcat Grant, Gary Bell, Billy Martin, and Jimmy Piersall. Surely both Lopez and Veeck took pleasure in watching the Yankees slide to third place.

However, the Yankees would come back strong and win pennants in the next five years, fighting off challenges of various degrees by the Orioles in 1960, Tigers in 1961, Twins in 1962, White Sox in 1963, and the White Sox and Orioles in 1964. In 1963 and '64, Lopez again finished second to the Yankees.

Having relived that 1955 pennant race for 50 years, I can only conclude that there was another factor that allowed the Yankees to overtake and pull away from us although we were the better team. I have become a believer in the "Yankees mystique." That's their secret—their ballpark with the many banners and ghosts of Ruth, Gehrig, and all the rest; their glorious history with great stars and far more championships than any team in baseball; and their famous pinstriped uniform, which is not unlike soft armor, all humbled opposing players. When the pressure was on and your team was racing to the wire with the New York Yankees lapping at its heels, the Yankees had a tremendous psychological edge.

That also explains why the Yankees beat the Brooklyn Dodgers in five of six World Series confrontations. The Dodgers had exceptional players over the years: Jackie Robinson, Roy Campanella, Gil Hodges, Pee Wee Reese, Billy Cox, Junior Gilliam, Carl Furillo, and Duke Snider. And they had outstanding pitchers: Ralph Branca, Rex Barney, Carl Erskine, Preacher Roe, Don Newcombe, Billy Loes, Hugh Casey, Clem Labine, Joe Black, and then Johnny Podres, the youngster who beat the Yankees in Game 7 of the '55 Series to finally reward the long-suffering fans of Brooklyn. The Dodgers matched up against the Yankees, were used to the same media exposure, and had an aura of their own, so at the time I couldn't figure out why they couldn't beat them. I should have considered damn Yankees luck and Yankees mystique and that the Dodgers lost so often to the Yankees that it had to affect their performances in subsequent Series. Usually one World Series defeat won't make you feel wary of returning the next year—for instance, I don't think the Indians' loss to the Giants in 1954 contributed to our poor September in 1955—but the Dodgers were beaten by the Yankees so many times that I think it became almost routine. So, when the Dodgers' Billy Loes, perhaps the flakiest pitcher of that period, was asked who would win one of those Series, he said with complete candor, "The Yankees in six games." Saying your opponent will win is tantamount to treason, so the aghast reporters asked, "How can you pick the Yankees in six? You're on the Brooklyn Dodgers!" Loes thought it over and changed his mind, saying, "OK, the Yankees in seven."

I didn't root against the Yankees in the World Series, but because I played in the National League, I was disappointed when the Dodgers lost to the Yankees. I always felt I could have been the player to get them past the Yankees. In fact, if I had been a free agent during my playing days and all the money was equal, my choice of city would have been New York and I would have gone to the Dodgers rather than the Yankees. Ebbets Field was a much better ballpark than Yankee Stadium for a right-handed power hitter, and I loved the fans. In 1953, it was rumored the Pirates were going to trade me to the Dodgers, and I was all for it, but instead they sent me to the Cubs. That was an unfortunate turn of events because I would have relished playing one full year in that intimate park to see what I could do. Surely an outfield of Snider, Furillo, and me would have been one of the most imposing in baseball. And we would have had an everyday lineup consisting of five future Hall of Famers, a should-be Hall of Famer in Hodges, and two others of All-Star caliber.

Although I never got the opportunity to beat the Yankees in the World Series, I had a vicarious thrill when my old team, the Pittsburgh Pirates, defeated the Yankees in a memorable seven-game Series in 1960, five years after I retired as a player. A few of my former suffering Pirates teammates were key members of the team. Bob Friend won 18 games, Vern Law won 20 games and was given the Cy Young Award, Elroy Face was a star reliever, and my roomie Dick Groat led the league in hitting and was voted the NL's MVP. That team also had Roberto Clemente and Bill Mazeroski, whose blast off Ralph Terry in the bottom of the ninth inning of Game 7 was the first walk-off homer to ever win a World Series. It went over left fielder Yogi Berra and way past where "Kiner's Korner" once stood.

That game had so many twists and turns, including an unforgettable moment in which a double-play ball skipped upward after hitting a stone and sharply struck Yankee shortstop Tony Kubek in the throat, leading to a Pirates rally and eventual victory. The stars must have been in a strange alignment because that's the kind of thing that usually happened to Yankees opponents. That pebble always would be called endearingly by Pirates fans, "Fogerty's Rock," to honor the team's groundskeeper.

Pittsburgh had one of the great celebrations of all time, and it wasn't unruly. You couldn't drive down the street, there were so many people walking around. Everyone was so happy because the city hadn't experienced any title in professional sports since the Pirates defeated the Washington Senators in the 1925 World Series. The Pirates hadn't even been in a World Series since 1927, when perhaps the greatest of all Yankees teams crushed them in four straight games. At last there was retribution. The 1960 Series and that final game really pointed out what baseball is all about because you never knew what was going to happen next. The Yankees were such a dominant team and scored about 500 runs, but the Pirates got the rings. Afterward, Mickey Mantle cried for the only time during his career. I think all the Yankees were devastated because they believed that for the only time in their dynasty years, they lost a championship while going neck and neck against an inferior team. They had always been able to pull out victories when they needed them, a hallmark of recent Yankees teams as well.

In World Series play, the Yankees rebounded from their 1960 defeat to Pittsburgh with an easy victory over the very good but overmatched Reds in 1961. The 1961 team, featuring Roger Maris and Mickey Mantle chasing Babe Ruth's home-run record, and Whitey Ford winning 25 games, was probably the best Yankees team of the entire era. It was managed by Ralph Houk, who was a great pal of mine from California. Stengel's reign came to an end after the loss to the Pirates, ostensibly because he turned 70. He responded, "I'll never make the mistake of being 70 again."

In 1962, soon after Stengel had completed his first year managing the expansion New York Mets, the New York Yankees won a seven-game Series over the San Francisco Giants, their previous crosstown rivals when the Giants had played in the Polo Grounds. Ralph Terry induced Willie McCovey to line out to Bobby Richardson for the final out in Game 7, with the tying run on third and potential winning run on second.

The Yankees' luck ran out in 1963 against the other New York team that had moved west, when the L.A. Dodgers' pitchers Sandy Koufax, Don Drysdale, and, once again, Johnny Podres completely shut down the Yankees' potent offense. Having beaten the White Sox in 1959, it was the second World Series victory in two attempts for the L.A. Dodgers, and the victories went to three pitchers who had started out in Brooklyn.

In 1964, the Yankees played in their 15th and last World Series of the era, and they lost for the fifth time. Bob Gibson recorded three victories, and the Cardinals beat the Yogi Berra–managed Yankees in an exciting seven-game Series. It had been the Cardinals who won the first postwar World Series, and now, fittingly, they ended the era with another championship in their first time back to the fall classic. After 1964, the Yankees finally went into dramatic decline, not winning another pennant until 1976 or another World Series until the following year. The Yankees had previous dynasties, so perhaps what they accomplished after World War II almost was taken for granted at the time. But put into the perspective of 20/20 hindsight, what they did in those 18 years seems nearly impossible.

There would be many great teams in baseball after 1964, including the Yankees of 1976–81 and the Reds' Big Red Machine of the seventies, but probably only two teams won enough championships to be called dynasties. One was the Oakland A's of the seventies, which won five consecutive American League West flags and three straight world titles before free agency kicked in and star players Catfish Hunter, Reggie Jackson, Rollie Fingers, Sal Bando, Joe Rudi, and Bert Campaneris went elsewhere. The other team has been the New York Yankees under Joe Torre.

⚾ ⚾ ⚾

Dynasties highlight every sport's history. Those championship teams—and their star players and opponents—both created and defined their eras, and we use them as our touchstones when looking back in time. But while they were dominant, opposing teams and their fans were too frustrated to feel appreciation. It's hard to live through the dynasties year after year if you don't root for those teams. That's why Tug McGraw, the always quotable onetime great reliever for the Mets and Phillies, advised, "Always root for the winner. That way you won't be disappointed." Even considering New York's surprise loss to the Marlins in the 2003 World Series, Yankees fans have rarely been disappointed since 1996, Joe Torre's first year as the manager.

The Yankees are *the* team, as they were in my day. When one considers that it was just two years after the calamitous 1994 strike that they began their run of five World Series appearances in six years—meaning they had to win two playoff series just to get there five different times!—they haven't been given enough credit for baseball's resurgence in popularity. In 1998, when fans really came back to the game, the Mark McGwire–Sammy Sosa home-run race was the primary reason, but the year's second-biggest story was the Yankees' winning 114 regular-season games and 125 overall after sweeping the World Series from the San Diego Padres. Fans stayed tuned in after McGwire and Sosa put away their bats.

Since then, the Yankees have been a major source of fan interest year after year. They have been at the right place at the right time with the best team. As it was in the postwar era, they are baseball's greatest attraction at the ballpark and on television—the one team that guarantees an audience. Fox executives probably attend church en masse during the postseason to pray for the Yankees to reach the World Series—because the huge number of Yankees fans and Yankees haters around the country assure high ratings. Even though the Yankees don't win every World Series, they have returned to the Fall Classic repeatedly, while other teams win only one appearance each and then make way for a new hot team. Although the Yankees have been under attack for the *financial* reasons they are able to dominate base-ball—while other Series teams try to hold on to most of their stars the next season, the Yankees actually add stars—they probably have also been base-ball's largest asset. Everyone benefits from the crowds the Yankees draw, the television audiences they generate, and the merchandise they sell when they are a winning team. When they had bad teams and interest waned, it was bad for all of baseball.

It is strange to recall that after the Yankees' 1964 World Series appearance, the team that had so much success since 1947 became mortal overnight. Something was definitely askew when the sports world's most famous franchise fielded innocuous players. Joe Garagiola commented, "When I covered the Yankees in the sixties, they had players like Horace Clarke, Ross Moschitto, Jake Gibbs, and Dooley Womack. It was like the first team missed the bus."

During the nine years CBS owned them, the Yankees couldn't escape the clutches of mediocrity. Only after George Steinbrenner, a shipbuilder from the Midwest, became the majority owner in 1973 did the team return to glory. A few years after the meager $10 million purchase, there was even a sign of renewed decadence, which hadn't been present on the team since Whitey Ford, Mickey Mantle, and Billy Martin went barhopping. It surely had much to do with Martin being the manager (although his firings became annual events). Of playing in the "Bronx Zoo"—which was the title of Sparky Lyle's humorous book about his raucous team—third baseman Graig Nettles made his famous remark, "When I was a little boy, I wanted to be a baseball player and join the circus. With the Yankees I've accomplished both." Steinbrenner loved all the publicity about himself and his charismatic players, good and bad, because it won New York City back from the Mets and, when they eventually won, made him somewhat of a savior—not a mere meddler.

Those Yankees won five division crowns and four pennants in six years beginning in 1976, three consecutive pennants from 1976 to 1978, and back-to-back World Series in 1977 and '78. From their exciting example, Steinbrenner came up with his recipe for assembling a great team. He would start with a core of homegrown stars (Thurman Munson, Ron Guidry), then sign high-profile free agents (Catfish Hunter, Reggie Jackson, Goose Gossage), and trade for All-Star-caliber role players (Chris Chambliss, Willie Randolph, Bucky Dent, Graig Nettles, Lou Piniella, Mickey Rivers, Ed Figueroa). On the field, there would be an intriguing mix of home-run hitters and contact hitters who were excellent fielders, more than one "ace," and a star reliever who would control the endgame. Everyone on his team had to be able to perform in the clutch, in the New York spotlight.

Steinbrenner's formula would have success from the beginning, but his team, even in the years featuring superstars Dave Winfield (free-agent signing) and Don Mattingly (homegrown star), could not reach the postseason after 1981. The eighties marked the first decade since before Babe Ruth put on pinstripes that no Yankees team won a world championship. That could almost explain Steinbrenner's impatience, which resulted in 17 managerial changes in his first 17 years. The Yankees finally made it to the postseason in 1995, Mattingly's final season, and they became world champions for the first time in 18 years when Joe Torre became their manager in 1996. At last, Steinbrenner had hired a manager with whom he could coexist, someone he did not think he could outmanage. He seemed to know that if on a foolish whim he fired Torre, who had remarkable success and was beloved and respected by the fans and the supercritical New York press, that would be the first change of managers that would get him permanently crucified. So Torre continued to manage, Steinbrenner continued to supply him with players, and the Yankees continued to win.

When Torre left the Angels broadcast booth to take the job that was offered to him by Steinbrenner and then-GM Bob Watson, I thought he was crazy and would end up as another quick casualty on Steinbrenner's managerial chopping block. I was wrong. He was able to handle it. He suddenly emerged as the great manager many people expected him to be when he was the skipper of the Mets, Braves, and Cardinals. He is now going to be known as one of the outstanding managers ever—a Hall of Famer. Despite having all "the horses," he has never had an easy job. He has exhibited a tremendous knowledge of the game, a golden touch when making decisions during big games, and the temperament to handle tough situations with his players and the press and to avoid major confrontations with his boss. For there to be harmony on this team of high-priced players, especially when many have been brought in from the outside (including Tino Martinez, Roger Clemens, Jason Giambi, Mike Mussina, Wade Boggs, David Justice, and Hideki Matsui), it has been imperative that he impress upon everyone that the Yankees are more important than any individual. Torre keeps the players humble. They recognize that he is a great guy, with a sense of humor and unflinching principles that include tremendous loyalty to them. So even the superstars respectfully listen to him and do their jobs. They regard *him* as the central figure on the team.

Interestingly, no Yankees detractors begrudge Torre for the Yankees' dominance since his arrival. Steinbrenner and his bottomless pockets are the targets. The current Yankees show what a team with the right combination of players can do if it dedicates itself to its fans, to the game, to each other, to the manager, and to winning. But because the Yankees are one of the few organizations that can afford a number of pricey stars at the same time, its owner is accused of buying titles. His budget of more than $180 million is much higher than that of any other team and makes the player payrolls of some small-market teams seem like chump change. His critics assert that winning at all costs has been such a focal point for Steinbrenner—the reason they think the Yankees organization epitomizes what's wrong with baseball today—that he long ago forgot what the word *budget* implies.

I understand Steinbrenner's thinking: prideful Americans want everyone to know our armed forces are second to none. Similarly, Steinbrenner wants everyone to think the Yankees are number one. When you go to war, you want to recruit the best men for your army; as owner of the Yankees, he goes after the best available players. His sole objective is to win, and if they don't help him do it, they're gone in a hurry. I can't help but be impressed by what he's accomplished. I can't really knock him because he does work within the system and is doing what all fans want the owners of their teams to do, which is to put together a team that will win year after year. But I recognize he can do it only because he has resources for players and capable front-office people that are unavailable to any other franchise.

The dramatic escalation of TV monies in baseball is creating problems of monstrous proportions because it benefits most the team that needs the least help—the Yankees. For years, Steinbrenner already made enormous profits because his team played in New York City and had spectacular media deals. Now, he and a group of powerful partners, including Goldman, Sachs, and Co., have created the YES Network to broadcast the vast majority of Yankees games (with the rest being sold at a steep price to a local affiliate). With all the local cable companies paying exorbitant fees to include YES on their services, untold millions have been added to Steinbrenner's coffers. In the fifties, Bill Veeck was the one owner who complained that the Yankees had too much of an advantage because of subsidiary rights. Now, owners, sportswriters, politicians, and fans are claiming Steinbrenner is ruining the game by buying his way to success with the immense revenues he gets from television.

Under Steinbrenner's free-spending policy, the Yankees stay on top by doing the following:

1. They offer lucrative contracts to superstar free agents.
2. They hold on to their own prized players when they become free agents. The philosophy is to keep the core intact and add to it. Yankees fans who have tired of hearing that they are rooting for a team of carpetbaggers point out that a number of their stars came up through the farm system—Derek Jeter, Bernie Williams, Mariano Rivera, Andy Pettitte, Jorge Posada, and Alfonso Soriano, for instance. But where the Yankees differ from other teams is that they can hold on to such players after they develop into stars and can command huge salaries— not just one or two of them, but *all* of them—simply by raising their budget.
3. The Yankees trade for high-salaried veterans, often during the season. For bait they often use minor leaguers whom they have

promoted as multitool future stars. In most cases, they have employed the old Dodgers trick of overhyping players so they can get great value for them in transactions.

4. They pay a lot to the fourth and fifth starters, so they can have an entire rotation of pitchers who would be aces or the second best pitchers on other teams.

5. They pay a lot to middle relievers like Jeff Nelson, Mike Stanton, Ramiro Mendoza, and Steve Karsay because they often pitch at the pivotal times in games. To secure set-up men who have the stuff to be closers elsewhere, they pay them nearly closer-type salaries.

6. They will eat big contracts for acquisitions that don't pan out and immediately dip into the piggy bank to try again.

The Yankees are a greedy team. When great players are available, they want to sign them to improve their team, make sure another team doesn't improve, grab headlines, and show the *Wall Street Journal* that the Yankees are as dominant in business as they are at baseball. There are no quiet periods; deals are always in the works; Steinbrenner's trigger finger is itchy.

The Yankees' unquenchable thirst for acquisition was brilliantly satirized in the humor newspaper *The Onion* in 2003, when a story claimed that "the New York Yankees have signed every player in major league baseball," which meant that the Yankees had rid themselves of all competition. Joe Torre's comment after his roster jumped to 750 players was, "This is a baseball town, and some of these fans think the Yankees are the only team in baseball. Now that we truly are, the pressure to win will be that much greater." This piece was more than witty; it hit the nail right on the head. It went on to say that the Yankees' pitching rotation prior to the mass signing lacked a clear *seventh* ace. Amazingly, this was close to the truth. At that time the Yankees not only had seven starters vying for the five spots in the rotation, they also made the gluttonous move of signing yet another starter, the disabled free agent Jon Lieber, for the *2004* season.

Can the Yankees sign anybody they want? It almost seems that way. Greg Maddux turned them down and chose to pitch for the Braves for millions less, but that was 10 years ago and he probably based his decision on wanting to play in the league that would allow him to bat. Otherwise, the Yankees always seem to get their man. Ask the Red Sox, who prior to 2003 were furious after losing out to the Yankees on two coveted free agents they had hotly pursued: Japan's most feared hitter, Hideki Matsui, and Cuba's best pitcher, defector Jose Contreras. When Boston management griped that the Yankees had too much of an advantage in pursuing free agents, Yankees management scoffed that the rival organization just had "sour grapes." The use of that term was interesting because Bill Veeck wrote that whenever he'd point out how the Yankees had too much of a financial advantage over other teams, Yankees management was quick to discredit him for his "rampant case of sour-grapeism."

If I were a free agent today, I would consider a number of teams, including the Red Sox (who play in a great ballpark for a right-handed power hitter); the Cubs (who play in my favorite city and schedule most of their home games in the afternoon, which I prefer); the Mets (who play in New York and aren't a stingy team); and the Braves (who have their act together and a winning tradition). I'd rule out San Francisco and Oakland because I hate cold, damp weather and the Dodgers because they became too corporate after the O'Malleys sold the franchise. So I wouldn't automatically pick the Yankees, although it's now much easier to hit home runs to left at Yankee Stadium than when I played.

But it's a fact that given the choice, most current free agents will sign with the Yankees, and often for less money than is offered by other teams. There are several reasons for this. A major one is that the Yankees are the most famous team in the world, perhaps the only American team foreign players know. The Yankees mystique is a definite attraction when the money offers are equal. Having a chance to play in America's most famous ballpark and don the uniform Babe Ruth once wore are major enticements. Players also like the idea of moving to America's most famous city and its media capital, where they can get a lot of attention and perhaps double their salaries with endorsements. If there is no fear of failure, New York is *the* place to play. Players who sign with the Yankees are excited by the combination of a big salary and signing bonus and the very real possibility they will play in a World Series and win a championship. Or they just want to play on the tradition-rich team that their father, favorite uncle, or Aunt Tootsie once loved. It seems like every player who signs with the Yankees mentions that they want to please some family member who idolized Ruth, DiMaggio, Mantle, or Mattingly. Being a Yankee seems to be a goal of almost every player, which makes it tough for other teams to outbid them.

So perhaps Boston has good reason to carp about the Yankees. The Red Sox have done a great job the past few years of hanging in there (and giving out big contracts despite having a small ballpark)—and they nearly beat the Yankees in the 2003 ALCS before Babe Ruth's ghost showed up late in Game 7. However, they have always seemed one player—perhaps one big free agent—behind the Yankees. What really must have gotten their goat is that after the signings of Matsui and Contreras, the Yankees engineered a three-way trade to make sure the White Sox and not the Red Sox got super starter Bartolo Colon from Montreal. That sneaky maneuver didn't break the rules of baseball, and other teams have done it on rare occasion. But if you think about it, when the team on top makes a transaction not to improve itself but to subvert a rival, it smacks of monopoly. As Veeck said about the Yankees management 50 years ago, Steinbrenner and his front office try to prevent healthy competition.

When I think of Steinbrenner and the Yankees, I think of Bill Gates and Microsoft, which also fights off competition and wins wars of attrition to remain on top year after year. Other companies constantly complain that Microsoft is a monopoly that engages in tactics to prevent them from becoming competitive, but at times they simultaneously invest a tremendous amount of money to upgrade their products to be equal to Microsoft's. Microsoft has money to burn, so it can afford to take a chance on upgrading products in the hope they will catch on with the public. But these other companies are taking a huge risk, because unless the demand for an upgraded product is tremendous, they will have difficulty staying on that high level. The Yankees, too, have money to burn because of television. But it's a different story with those other teams that invest a lot of money to compete against the Yankees. Unless they win immediately and their attendance rises and stays high, they will have lost a great deal of operating money.

To compete at the same level as the Yankees, teams have rolled the dice and splurged, hoping to capture lightning in a bottle. The Florida Marlins signed a bunch of free agents and won the world title in 1997, but then they had a fire sale of all those players much like Connie Mack used to do with high-salaried Athletics. Seeing that championship team break up without even defending its title was disheartening, but at least Florida's fans got to experience a world title (six years before an upstart Marlins team with a relatively small budget gave them a much more unexpected second championship). So did Arizona's fans in 2001, just four years after the Diamondbacks came into existence. They drew more than 3 million their first year but then had a precipitous drop in attendance. Then they decided to build the team up by spending money. If you spend the money, you can change your ballclub overnight, and that's the route they chose. They had to ask players to take deferments. Eventually that will catch up to them, so I'm sure they're asking, is it worth it? To win the championship, Arizona brought in high-priced Curt Schilling, and he and Randy Johnson pitched the team to a title over the Yankees in what Fox's Tim McCarver, my onetime broadcasting colleague with the Mets, considers the greatest World Series ever. But Arizona fell further into debt because it couldn't really afford both players. When the team faltered in 2002 and started slowly in 2003, and attendance dropped, Schilling was put on the market. If it had been the Yankees, which has no money worries, Schilling would have been offered a contract extension, and other high-priced players would have been added for another run at the flag. That's the difference.

Sometimes a hurried attempt to reach the Yankees' level will fail miserably. The Mets are the perfect example. After they fell short of dethroning the Yankees in the 2000 Subway Series, they decided to make major changes and bring in a lot of new faces—although few players in the history of the Mets have gotten better when they came to the team. Five good-bet players in 2002 didn't pan out, and the Mets got stuck in the cellar with their enormous multiyear contacts. GMs get bad breaks. The Orioles are another team that paid a lot of money for players but got few dividends. You don't know if the players you're getting will be as good as they were on their previous teams or if they will avoid injuries. If teams that try to win quickly by spending a lot of money flop, they could spend years trying to unload players and rebuild.

It's hard for teams to build from scratch anymore. Bringing up players from the minors isn't enough. You have to do it through the draft, trades, and signings—spending money. Teams that don't change don't win. The team that has done it best has been the Atlanta Braves. Under manager Bobby Cox, they have been in every postseason since 1991—not even the Yankees have done that. It has been an unbelievable achievement. What management did well was make changes but retain their star pitchers Greg Maddux, John Smoltz, and, until 2003, Tom Glavine. They have always been a fundamentally sound team with strong pitching and a few stars—like Chipper Jones, Andruw Jones, Javy Lopez, and trade acquisition Gary Sheffield. The only reason the Braves haven't received more acclaim is that they have been a postseason disappointment, losing in four of their five World Series appearances and, despite their pitching, too often not making it there at all. That they twice lost to the Yankees and blew a 2–0 lead in 1996 has kept them in the Yankees' shadow as the second best team of the era. They seemed awed the second time they played the Yankees in 1999, almost as if they *expected* to lose. Defeat causes insecurity, just as success breeds success. I'm sure the Braves felt that, as did the Brooklyn Dodgers after several Series losses to the Yankees during the late forties and early fifties.

The Braves and Seattle Mariners have stayed among baseball's elite despite wholesale personnel changes because their shrewd general managers John Schuerholz and Pat Gillick have replaced key players with equivalent talent. They have made smart moves and free-agent acquisitions, including Japanese superstar Ichiro Suzuki by the Mariners. However, the Cleveland Indians, a onetime powerhouse, have been experiencing hard times because they went a different route. When the Indians built Jacobs Field, they sold out for a few years although Cleveland wasn't considered a great baseball town. The Indians had great teams at the same time as the Yankees and even beat them in the 1997 AL Division Series, but they let everyone go and went downhill while the Yankees stayed at the top

134

because of a continual infusion of talent. The Indians disassembled their team and got rid of their top draws, which I don't understand. That was a terrible miscalculation, because it has caused them to suffer a huge attendance drop. The Indians are going to have a hard time coming back, because when they lost their great players they didn't get much in return. They can put hope in their prospects, but I don't agree with the old adage, "He's young and will only get better." That's not usually true. Young players are often already at their peaks—exposure is their downfall.

When John Hart was the Indians' GM, he gave long-term contracts to good young players and kept them there for several years. That was a smart move. He locked them in at good rates *before* they became stars and could ask for much more. That has become common practice now, but new GM Mark Shapiro doesn't want to do that; he wants to wait for the prospects to develop. His isn't the way to win back disgruntled fans. Only if you win will you have fans—that law in baseball has never changed. In football, you can lose all 16 games and still have packed houses, but in baseball, if you are in last place too long, you aren't going to draw people, except if you're a team with a cult following, like the Cubs or the Mets of the sixties. Teams need good, popular players to increase attendance. When they get rid of them and get little in return, it spells doom.

I don't believe teams come into a season thinking the Yankees are going to win for sure, but they do know the Yankees have the advantage and are the team to beat. So everything is planned with the Yankees in mind, from budgeting and signing players to getting a lefty reliever to handle the Yankees' top left-handed hitters with the game on the line. But teams need success in a hurry because the rules of baseball work against maintaining winning teams. Without the reserve clause, no owners can assemble a contending team and keep it together for a long period of time—except by paying the star players a great deal of money. The Yankees do that despite a luxury tax; but small-market teams like the A's can't afford it, so they lose their star players.

Teams like Oakland, Anaheim, and Florida have had success with young players who develop very quickly. But the problem is that once a team has success, you have to give all the players huge increases in salary and multi-year deals. And you can't do that unless you're a team like the Yankees, Mets, and Dodgers, who have large budgets. The A's lost one AL MVP, Jason Giambi, to the Yankees, who paid him $120 million for seven years; and the next year, they said they couldn't re-sign their new AL MVP Miguel Tejada to a long-term deal. A's owner Steve Schott explained, "The system is broken down when only two or three teams can pick a player of Miguel's caliber and sign him to an eight- to ten-year contract and pay him the money he deserves. The small-market team with the system we have just can't afford him." After losing Giambi, the A's didn't even make Tejada an offer. The A's have been the one small-market team to contend because they have made extraordinary draft choices, including starting pitchers Tim Hudson, Mark Mulder, and Barry Zito. But once these men play enough years to be free agents, they will probably leave Oakland for greener (as in money) pastures, one player at a time, year after year. How fair is that?

A's GM Billy Beane has gained a lot of notoriety by putting together top-notch teams through the draft, signing reasonably priced free agents, and making creative trades. His modus operandi is to acquire players for less money than they're worth and to get rid of players for more than they are worth. He shuffles players in and out, trying to get a winning team for less than $50 million. He's a shrewd guy who builds around pitching and goes after batters with high on-base percentages. He de-emphasizes speed and wants hitters who walk and put the bat on the ball. You have to be creative like Beane to have success as a small-market team, but nobody has done as well. Having spent most of my career on a team run on a tight budget, I realize how frustrating it is for small-market teams to compete today and how it wears on players who want to win and not just make the team.

The system must be fixed, or small-market teams will continue to lose their best players almost every time. You have to put in some restrictions so, figuratively speaking, the guy who can't run as fast has a chance to win the race anyway. When you choose up sides you try to find balance—the first guy gets one pick, the next gets two picks. That idea has to transfer to baseball in some form. The draft is one equalizer, especially if teams who lose players to free agency can pick up high picks from the teams that sign them. However, with draft picks you have to be lucky as well as intelligent, and you're often prevented from drafting too high because you don't have the budget to sign top picks.

Baseball is that strange creature that has competition among owners who are in actuality partners. If all the other teams shut down, then what could the Yankees do? They need a second team to play against. The Yankees are in a league with other teams, so they should treat them as equals. How can you argue against that? It gets sticky when the small-market visiting team wants half of the TV revenue—and that's when discussions come to a screeching halt. The logical answer would be to put the local TV money into a pot and distribute it evenly. Then, for instance, a visiting team would share all the income with the Yankees, minus their expenses for operation. But owners doing well don't want to share their profits.

The Yankees certainly don't want to share that money. They don't want to give up $15 million to $25 million a year. None of the owners with good television deals want to give up that revenue. I can't blame them. I don't believe in revenue sharing. If one team like Montreal gets no money for local TV rights and another gets $8 million and another gets $60 million, how do you split that up? You can't ask other teams to dish out money so a free agent will stay with his original team. Why should the Yankees share their money with any other team? That's socialism, and I've never seen that work anywhere in the world. Our country is based on capitalism, and that's why the Yankees are so strong.

Now they've tried to achieve some degree of parity with a luxury tax and giving money to owners of small-market teams. The "luxury tax," which goes into effect if owners go beyond a certain payroll limit, should impede individual owners like Steinbrenner from acquiring too many high-priced players. But it hasn't worked that way. Steinbrenner has been willing to pay the tax if he has the chance to sign a coveted player on the market. When he promises to cut salaries, obviously he isn't referring to his players—instead he might choose to get rid of people in the front office.

Another problem is that not all owners who receive a share of revenues put that money back into baseball. In some cases, it goes into their own pockets to offset their losses. The collective-bargaining agreement didn't stipulate that the money must be used to acquire new players. So can Major League Baseball simply tell an owner what he should do with his money? Maybe it can: if you give him the money, you should be able to tell him what he must do with it. The money is shared specifically to create competition, so the owners who get it should have to use it for that purpose. Perhaps they are saying they will pocket the money until they are breaking even and then if there is money left over, they will use it for players. But that doesn't solve anything.

So how do you equalize things? Giving visiting teams a higher percentage of ticket price revenue should help. I think it's about 65-35 now, and if it goes a bit more in favor of visiting teams, that will help defray some of the costs of small-market teams. Otherwise no one has an answer. Smarter people than I are considering the problem. Bill Veeck, who wanted the Yankees and other teams to share their TV revenues with his struggling Browns, had the right idea: it takes two to tango. Should the local TV money be split between the home and visiting teams? And if so, how? Should it be based on each game? Or should the ratings for that game be the determining factor on how much money should be divided between the two clubs, as they do for paid attendance? These options must be considered before a solution can be found. All for one won't work; one for all might. And I'd say that any solution regarding the division of local television money should be arrived at by owners, outside the auspices of the players' union.

But let's say someday all monies will be shared equally. At least that would do away with complaints by teams that they have no money to compete, but there would still be bad teams because not all owners operate as well as others. The Yankees have been fortunate in that they have had very smart people making the deals and calling the shots while under their boss's constant scrutiny. Steinbrenner hires outstanding front-office people such as Al Rosen, Bob Watson, Brian Cashman, and Gene Michael. Al Rosen told me that when he worked for George in the late seventies, he discovered that he was supposed to work for him 24 hours a day. On Christmas every team closed its offices and let everyone take three or four days off— every team, that is, except the Yankees. Rosen had to be in the office with Steinbrenner on Christmas, like Bob Cratchit with Scrooge. Christmas is not a holiday as far as Steinbrenner is concerned. When Rosen quit during the All-Star break in 1979, he sent Steinbrenner a note that said he loved him but didn't love working for him. I know Steinbrenner only socially, and I must say that he's a lot of fun to be around. But I wouldn't want to work for him, either.

However, I think I would have liked playing for him. Remember that I played in Pittsburgh for Branch Rickey, who was too cheap to pay fair salaries or acquire good players so we could be contenders. There's nothing worse than playing for a bad team over the years, and I was living proof of that. It was tough. I know many people in baseball dislike Steinbrenner's methods in maintaining high performance on and off the field, but I think I'd have the same response as most current Yankees players when they are queried about their boss. Most defend him by saying, "All George wants to do is win." If you're a player, you have to think that's a very admirable quality. You can't ask anything more from an owner.

Chapter **6**

Chasing **Babe Ruth**

O f all that has been said or written about me in my life, my favorite quote came from a man who didn't even know my name. A few months before his death at the age of 53 in August 1948, Babe Ruth remarked to reporters, "That *kid* in Pittsburgh might break my homer record."

It didn't matter that Ruth didn't know my name, because he called everybody *kid*; it was enough to learn that my childhood idol even knew about me and that I was hitting a lot of home runs. After all, Babe Ruth was by far the greatest baseball player of all time. Still is. Through the sheer force of personality and a never-ending barrage of balls sailing out of ballparks, he single-handedly resurrected the sport that many thought had been irreparably damaged by the Black Sox scandal. He also changed the way the game is played. No one today can imagine the impact Babe Ruth had on the public—no ballplayer has ever come close. He didn't seem to mind if I broke his magical 1927 record of 60 homers because he was far bigger than a single record. In fact, he dominated the home-run section of the record books. Even with the eventual loss of almost all of his records by the early 21st century, his fame wouldn't be at all diminished.

I made no attempt to contact Babe Ruth after his generous, extremely motivating words. He had no way of knowing it, but we had already met. When I was in high school, I became one of thousands of kids who shook his hand and decided that was the defining moment of their childhoods. The president of the United States didn't mean anything; Babe Ruth was important.

My meeting with Ruth happened through another Babe—Babe Herman, the one time major league outfielder who was working as a scout for the Hollywood Stars of the Pacific Coast League. Herman hit .324 in a 13-year career, including .381 and .393 in back-to-back years for the Dodgers, but was most remembered for misplaying fly balls and once trying to stretch a double into a triple and finding that two of his teammates were already standing on third base. I caught Herman's eye when he sat in the stands and watched my semipro games at Wrigley Field in South Central Los Angeles and the home of the Stars, Gilmore Field, which was located on Beverly Boulevard near the famous Hollywood Farmer's Market, about three miles from Hollywood and Vine. He saw my potential. As a kid, I couldn't afford a Louisville Slugger, and Herman had a whole mess of them with good, aged wood. He probably walked away with them when he played with Brooklyn from 1926 to 1931 because no team gave away equipment. He really wanted to sign me for the Stars, so he gave me a bat or two.

Then one morning, he asked me, "How would you like to meet Babe Ruth?" As soon as I shouted yes, he whisked me over to Wrigley Field. The twenty-five-thousand-seat ballpark was being used as Yankee Stadium in scenes being filmed for what would be the classic 1942 movie bio of Lou Gehrig, *The Pride of the Yankees*. The movie starred Gary Cooper, for whom Herman was the stand-in in some of the baseball scenes. I was wild about movie stars, but I didn't care about him that day. The only person I wanted to meet was Ruth, who had come out to California to make a cameo appearance in the picture.

So Babe Herman took me onto the field and introduced me to Babe Ruth. It was between takes and Ruth was in a Yankees uniform with a No. 3 on its back, bigger than life. I wasn't nervous because he had a reputation for being nice to fans, particularly to kids because of his youth spent in an orphanage. True to form, he was friendly to me even though he had no idea who I was. He called me *kid* then too. It didn't matter—Ruth was the biggest man in the world as far as I was concerned, and that brief moment was a great thrill I'd always cherish. (Incidentally, I still didn't sign with Herman. His argument was that I'd make more money when I was sold by the Stars to the majors because "Son, you're going to make it big." But I didn't fully trust the Stars' general manager. He promised me that if he eventually sold my contract to a major league team he would give me 50 percent of the money he received in the transaction, but I worried that he wouldn't tell me the true amount and I'd get shortchanged. So I thought about signing with the Yankees. But wanting to reach the majors sooner, I instead signed with the Pittsburgh Pirates through scout Hollis "Sloppy" Thurston for $3,000. In 1940, that was the highest sum ever given out in southern California and an enormous amount to my mother and me, considering she was making half that as her yearly salary.)

When Hank Greenberg became my Pirates teammate in 1947 and I started hitting a truckload of homers under his instruction, he too told the media that I might break Ruth's record. That meant a lot to me because Hank, with the Detroit Tigers in 1938, and Jimmie Foxx, with the Philadelphia Athletics six years earlier, came closest to doing it when they hit 58. Foxx, who Lefty Gomez claimed had muscles in his hair, actually smashed 60 homers, but he didn't tie Ruth because he lost two to rainouts. Greenberg, who had a number of multihomer games in his big year, seemed to be in good shape when he needed only two more homers with five games to go. But he was shut out against the St. Louis Browns and then had the misfortune of having the Indians move the season-ending series with the Tigers from the hitter-friendly League Park to Municipal Stadium. Cleveland Municipal Stadium was so immense that even after future Indians owner Bill Veeck brought in the fences years later, it *still* took a mighty wallop to send the ball out of the park.

Hank didn't like to talk about his quest to break Ruth's record. However, he said two significant things in response to conjecture that he wasn't given a fair chance to reach 60 homers because of favoritism by opposing owners, managers, and pitchers for Ruth. In regard to moving the venue, Hank said it wasn't done to stifle him but to accommodate many more fans than the thirty thousand that League Park held. He made no mention of the fact that the final game was called after six innings on account of darkness, depriving him of one and possibly two more times at the plate. Hank also discounted reports that contended he was not pitched to once he got too close to the record. That he got three or four hits in one late-season game—and one ball that left the park just a few inches into foul territory—indicates he was probably correct.

Hank wasn't one to complain or make excuses, so he never told me if being Jewish was a factor in his coming up short of a new record. When I hit over 50 homers, I got a lot of negative mail, including some saying I'd be killed if I passed Ruth, so who knows what feedback Hank got from fans when he got much closer than I did, especially being Jewish in those days. I'm sure there was strong bias against a Jew being the home-run king, and I would think he felt added pressure.

Hank didn't break Ruth's record, but he wanted me to. So he changed me from being a player with some power to a homer hitter who both he and Ruth thought could reach 61 homers in a season.

When I signed with Pittsburgh and then played in its farm system before the war, I was never told that I had to hit home runs to play in the majors. When I stuck with the parent club in 1946, I didn't try to hit balls out of the ballpark because that would have been career suicide in mammoth Forbes Field. I just wanted to hit well enough to earn playing time. Major league baseball turned out to be harder than I expected, and I was in a bit over my head my rookie year. I batted only .247 and led the league in strikeouts. But I did beat out Johnny Mize, the first baseman for the Giants, for the National League home-run title with 23 to his 22. I was lucky to win because Mize missed more than 50 games with a broken arm. I didn't realize my relatively low home-run total would mean so much to Pittsburgh fans, but I was the first Pirates homer champ since 1902 and tied Johnny Rizzo's team record for most homers in a season.

When Greenberg arrived the next spring, he helped me convert to being a pull hitter because the ball wasn't live then, and homers to the opposite field were few and far between. He also wanted me to take advantage of "Greenberg Gardens," the new bullpen area behind the makeshift left-field fence that the Pirates put up for his benefit. Before the Pirates installed that fence 335 feet from home plate, which was a normal distance, the only two ways for anyone to homer to left were to pull the ball directly down the line or hit it *over* the high scoreboard. If you hit the scoreboard it would bounce back on the field and be in play. Reaching the fence in center, 457 feet from home, wasn't likely. So before Greenberg's arrival and the construction of the shortened fence, Forbes Field was not the place to break the homer record. So if I had broken it, there's little doubt that Ruth fans would have insisted the reason was "Kiner's Korner," as it came to be called. They ignored the fact that the lefty-swinging Ruth had a big advantage when he hit 60 homers because the house that he built in the Bronx had a short right-field fence.

With Greenberg as my tutor, I learned to pull fly balls to left field that had the potential of going out of the park. That became my new objective in hitting. I had a pretty upright stance, holding my hands high to compensate for a high fastball. I started out using 35-inch bats of between 33 and 35 ounces, which was what most hitters of the day swung. In time I would use heavier bats, from 37 to 42 ounces, depending on the pitcher. I tried to make contact at about 80 percent of my ability for swing speed so that if I did hit it on the good part of the bat and picked the right pitch to hit, the ball would fly off into the distance with a lot of backspin.

While trying to implement what Greenberg was preaching, I started off terribly in 1947, with only three homers by the end of May. I didn't lose my confidence, but my manager Billy Herman would have sent me to the minors if Hank hadn't gone directly to our majority owner, Frank McKinney, to plead my case. So I stayed in the big leagues and had a great year. I hit .313, which would be a career high, scored 118 runs, and drove in 127 runs—the first of five consecutive years I would have more than 100 in both categories—and I led the league for the first time in slugging percentage.

In July, I set the Pirates' single-season record with my 24th homer of the season. In August, I equaled major league marks by hitting homers in four consecutive at-bats—three coming in one game against the Cardinals—and hitting five homers in two games, six homers in three games, and seven homers in four games, which tied Tony Lazzeri in 1936. Then in another hot streak in September I belted eight homers in four games to break Lazzeri's record and move ahead of Johnny Mize in a very tight home-run race. That may have been my greatest home-run feat, and it was written up a lot.

However, my biggest thrill came six days later, when, in just my second year, I became only the second National Leaguer to hit 50 homers in a season. I felt that put me in a special echelon. Johnny Mize would hit his

50th two days later to join me and Hack Wilson, who set the National League record of 56 in 1930.

Papers ran a tally of what we did each day. In fact, there was a tremendous amount of press coverage of the race. Fans knew about it all over, but Pittsburgh and New York, where Mize played, were where it was really played up. In addition to all the dailies in New York, the Associated Press and United Press International came out of New York, and their stories went out all over the country. So I became well known and got a lot of mail, including hate mail. I became a big celebrity in Pittsburgh, and attendance improved dramatically. Unfortunately, it was a small town, so I couldn't go anywhere without drawing a crowd, and sometimes I had to make like Greta Garbo and stay in seclusion. Oddly, New York was the only place where people left me alone.

Mize and I had pictures taken together when our teams played each other. We became friends years later, but at the time I thought he was gruff and not easy to get along with. There was no animosity among home-run hitters in general, but there was no mutual admiration society either. I felt neither hatred nor compassion for Mize when we competed for homer titles. I really wanted to win, but my nature was to just let the chips fall where they may.

Mize set his sights on winning. He even hit first in the lineup to get some additional at-bats. Billy Herman offered to bat me first, too, but I didn't want to jinx myself so I stayed in the cleanup spot. (It helped me that Greenberg batted fifth, one of the few times in my Pirates career I had an RBI man protecting me.) Mize and I went back and forth until we each hit number 51. And then, surprisingly, we both went cold and didn't homer again for the last few days of the season. Toots Shor's restaurant was located at 51 West 51st, and Toots claimed we did it on purpose.

When the season ended, my total had jumped by 28 homers, and I won my second consecutive homer title, tying Mize. After June 1, I hit 48 homers, which had to be some kind of record. Everyone recognized that it wasn't a fluke because I homered at a terrific clip for a long enough period of time. Any way they looked at the numbers, it showed that if I had homered at the same pace in April and May, I would have shattered the homer record. So that is why Ruth, Greenberg, and others thought I had a legitimate chance in future years.

After I hit 51 homers I wanted to do it again. But Zack Taylor, who was a coach on the 1947 team, insisted publicly that I'd never again hit 50, or even a significant number of home runs. His reasoning was that I hit my homers after I got signs on what pitches were coming from our third-string catcher, Billy Sullivan, and Sullivan's major league career had ended after the '47 season. Billy didn't play much, but he was a master at breaking down the codes that teams used. I'd get to second and I'd memorize the pattern of signs and pitches I'd see, for maybe six or seven pitches, and then I'd tell it all to Billy and he'd process it all and break down the code. Such things were common on most teams; in fact, when Greenberg played on the Tigers, his manager Del Baker signaled him what pitches were coming. Of course, knowing what pitch is coming and hitting the pitch are two different things, so I didn't buy Taylor's vision of my future.

It may have surprised Taylor that I made my first All-Star team in 1948 and drove in 123 runs, as we jumped to fourth place and had the only winning record in my years with the team, 83–71. If not, then maybe my homering at one point in 17 of 35 games might have done the trick. Or my going deep on eight successive Sundays. (I loved Sunday doubleheaders because they gave me a chance to hit eight or nine times and find my groove.) I am sure Taylor didn't expect me to capture another homer title, again tying Johnny Mize—meaning that over a three-year period I hit only one more homer than the "Big Cat."

But Taylor might have felt somewhat vindicated because my homer total dropped from 51 to 40 and my average fell 48 points. What happened to me happens to many others after they have monster years. Doing it two years in a row is very difficult. Hack Wilson played in 43 fewer games the year after he hit 56 homers, drove in the all-time record 190 runs (later changed to 191 RBIs), and batted .356. But that doesn't explain why he had only 13 homers and 61 RBIs and batted just .261. After hitting 61 homers in 1961, a drained Roger Maris would drop to 33 in 1962. Even Barry Bonds would hit 27 fewer homers in the year after he slugged 73 (although it must be pointed out that he upped his average from .328 to .370 and walked a record 198 times).

After I hit just 23 homers in 1946, no one was that worried about me in 1947, so they pitched me the same way. I sneaked up on them and hit 51 homers before they realized I was for real. I got smarter and they didn't. But in 1948, they wised up and it was harder for me to hit home runs. One reason is that Greenberg was no longer batting behind me, so I was walked more than 100 times for the first of seven consecutive seasons.

To be a good hitter, you must always change. In 1949, I changed again. I knew the pitchers better and how they worked me, and I remembered Greenberg's advice to be more selective and lay off pitches I couldn't hit with authority—even if they were strikes. You want to handle the pitches you get and knock them out of the ballpark. It's more mental than physical.

I hit 54 home runs in '49. Johnny Mize was going downhill, so I didn't have any real competition for the home-run crown. I finished with 18 more than Stan Musial, the second-place finisher. I became the first National Leaguer to hit more than 50 homers twice, which didn't mean as much to me as hitting 50 the first time but was probably a greater achievement. I hit 16 of those homers in September and again had homers in four successive at-bats. My 54th homer went over the scoreboard clock at Forbes Field.

Again I received a lot of mail during the season, including many with threats. "Don't break the record!" read their printed warnings. "Ruth is the idol of us all!" People from all over the country made it quite clear that it was sacrilegious and unpatriotic to even *think* of surpassing an American icon. Twelve years later, fans would react to Roger Maris with similar rage when he was in a more legitimate position to break the record. They needn't have worried about me. I would never get closer to Ruth's single-season home-run record than I did in 1949.

Around that time, I contributed to an article for the *Saturday Evening Post* that was titled, "The Home Run I Would Hate to Hit." I told the writer of the piece that I would hate to break Babe Ruth's record because of the great admiration the fans had for him and because he was such a big part of the game. That was a big fat lie. I never admitted it in public, but prior to a season it was a goal of mine to hit more than 60 homers. Yet when questioned, I would "humbly" tell reporters that it didn't matter to me if I ever equaled Ruth. The truth is that I would have loved to have broken his record, but I never got close enough to do it. What made it too difficult is that many pitchers wouldn't throw me strikes. Some games I'd be walked almost every time up. Consequently, I was never on Ruth's pace. I would finish the season with big Septembers and my final total would be fairly close to his, but I was never a serious threat. It didn't help that Ruth hit 17 homers in September of his record year.

Another enormous obstacle was that the old stadiums in the National League weren't friendly to right-handed power hitters. The only two parks that were good for home-run hitters were Ebbets Field and Forbes Field, after they constructed "Greenberg Gardens."

Ebbets Field was a fantastic place in which to hit because it was short all the way around, the reason it was called a "bandbox." Down the line in left it was 348 feet, and left-center field was only about 375 feet. I hit a lot of homers there and would have hit many more if they hadn't had such great pitchers. It was my favorite stadium. A cigarette company put up a mechanical sign that would dispense a carton after a home run—unfortunately it didn't do that for me, only for Dodgers who went deep.

Cincinnati's Crosley Field was the only other park where you could homer to center, because it was only 387 feet away. But otherwise it wasn't a good park for me. It was built on a river bottom, so there was no breeze during the day and balls didn't carry. Also, there was a big scoreboard in left center that would prevent homers in that area. When Frank Robinson slammed 38 homers as a Reds rookie in 1956, I was really impressed. Ted Kluszewski, a former football player who cut off his sleeves so his muscles would show, slugged a lot of homers there. He was left-handed, but he hit the ball the other way too. One year he hit 49 homers and struck out only 35 times, which shows what a great hitter he was.

St. Louis' Busch Stadium, which was called Sportsman's Park until the Browns' owner sold it to the Cardinals and Anheuser-Busch president Augie Busch in 1953, wasn't bad for hitters despite the stifling heat. Left field was about 350 feet, and it was more than 420 feet in center, but the ball carried very well because of that heat. In 1929, they put up a 33-foot-high screen in right to guard against homers into the lower deck of the pavilion area (where in the fifties fans sat for 90 cents). It was kind of like the Polo Grounds in that it was hard to hit the ball in the lower stands, but if you hit the ball high and far enough it would land on the roof. They took the screen down, but it didn't enhance homer hitting much because it was hard to hit a line drive far enough to reach the seats.

Shibe Park in Philadelphia, which was renamed Connie Mack Stadium in 1953, was a good place for hitting. It was a long way to the fence—468 to dead center—but the ball carried well to left. It was the rare park where it was harder to homer to right, because there was a very high screen above the right-field fence.

Wrigley Field in Chicago was very hard on hitters in my day because the center-field bleachers weren't blocked off to fans. The white ball leaving the pitcher's hand would blend in with the white shirts, and you'd lose the ball on its way to the plate. It was lethal. Players complained about it, so as the NL player rep I had to convince the Cubs' GM Jim Gallagher to block out those seats in center. He thought it would cost the team money, but in those days the Cubs didn't draw so many fans that some would be turned away because of the reduction of seats. So Gallagher agreed, and it has been a good park for home runs to this day.

Braves Field, the home of the Boston Braves, was very tough because it was deep in left and center and the wind usually blew in. It was short in right, and they had what was called a "jury box" beyond the right and right-center-field fence where the pitchers warmed up. The Braves moved to County Stadium in Milwaukee in 1953, and that was a good park, where Aaron and the left-handed Eddie Mathews thrived as power hitters. Pitching staffs often determined whether it was a good park to hit in and the Braves had Warren Spahn, Lew Burdette, and Bob Buhl, so it wasn't great for visiting hitters. I played there only two years.

The Polo Grounds was the worst. It was only 257 feet down the right-field line and 279 feet down the left-field line, but it was huge everywhere else. It was 445 feet to the front of the bleachers, which was a tremendous distance, and it was 483 feet to where the clubhouse stood. They had two decks in the outfield, and one way you homered was to hit a high fly—you would think it would be caught by the outfielder below, but it would land in the upper-deck overhang. Bobby Thomson's homer to win the 1951 pennant was unbelievable because it was awfully hard to hit a line drive that hard into the lower deck at the Polo Grounds.

Branca threw an inside pitch, which made Thomson's homer possible. When I started to hit homers, I never got inside pitches at the Polo Grounds. It was frustrating because they would pitch me low and outside and make me hit the ball to center where there were acres patrolled, beginning in 1951, by Willie Mays. He could track the ball down anywhere. So it wasn't an easy park for me to hit in, although I hit more homers off the Giants' Larry Jansen than I did off of any other pitcher.

Probably the longest ball I hit at the Polo Grounds was off Sheldon Jones. Thomson, who played center before Mays, almost ran it down, and it short-hopped the fence at 483 feet. The runner on first held up so I couldn't get an inside-the-park homer. So I had hit the longest triple in the history of that ballpark, maybe in history. And Mays might have caught that ball.

Mays managed to hit a lot of homers at the Polo Grounds. He pulled homers the first few years, and when they pitched him outside he went the other way, to the shorter part of the field. He was one of the few guys who had enough power to do that. I hit the ball that way only on checked swings.

Some of those old ballparks were so difficult for me to hit homers in that I was always glad to come back to the friendly confines of the stadium named after 18th-century general John Forbes. It was there that on May 25, 1935, Babe Ruth, then playing with the Boston Braves, hit the final three homers of his career. His 714th and last homer was the first ball ever to clear Forbes Field's right-field roof.

Although I came to the conclusion that breaking Ruth's single-season homer record was an unrealistic goal, I thought the National League record of 56 by Hack Wilson was within reach. In fact, I would have had 55 homers in 1949, but one I hit off the Boston Braves' Johnny Sain was rained out. I never met Wilson or saw him play, and all I really knew about him was that he was a very short guy who weighed more than 200 pounds and was a drinker. Supposedly a manager once took Wilson aside and demonstrated the severity of alcohol on the body by dropping worms into a glass of whiskey and a glass of water. When the worms in the whiskey stopped moving, the manager pointed to those still swimming in the water and asked Hack what he had just learned. Wilson replied, "If you drink whiskey, you won't have worms."

I would have loved to have taken away Wilson's homer record and left him with his remarkable single-season RBI record, which I couldn't see anyone ever breaking. I never said publicly that I targeted his record either, but it's disappointing I never beat it, especially because I would have held the record for decades to come. Wilson's NL record wasn't broken until 1998, when the Cardinals' Mark McGwire and the Cubs' Sammy Sosa obliterated Maris's major league record by clouting 70 and 66 homers, respectively.

Even though I recognized the futility of chasing Ruth's single-season home-run record, I was still in contention for breaking another of his significant homer records. With my fourth consecutive home-run title, I had a shot at his major league record of six in a row.

In 1950, when I was voted the Player of the Year by *The Sporting News*, I won my fifth consecutive title with 47 homers, beating the Cubs' Andy Pafko by 11. In one memorable game against the Dodgers, I hit for the cycle, had two homers, and drove in eight runs. Wally Westlake hit more than 20 homers and drove in close to 100 runs for us, but nobody else could do better than 8 homers or around 50 RBIs. We were a last-place club, so once more, I wasn't pitched to and I just missed getting 50 homers for the third time.

In 1951, I tied Babe Ruth's record with my sixth consecutive home-run title. There's an amusing story that goes with it. I hit 42 homers that year, but the Dodgers' Gil Hodges had 40 and could have tied or even passed me in the storied third playoff game versus the Giants to determine the National League champion. Our season was over and our announcer, Bob Prince, was visiting the Polo Grounds and sitting next to Giants announcer Russ Hodges during his live radio broadcast. When Bobby Thomson hit the game-ending "shot-heard-around-the-world" homer to beat the Dodgers, Hodges did his famous call, "The Giants win the pennant! The Giants win the pennant! The Giants win the pennant!" Then he was so distracted from wanting to rush down to the clubhouse to mingle with the champions that he turned the microphone over to Prince. So during all the excitement after one of the greatest games of all time, Prince interjected, "And Ralph Kiner is still the home-run king of the National League." What he said had no bearing on anything that was going on and I'm sure nobody listening cared, but it went out over the air. People would later say to me, "What the hell were they talking about *you* for?"

In 1952, as I went after a record seventh consecutive homer title, I found myself involved in yet another down-to-the-wire race. This time my competition was the Cubs' Hank Sauer, who would be voted the National League's MVP. I was one homer behind Sauer after 152 games, 37 to 36. Our last series was in Cincinnati, and we were scheduled to play two games.

Rather than taking the train with the rest of the team, I flew to Cincinnati at my own expense so I could get a good night's sleep. Before the first game, I asked our young shortstop Dick Groat to pitch batting practice to me for about an hour and a half, which he was very happy to do. And it paid off. I hit my 37th home run to tie Sauer, who didn't homer that day. But on Sunday I didn't hit a homer, so that left him with an opening. We got on the train going back to Pittsburgh before I was able to get any news about Hank's final game. I didn't know if he had homered and won the title outright. I was anxious, of course, because I wanted to break Babe Ruth's record, so when the train stopped in Indianapolis I jumped out and found the stationmaster. Through Western Union, I discovered that Sauer had *not* homered and we ended up tied. So I had broken a major record held by my idol Babe Ruth! When I got back on the train I ordered champagne for all the players to celebrate.

In 1953, even before I was traded to the Cubs, it was obvious that my home-run title streak was ending. I had no chance to keep it going after I hit only seven homers in 41 games for the Pirates. Although disappointed to leave Pittsburgh, I did better after I arrived in Chicago and wound up in fifth place in the league. Eddie Mathews won the title with 47 homers; Duke Snider, Roy Campanella, and Ted Kluszewski all hit more than 40; and I had 35. I wasn't disappointed that my seven-year run was over, because it wasn't as if I lost the race in September. I was often asked if I was relieved that I'd no longer have to experience the pressure of keeping my streak alive. My answer was: "What pressure?" I never felt added pressure—either that, or we players lived with pressure better in those days.

It seems strange, but when I was winning the seven titles, I never thought about my place in baseball history or the Hall of Fame. All I was doing was chasing Babe Ruth.

During my time I didn't think anyone else had a chance of breaking Ruth's single-season home-run record. I was ahead of everyone else as far as home runs were concerned. Mize was getting old. Ted Williams walked too much. Joe DiMaggio played in Yankee Stadium, which was a bad park for right-handed power hitters. Musial didn't become a power hitter until he was making more money than I was, and he still never hit more than 39 in 1948, and that year I beat him by one.

During the fifties, a number of new sluggers emerged: Mickey Mantle, Willie Mays, Eddie Mathews, Ted Kluszewski, Ernie Banks, and, later, Frank Robinson, Rocky Colavito, Harmon Killebrew, and Orlando Cepeda. But only Mays, with 51 in 1955, and Mantle, with 52 in 1956, hit more than 50 homers in a season, and neither challenged Ruth's record any more than I had. It took them a few years to develop into homer hitters, but they became the two guys I thought had the most potential to hit 60 home runs in a season. Mantle had the advantage of being a switch-hitter with awesome power from both sides of the plate. Mays was hindered by playing first in the Polo Grounds and then in Candlestick Park in San

Francisco, where he was forced to hit opposite-field homers because of the windy conditions. Both Mantle and Mays hit more than 50 homers again during the sixties, by which time the season had expanded from 154 to 162 games.

In 1961, everyone thought Mantle had the better chance than his teammate Roger Maris of breaking Babe Ruth's record. He was right there with Maris into September when he got a debilitating cold and then a bad infection after a "shady" doctor injected him with a mysterious substance. So Mantle's quest came to an unceremonious end, with him stuck on 54 homers. Then Maris had to finish on his own without anyone else pushing him or sharing the attention of the press. Maris would miss having Mantle batting behind him in the fourth slot and protecting him down the stretch. Interestingly, he didn't receive one intentional walk all season—even after Mantle was gone and he was approaching the record. I would think pitchers wouldn't want to be associated with giving up famous home runs, but a few years later I interviewed Jack Fisher, who yielded Maris' 60th homer (as well as Ted Williams' 521st and final homer in his last at-bat), and Tracy Stallard, who gave up Maris' 61st homer, and they were proud. They didn't think it was shameful or an egregious error. It wasn't like giving up a pennant-winning homer.

Maris had a beautiful left-handed swing that was ideal for Yankee Stadium's short right-field fence. In fact, he got a number of homers by hooking the ball down the line and over the fence in the right-field corner, which was only 296 feet away. So I knew he had the capability of hitting a lot of home runs. But I didn't think he would break Ruth's record. My theory at the time was that if anyone broke the record, he would have to be well ahead of the record pace going into September and then coast past sixty homers with three or four homers to spare. If Maris was forced to try to break Ruth's record by only one, the pressure, as I told the press, would be too immense.

Any player who was a threat to Ruth would be under intense pressure, but what Maris was subjected to was more than anyone could have handled. First of all, he received tons of hate mail. All of it was pro-Ruth, but in many cases it was also pro-Mantle. It seems that if any Yankee passed Ruth, the fans wanted it to be their favorite son. This was an ironic sentiment considering that until Maris put on the pinstripes, Mantle had always been the main target of the hometown boobirds, who never wanted him to forget that he wasn't Joe DiMaggio.

Maris also was experiencing unrelenting pressure from the New York media, which demanded stories every day, even if the only story was that he hadn't homered. The media was much larger and more hostile than when Ruth set his record or when I played. Having come from North

Dakota, the shy Maris had no idea why so many reporters would keep inter- rogating someone who made it clear that he wanted no publicity. (Even after breaking the record, Maris did very little to capitalize financially on his accomplishment. But he did hit pay dirt after he was traded to St. Louis a few years later and made one of the best deals in baseball history when he persuaded Cardinals owner Augie Busch to give him a Budweiser franchise in Florida if he played just one more year.)

Unfortunately, nobody in the Yankees front office made any effort to help Maris deal with the press, so he was forced to experience very public meltdowns. If that weren't enough, baseball commissioner Ford Frick, who had been a friend of Ruth's, revealed his anti-Maris bias. He created a tremendous amount of controversy when he announced that unless Maris broke Ruth's record in 154 games instead of the 162 games that the expanded American League scheduled for the first time in 1961, an aster- isk would be placed next to Maris' total in the record book. So with nega- tivity swirling around him, it's not surprising that Maris, despite being a laid-back individual, had such psychological problems that hair started to fall out of his crew cut.

Yet he did not crumble. Maris, who had 59 homers after 154 games (to tie Ruth's 1921 total for second most), proved I was wrong in theorizing no one would beat Ruth by just one home run. He did so by lining a Tracy Stallard fastball into the right-field stands at Yankee Stadium on the last day of the season, as his team won its 162nd official game by the fitting score of 1–0.

When Maris went for his 61st homer, there wasn't nearly a packed house. Many New York baseball fans didn't even watch the game on television or listen to it on the radio. This leads one to believe that the press was making a bigger deal of what Maris was doing than the fans were—or that when Mantle went down, the great story lost its hero. Hank Greenberg and I were playing tennis in New York when Maris hit his homer. Hank asked someone with a radio what was going on, but he wasn't really that interested. I was the same way. I was thinking it was anticlimactic because of the extra games.

I happen to have agreed with Frick; 162 games is definitely different from 154 games. In those extra eight games, a batter probably gets 35 to 40 more opportunities. You want someone to break a record under the same condi- tions, with no advantages. My reaction at the time is the same as it is now: OK, Maris broke the record, but he didn't *really* do it because he played more games than Ruth—and baseball itself changed with expansion to favor hitters. But I don't want Maris to have an asterisk by his name for the simple reason that I don't want the entire record book to be full of asterisks, noting every record broken after baseball went to a 162-game schedule. It's best if they just leave it alone.

Maris' great accomplishment was to hit his 61st homer under extremely difficult circumstances, on a pressure-packed final day, when no other runs were scored in the game. Ruth's 60-home-run mark reminds me of the four-minute mile. No one thought it could be broken before 1954, but once Roger Bannister did it, all the other milers knew it was possible and everyone started going under four minutes. Which is why it's so surprising that no one would pass Maris for another 37 years. Perhaps we underestimated what he did at the time, thinking that with the schedule at 162 games and the dilution of pitching talent because of expansion, the record would be broken every couple of years. Amazingly, Maris would hold onto his record three years longer than did Ruth.

Between Roger Maris' 61 homers in 1961 and Mark McGwire's 70 homers in 1998, several players made a run at a new record but fell short. In 1969, 23-year-old Reggie Jackson of the Oakland A's had 37 homers by the All-Star Game, which was a record. He was so young, strong, and confident that it seemed likely that he would pass Maris. But most pretenders hit roadblocks sometime during the season, and Jackson did nothing for the rest of the season. It was jarring how badly he slumped. He finished with 47 homers, and it's interesting to note that in the next 18 years he never hit more than 41 homers in a year. Many home-run hitters strike out a lot, but you can't strike out as much as Jackson, who whiffed 142 times that year. If you don't make contact, the chance of hitting the ball out of the ballpark is zero. Ruth was known as a strikeout king, but the most times he ever struck out in a season was 93. I think I averaged about 65 times a year. McGwire struck out a lot while he pursued Maris, but he had the luxury of knowing that if he made contact, the ball would go about 500 feet. He went one month with no hit other than a homer—it's ridiculous that he never had even one single. When Barry Bonds hit 73 homers in 2001, he also seemed to homer every time he made contact. Like McGwire, he was willing to take walks; unlike McGwire, he rarely struck out.

Matt Williams of the Giants always struck out a lot, but in 1994 he was a true candidate for immortality when he had 43 homers after only 112 games. However, that's when the season was aborted by the players strike. I didn't think we were deep enough in the season to say positively that he'd break it. A lot of guys had gotten off to great starts, but as McGwire would tell reporters four years later, nobody should make a big deal of it until a player has 50 homers going into September. At the time Williams challenged the record, many of us thought he would hit a roadblock, as did Jackson and many other players who hit a lot of homers between April and mid-August. But if the record at the time had been 65 or 70 and Williams would have seen that players were capable of passing Maris' mark, I think he would have hit at least 62. Sixty-two homers seems like a reasonable goal now that McGwire, Sosa, and Bonds have done it.

McGwire came close to catching Roger Maris in 1997, when he hit 58 homers while playing for the A's and Cardinals. So it was evident he was a genuine threat to break the record, which is why a large contingent of sportswriters poured into the Cardinals' training camp the following spring. Then from the first day of the 1998 season they began following him everywhere but into the bathroom. They waited for McGwire to hit a lull and for calls from their editors to return home and start writing about other stories, perhaps about the Yankees' 114-win season. But he never did, and they never did. As the season progressed, an equal number of reporters were dispatched to follow Sammy Sosa, who was matching McGwire homer for homer.

When McGwire came into the National League, people asked me if he reminded me of anyone I ever saw. I said, "Me!" I had the ability to hit fly balls with backspin that would start out like catchable balls and then carry out of the ballpark. That's how Mark McGwire hit. His homers had an extra surge, like going into a second gear as they approached the fence. And they kept going.

Sammy Sosa occasionally hit moon shots, but his fly balls rarely had that surge. He homered for the simple reason that he is a big, strong guy with quick hands who hits the ball in the air. He homered often to right-center, where the ball carries really well in Wrigley Field. Sosa, who had never hit more than 40 homers a season before 1998, became a great homer hitter when he got smart enough to not swing at the low outside curve, which no one can hit out of the ballpark. He replaced strikeouts with long drives. (In 2003, Sosa's accomplishments became suspect when cork was discovered after his bat shattered during a game. Sosa's excuse, which allowed him to escape with a short suspension, was that he had accidentally used a batting-practice bat. His story could be believed only by the optimist who still leaves the back porch light on for Jimmy Hoffa.)

When I was hitting a lot of home runs over a few games or a week or even a month, I'd think, "How long can this last?" With McGwire and Sosa it lasted all year (as it did with Bonds in 2001). They never slowed down; they never had prolonged slumps when they didn't homer at all. Every time McGwire threatened to pull away, Sosa would go on a tear and either catch him or edge ahead. In one month, he hit a record 20 homers to overcome a 15-homer deficit. It was as if it were all scripted and they homered on cue, day after day, going back and forth. And the homers themselves were awesome, mighty blows hit by mythical figures. Nothing came cheap—except, interestingly, McGwire's 70th homer on the final day of the season, a poorly struck ball that he somehow muscled just over the top of the left-field fence.

Like everybody else, I was riveted by the McGwire-Sosa race. It was one of the great events ever in baseball, wonderful theater that transfixed a nation and revitalized interest in the game by fans who were outraged by the '94 strike and no postseason. Because it was played up every day by the media, it reminded me of the 1947 home-run race I had with Mize. But we were approaching 50 homers, not a record 62 homers. And while we made sports headlines, McGwire and Sosa made headlines on the front pages of newspapers across America. The first thing people looked for when they got a paper each day was whether they had homered. Usually they had. I wasn't surprised by how much the media played it up because it was a big cultural event. I don't think any record in sports has come closer to capturing the fans' interest than the single-season home-run record. I don't think any baseball fan who is worth his or her weight doesn't know who holds the record.

The two players handled it with class, keeping it friendly but competitive. McGwire didn't enjoy the experience as much as Sosa, who loved being on center stage with the media and finding popularity with fans. McGwire became close to the Maris family and probably had mixed emotions about taking away the one record that guaranteed Maris lasting fame. He may have been goal-driven, but he felt a bit guilty about what his goal was. So he was more workmanlike in his approach than Sosa, not happy-go-lucky about the occasion. He was much tenser, at least until September when he finally admitted he was going to hit more than 61 homers. At that point, he understood why the reporters had been trailing him all season and the whole country was so interested in the race. He also saw how much more fun Sosa was having by being friendly to the press, so he realized it might be a good idea to emulate Sosa. Then, finally, he lightened up and enjoyed himself.

It was harder for McGwire because he was chasing Maris, while Sosa seemed to be chasing McGwire. Sosa seemed pleased to be second to McGwire at passing Maris and at finishing behind him at season's end, 70 to 66. If it had been reversed, I think McGwire would have been very unhappy if he hadn't reached 62 homers first or ended up with the homer title and new record.

As I said earlier, I had predicted that whoever broke Babe Ruth's record would have to do it by several homers so that the pressure wouldn't be too great at the end of the season. Although Maris proved me wrong, McGwire and Sosa did follow my blueprint, zooming past 61 homers in mid-September and eventually beating the record by large margins. Having proved Maris' mark was attainable, McGwire and Sosa passed it again in 1999, hitting 65 and 63 homers, respectively. And in 2001, while McGwire battled injuries and slumps, Sosa set a record with a third season with more than 60 homers. But Sosa wasn't even in the hunt that year with his 64 homers. Barry Bonds, who had never even hit 50 homers before, slammed an incredible 73, and, impossibly, usurped McGwire as the single-season record holder after only three years. Like McGwire and Sosa in '98, he didn't feel added pressure because he always remained well ahead of the record pace. Surprisingly, the aloof Bonds seemed to enjoy himself at his postgame press conferences during the season.

Bonds crushed 73 homers without anyone pushing him, becoming the first record holder to do it that way since Ruth. As Ted Williams said, hitting is the most difficult thing in sports, but at times it seems like Bonds found the secret. He has all the components to be a great hitter, with the ability to pull it off. There is nothing about his swing to criticize. It is one of the greatest swings I've ever seen. He has a fast, short stroke and superb hand-eye coordination. He has always been an outstanding hitter, but becoming more selective has made him even better in the past few years. The secret to being a great hitter is to get pitches you can handle, and Bonds is extremely patient while waiting for his pitch. He walks rather than chase balls. People say he doesn't get anything to hit, but most batters swing at what he lets go. Pitchers try to make all batters swing at what they only think goes across the plate in the strike zone, but Bonds doesn't fall for the illusion of a strike. He doesn't have a lot of checked swings. He gets the benefit of calls, but all good hitters do.

What is truly amazing about Bonds is just when his career seemed to be in decline, he went on an exhaustive, five-hour-a-day conditioning program and came back more dangerous than ever. As I have said, if you add 20 pounds of muscle to someone who has super eye-to-hand coordination, he can't really be pitched to. Bonds is a good case in point. He can swing at almost any pitch in the strike zone because now that he is bulked up, if he makes good contact, it no longer ends up in an outfielder's glove but flies over the fence to all fields. He even chokes up on a very light, whippy bat, which, wrote the *San Francisco Chronicle*'s Ray Ratto, is made of mahogany and plutonium.

I have never seen anything like what Bonds did in 2001. Neither had most opposing managers because they were doing a rare act with regularity—walking him intentionally even if he represented the tying or winning run. Athletics manager Ken Macha explained that he did it because he assumed that if he pitched to Bonds he'd homer every time up. It's hard to argue with that logic.

My only objection is that Bonds wears pads on his right arm to keep from being hurt if he is hit by a pitched ball. Intimidation is a part of pitching, so Bonds and other batters should not be permitted to wear armor that eliminates the fear factor. Because he's confident he won't feel anything, he doesn't bail out on inside pitches and can make contact. That gives him too much of an advantage.

I think before Bonds is through he will also hold the career home-run record. For a while it looked like Ken Griffey Jr. would be the one to pass Henry Aaron's 755 career homers, but injuries have taken away a few of his prime years. Sammy Sosa could do it, although he might have trouble continuing to hit 40 or 50 homers a year for as long as it would take. But the easy bet to pass Aaron first is Bonds; he is already at 658 homers and shows no signs of slowing down. At an age when most players go downhill, he has actually gotten better. Usually by the time you learn how to make the most of experience, it's too late, but not with Bonds. If he wants to play long enough to pass Aaron, then that's just what he'll do. He's the type of player who can dedicate himself to working hard and ignore all the distracting outside influences. Now 50-homer years aren't unusual, so if Bonds doesn't hit 32 or 33 homers each year for the next three years and pass 755 homers, everyone will be surprised. I know Aaron expects it to happen.

When I was a young kid and all during my playing career, Babe Ruth's record of 714 home runs was considered invincible, much like Cy Young's 511 victories. So safe was the record that nobody even protested that Ruth would have hit many more home runs if he hadn't pitched for more than five seasons with Boston. (Even in the dead-ball era, he would have hit a lot more homers—it was a game of singles then, but it was still that in the twenties, except for Ruth.) As the years passed, there was a growing consensus that nobody would break Ruth's record. Then Hank Aaron shattered it.

No one who watched Aaron's career with the Milwaukee and Atlanta Braves thought he had a chance to pass Ruth. It wasn't even a consideration because, despite winning four home-run titles, he never hit more than 47 homers in a season—and that came when he was already 37. But Aaron played 23 long seasons, and he also knocked out 45 home runs once, 44 (his uniform number) four times, 40 twice, and at least 20 in 20 consecutive years. Remarkably, he hit 40 homers at the age of 39, when he had fewer than 400 at-bats. Hank had a marvelous body and was able to play a long time, and year after year he got closer, until he finally broke the record in 1974. And because of the DH, he got to play two seasons with the Milwaukee Brewers and jog around the bases 22 more times.

Aaron was as great a player as Willie Mays and certainly as fearless, explaining years later that "the pitcher only had a ball; I had a bat." But he always was second to Mays in the eyes of fans and historians. The reasons were that he played with less flair than Mays, didn't have his power, and played far from the New York spotlight in Milwaukee. So it was a bit of a surprise that Aaron passed Mays on the homer list and became the prime challenger to Ruth's record. It certainly was a surprise to Mays. When he was asked about Aaron breaking Ruth's record, Willie said defiantly, "He has to pass *me* first." At one time Aaron was nearly 100 home runs behind Mays, but he did pass Mays first. And he kept going while age suddenly caught up with Mays, who had to retire after the 1973 season with 660 homers. By that time, Aaron had 713 homers, just one behind Ruth.

Waiting through the winter to resume his obsessive chase of the home-run record was an ordeal for Aaron. He continued to get frightening, racist letters that warned him of an unhappy fate if he didn't retire immediately. But he kept playing and tied Ruth by dramatically homering in his first at-bat of the new season off the Reds' Jack Billingham. Then in his first home game of the season, on national television, on cue, against the Dodgers' left-handed Al Downing, who also had number 44 emblazoned on his uniform, he hit a long fly to left that landed in reliever Tom House's glove in the Braves bullpen. He had broken Babe Ruth's unbreakable record.

When I played we talked about hitting our next home runs, not about hitting 500 career home runs. Only Babe Ruth, Jimmie Foxx, and Mel Ott had done that in the history of baseball. Gehrig had even fallen short, with 493. When I retired after the 1955 season, I was sixth on the all-time list with 369 homers, with Ted Williams being the only active player ahead of me. Now I'm about 50th. Of those who played between 1946 and 1955, I would be passed by Aaron, Mays, Killebrew, Mantle, Banks, and Mathews—all of whom eclipsed 500 homers—as well as Musial, Snider, Kaline, and Hodges. If I hadn't hurt my back and had played as long as Aaron, Mays, and Musial . . . well, it's easy to do the math. But at the time, 500 homers wasn't anyone's goal. DiMaggio was content to retire with 361, Mize with 359, Berra with 358, and Greenberg with 331. Obviously, 500 homers wasn't a requirement for eventual Hall of Fame induction. However, it would eventually become a milestone that guaranteed a free ticket into Cooperstown. That may change now that 500 homers is becoming all too common—Fred McGriff may be the test case when he is voted on five years after his retirement.

Also becoming commonplace today are 50-homer seasons. That is so strange to me. It was such a big event when Johnny Mize and I went over 50 homers in 1947 because only Hack Wilson had done that in the National League, when he hit 56 in 1930. Mize and I became just the fifth and sixth players to hit 50 homers, and it was only the eighth and ninth times it had been done. In the American League, Ruth had hit 54 homers in 1920, 59 in 1921, 60 in 1927, and 54 in 1928; Foxx had hit 58 in 1932 and 50 in 1938; and Hank Greenberg had hit 58 homers in 1938. In fact, 1938 was the only year prior to 1961 that two players reached 50 homers. In stark contrast, *four* players hit at least 50 homers in both 1998 and 2001.

When I hit 54 homers in 1949, I joined Ruth and Foxx as the only players to hit 50 homers twice, and I became the only National Leaguer to do it before Willie Mays in 1965. As mentioned, only Mays and Mantle had

50-homer seasons in the fifties. So in all the years with 154-game sched-
ules through the 1960 season, 50 homers was passed only 13 times by a
total of eight players; and only three of us did it more than once.

Fifty homers would be reached only five more times before 1995, the year
ballplayers went on a rampage and began hitting a rabbit ball out of the
ballpark with relative ease. Maris and Mantle exceeded 50 homers when
they made their run at Ruth in 1961; Mays hit 52 homers in 1965; George
Foster smashed 52 homers in 1977; and Cecil Fielder had 51 in 1990. So 50
homers were hit 18 times in all the years before 1995, by 11 players.
Consider that from 1995 to 2002, a mere seven years, 50 homers also would
be achieved 18 times, by 10 players (Albert Belle, Mark McGwire, Brady
Anderson, Ken Griffey Jr., Sammy Sosa, Greg Vaughn, Barry Bonds, Luis
Gonzalez, Alex Rodriguez, and Jim Thome). Contributing to the continuing
onslaught are a very lively ball; smaller ballparks; bad pitching because
there are so many teams; more flexible, smaller bats—Bonds uses a small
bat and chokes up—and a questionable approach to hitting in which batters
take full swings even if they have two strikes. And more muscle.

If you looked up old players you would notice that their weights didn't
change from year to year, but nowadays there are many players who bulk
up and whose weights jump considerably. Barry Bonds and Sammy Sosa
used to be thin, but now their arms and chests are massive. Mark McGwire
was skinny too when he hit 49 homers as a rookie. He probably weighed
around 200 pounds. But he put on about 40 pounds of muscle. In my day,
organizations commonly ordered players to not lift weights because they'd
become musclebound. Well, that has changed 360 degrees, and teams now
promote weight training. And now that players are much stronger, the
whole approach to hitting home runs has changed.

I would have loved to have hit 57 or 61 home runs in a single season,
and those numbers were targets. But if I had made breaking Hack Wilson
or Babe Ruth's records my *priority*, I still couldn't have done it under the
conditions in which I played—unless I had been traded to the Dodgers and
played half my games at Ebbets Field. But could I have become the home-
run champion if I knew then what I know now? I think it would have
enhanced my chances. I'd certainly go to a lighter and quicker bat now that
I know about the importance of bat speed in propelling a ball. And I'd take
full advantage of current training methods that include extensive lifting. It
has helped today's players, so why wouldn't it work for me?

Where I might be left behind, however, if I played today and chased
current home-run records—if McGwire's 70 home runs was reachable, than
so must be Bonds' 73—is that I would draw the line on using steroids and
other performance-enhancing substances. I'm sure some of my competitors
would not. Both the banned drugs and the over-the-counter stimulants

would, in my mind, take away from any record I set. And, while I might break the record today, what effect would that stuff have on my health down the line? When you see some of the histories of people who used steroids and see how their bodies deteriorated later on, you must have second thoughts about using them just to reach a record. It's akin to selling your soul to the devil because in time you will pay.

I think my life would have changed to some extent if I had broken the single-season home-run record, but not considerably. Today the return would be so much bigger; it would be tremendous in regard to endorsements alone. (McGwire wasn't that interested in endorsements, so Sosa took them instead and walked away with about $10 million.) There wasn't much of that waiting for me even if I did pass Babe Ruth. But I did hit a lot of homers, acquired some lasting fame, and wasn't deprived of anything I wanted to do. I took advantage of that. Moreover, I still have my name in many of the home-run lists in the record book, and I still hold the record for most consecutive home-run titles. No one can ever take that away from me. Well, on second thought, actually they can . . .

Chapter **7**

The **Celebrity** Connection

As a rookie in 1946, I really looked forward to visiting New York City. I had been there only once before, when I was with the Albany Senators in 1941. We were busing to Albany from our spring training camp in Barnwell, South Carolina, and stopped off long enough to watch the Giants play in the Polo Grounds, which was uptown between 157th and 159th Streets, by the Harlem River. That was the first regular-season major league game I had ever seen, and it made quite an impression. I hoped to make the majors and play at the Polo Grounds; I had no idea I'd eventually broadcast there for the second residents of the ballpark, the New York Mets.

During that short visit, I didn't have the opportunity to venture into the city, so when I returned five years later I couldn't wait to stay in a big hotel and have a night on the town. I thought nothing of standing in line at the Stork Club, like everyone else. By the end of my second year, I no longer had to stand in line anywhere. After hitting 51 homers and tying for the title with the city's hometown hero, Johnny Mize, I was treated much differently. When I'd go to nightclubs I'd be given the star treatment. That meant I'd be whisked past the line and escorted directly to a front-row table, and then whoever was headlining the show would acknowledge me to the audience during their acts. That also happened in Pittsburgh and the other major league cities. And that would be true during off-seasons in Las Vegas, which was becoming the other big playground of the time. That's how I got to know many performers.

The public may have seen me as a celebrity, but when I made my first few All-Star teams, I found myself impressed by the more famous players around me. At the 1950 game in Comiskey Park, the clubhouse boy, Yosh Kawano, came up to me when he noticed my anxiety. I had known him since I was a kid because we grew up in the same area. He told me, "Ralph, don't worry about a thing. Joe DiMaggio is in the other clubhouse, and I can swear to you that he puts his pants on one leg at a time." That statement put it all in perspective—which could be why I was able to hit a game-tying homer in the ninth inning, probably the biggest thrill of my career. Stars may put up big numbers, but they are still just human beings, not gods. That is

161

an important and often difficult concept for young ballplayers to grasp. So many fail in the big leagues simply because they can't stop feeling awed and intimidated by the star players they idolized before they reached the majors.

The only people I still regarded as celebrities were entertainers, and movie stars were at the top of the heap. Growing up in California during the thirties and forties, I was in awe of motion picture stars, much more than ballplayers other than Babe Ruth. As a young kid, anytime I was anywhere near Hollywood, I'd keep my eye out for famous actors and actresses, but it was to no avail. However, my luck changed when I got a little older. When I played at Gilmore Field I would search the box seats and occasionally spot Jack Benny, Groucho Marx, and other famous celebrities. I never thought I'd meet any of them, much less befriend them, but I would through baseball.

When I began to meet entertainers, including movie stars, during the early part of my baseball career, I was as impressed by them as any young man would be. But what I discovered, amazingly, is that most of them were just as starstruck when they met me. To movie stars, the real celebrities were athletes—not football, basketball, or hockey players back then, but golfers, star tennis players, boxers, and, above all, baseball players. So many were huge baseball fans and thought my experiences and achievements on the diamond were far more interesting and significant than their own in front of the cameras.

Once I was on an overnight flight from New York to California and Bud Abbott and Lou Costello were among the other passengers. I'd seen their movies and hilarious nightclub act that included their classic "Who's on First?" routine, and I wanted to ask them a million questions. But they were determined to talk to me about baseball, so that's what we did in the lounge all the way to Chicago, where we stopped to refuel. Abbott then went to his seat to get some sleep, and Lou and I continued to talk baseball. I had paid $100 for a berth, so eventually I went to use it, leaving Lou alone. When we were getting off the plane, I asked him, "When did you go to sleep?" He said sheepishly, "They put me to bed when I asked the stewardess if I could go outside for a breath of fresh air."

Few ballplayers in those days met or associated with celebrities. I was the rare exception because I gained national fame from hitting home runs; I spent the off-season in southern California; I played golf and tennis, which were the most popular sports activities of Hollywood stars; and, most significantly, I had Hollywood's top box-office attraction as the minority owner of my team. In 1947, the Pirates were sold for about $1 million to Frank McKinney, John Galbreath, a local attorney named Tom Johnson, and Bing Crosby, who purchased about 5 percent of the stock. Maybe Crosby wanted to be involved with a baseball team just as a hobby, but I had no trouble with that because most *majority* owners in those days did it for that reason.

162

I do know he was a big baseball fan. In fact he was a *sports* fan who had founded the Del Mar racetrack and was the entertainer most associated with golf. In 1937, he had initiated the Bing Crosby Clambake at the Rancho Santa Fe course, near San Diego, and gave out decent prize money at a time when the pro golf tour was small potatoes; Sam Snead won the inaugural one-day event. The same year he bought into the Pirates, he moved his tournament, which was renamed the Bing Crosby National Pro-Am, to the Monterey Peninsula, 100 miles south of San Francisco. In a couple of years I'd begin playing in that tournament; years later I'd help broadcast it.

The Pirates trained in San Bernardino, California, and Crosby would come up from Los Angeles to watch us work out. He'd put on a Bucs uniform for publicity shots of him playing catch or swinging a bat, but he never joined in the workouts, although he was a superb athlete. In fact, he had been a diver at Gonzaga College. At the end of spring training, the team would travel the 50 miles south to L.A., and Bing would throw a party for us at Chasen's, emceeing and singing songs with that effortless baritone voice that Louis Armstrong said "was like gold being poured into a cup." To have such a famous film and recording star do that made us feel special. One parody he'd sing began: "Nothing could be finer than to be with Ralphie Kiner on the ballfield." It wasn't "White Christmas," but each spring, I'd look forward to hearing that.

Bing attended our opening series in Pittsburgh in 1948. The Pirates' popular announcer Rosey Roswell invited him into the radio booth and coaxed him into doing some play-by-play. I got hold of a pitch and Bing started saying, "There's a fly ball to deep left field and . . ." Suddenly Rosey grabbed the microphone out of his hands, so he could do his famous catchphrase for homers, "Open the window, Aunt Minnie!" On cue, his assistant dropped a pane of glass so it sounded like a ball crashing through a window. Then Rosey added, "She never made it!" That may have been the only time in history that anyone took a microphone out of Bing Crosby's hands.

Over time, in Pittsburgh and California, Crosby introduced me to a number of stars, including his *Road* pictures partner, Bob Hope. He inspired Hope, who grew up in Cleveland and was a big sports fan, to be part of a 10-man syndicate led by Bill Veeck that purchased the Indians in 1946. Or had Hope's business venture inspired Crosby to buy a share of the Pirates a year later? That they each owned a part of a major league ballclub provided great material for them, and they inserted bits into their radio scripts, along with their jabs about each other's golf play. For instance, Hope bragged to Crosby that only in the American League did pitchers throw overhanded. So their baseball "rivalry" provided a lot of laughs.

After the 1949 season, I went back to Alhambra and stayed with my mother in the house she'd had built when I was in high school. One day, I paid a visit to Crosby in his office on the Paramount lot, and my timing was impeccable because he asked me if I'd be interested in having a date with Elizabeth Taylor. He explained that she needed someone to accompany her to the premiere of the Gregory Peck war film *Twelve O'Clock High* at Grauman's Chinese Theater on Hollywood Boulevard. Of course, he didn't have to ask me twice.

By then, I had dated several women in the entertainment industry, though only one had any degree of celebrity. Her name was Monica Lewis, and her big claim to fame was that she sang the Chiquita Bananas ditty "Don't Ever Put Bananas in the Refrigerator." She was being interviewed, and when asked to name her favorite baseball player she said, "Ralph Kiner." So I called her up at the theater where she was performing and introduced myself. After that we saw each other for a while.

However, nobody I had dated had remotely the fame of Elizabeth Taylor, and I was nervous about meeting her. She was 17 and was being touted as one of the most beautiful actresses in Hollywood. After being a child star, she was on the verge of making the transition to romantic leading lady in *Father of the Bride*, as the daughter of Spencer Tracy and Joan Bennett. Life would imitate art, because before she turned 18, she'd leave home and marry wealthy hotelier Nicky Hilton. However, at the time we went out—I believe she also dated Howard Hughes that year—she still lived with her parents in a small suburban home, and that's where I picked her up in my Cadillac convertible. I mention the car because it would play a major role in our evening together.

The premiere of *Twelve O'Clock High* was a star-studded gala affair with searchlights along Hollywood Boulevard and makeshift bleachers there for fans to watch the movie stars arrive and leave on a red carpet. Of course, when we pulled up and got out of the car all the fans went wild for Elizabeth and hadn't any idea who I was. I'd hit all those home runs, but major league baseball wasn't played west of St. Louis yet. We arrived late, so I let a parking attendant take my car and thought no more of it. We were the last of the invited guests to enter the theater.

When the movie ended, everyone filed out of Grauman's and lined up for their cars. One by one, the big stars were announced and their cars were brought up to them immediately. They'd wave to the crowd and depart. I moved to the front of the line and said to the attendant, "I would like my car paged, please; my name is Ralph Kiner." So the attendant paged "Ralph Kiner's car." And Elizabeth and I stood there waiting. Ten minutes later I inquired about my car. Ralph Kiner's car was paged again, but it never arrived. Now I was really hot and marched up to the attendant and snapped, "Dammit, my car isn't here and I'm waiting with Elizabeth Taylor!" And he said, "Well, your chauffeur must have fallen asleep." And I said, "I don't have a chauffeur, I'm driving myself." And he said, "In that case, your car is out there . . ." and he pointed with a very long finger in the general direction of a huge unattended lot a block or two away. So after hearing the bad news, Elizabeth, in her fur, gown, and heels, and I, in my tuxedo, trekked all the way to the lot. Of course I was embarrassed, but thankfully she was a great sport and didn't put on any Hollywood airs.

Finally we found the car and drove over to Romanoff's, where there was an after-movie party with a lot of celebrities in attendance. I was sitting with Elizabeth when Louella Parsons, the Hearst gossip columnist who could make or break an actor with a few strokes of her poison pen, came over to us. She said hello to Elizabeth and . . . she had no idea who I was. We told her I played for the Pittsburgh Pirates, and she nodded. It so happened that the Pittsburgh Steelers were in town to play the Rams at the Coliseum that Sunday, so she told me, "I hope your team wins tomorrow." I thanked her.

I managed to drop off Elizabeth at her home without further incident. And that was it. I have vivid memories of that night, but if I ever need real proof that I had a date with Elizabeth Taylor I can look it up quite easily, because it was written up in all the newspapers. It's too bad that night was such a mess because I never had the courage to ask her out on a second date. In fact, I never saw her again except in the movies.

I would date a few other Hollywood actresses, but the only one who was well known was Janet Leigh. Oddly, I didn't meet her in California but in Pittsburgh, and Crosby had nothing to do with it. Bob Cobb, who was a friend of (but no relation to) Ty Cobb, owned the famous Brown Derby restaurant in Hollywood (where he created the Cobb salad) and the Pacific Coast League's Hollywood Stars, who had a working agreement with the Pirates. Cobb was married to actress Gail Patrick and had show business ties, and when the 1951 Paul Douglas–Janet Leigh comedy *Angels in the Outfield* was about to be filmed, Cobb arranged with his chum Branch Rickey to use Forbes Field as the backdrop and the Pirates players as background scenery.

Shooting took place during the regular season, and the baseball scenes in the movie of the Pirates and their opponents are from real games. Janet and other cast members were planted in the stands and filmed while watching us. Knowing Rickey, I'm sure he got paid a smart sum, but there was no union then, and we had to do our cameos for free. Maybe that's why they didn't ask me to play myself, although I was in my uniform. Instead I played a character called Tony! I played first base 58 times in 1951, the only time in my career I played anywhere but the outfield, and that's where I—I mean Tony—was photographed on the field. Only the filmmakers were so unfamiliar with baseball that they shot me in reverse and didn't know the difference, and in the movie, Tony is a lefty. ("Lefties" weren't popular in

Hollywood in the early fifties, so maybe that accounts for why I was never asked to be in a movie again.)

Ballplayers, especially on a club so bad that angels were its best hope, weren't used to having beautiful young blonde starlets hanging around the park. So everyone noticed Janet a lot more than they did Paul Douglas (who played our manager). She certainly got my attention, and one day prior to a game, during a break in filming, I went up to her near the batting cage and introduced myself. We just started talking. I wasn't intimidated by her stardom, and what made it easier was that she was a real down-to-earth girl who even knew who I was. Maybe she followed baseball closely, but it's more likely she simply took the trouble to get some personal information on the Pirates.

When I asked Janet to dinner she accepted. And that was the beginning of our brief romance—a *good* romance. We went to private clubs, out of the public eye, but even so we made the headlines. Fortunately, there was nothing derogatory written about what was going on, perhaps because we were both single and enemy-free. We were together about three weeks. It was unusual for ballplayers and movie stars to date, but we never got around to discussing problems we'd encounter if our relationship lasted. I've thought of it many times since and concluded it probably wouldn't have worked. But at the time it was serious—at least on my side—and I thought there was a good chance it would continue. Then I left on a road trip with the team, and she went to Chicago. We had plans to meet and do this and that. But the next thing I know, I am reading the paper and come upon a tidbit about how Janet and Tony Curtis had announced their engagement. I think he was in Europe and rushed back home because of the publicity we got. In fact, they got married about a month after she left Pittsburgh. So I doubt I made a big impression on her.

I was surprised. I thought, there's another one I lost. But I wasn't too disappointed. Soon I proposed to Nancy Chaffee, when she came through Pittsburgh while on her way to New York to fly to England to play at Wimbledon. We would get married in October. So apparently Janet and I were both ready to tie the knot when we dated in Pittsburgh, but the story line sure got switched in a hurry.

In the off-season, Nancy and I invited Janet and Tony over to our new house in Rancho Mirage. So the four newlyweds hung around the pool. It was all very civil and friendly, and Tony even showed me magic tricks he was learning for the movie *Houdini*. Janet and I never discussed anything personal that day. That was the last time I ever saw her.

But that was not the end of the story. The epilogue came 34 years later. In the summer of 1985, my wife DiAnn and I were at Veterans Stadium in Philadelphia. After the game, we were in the press room and Jamie Lee

Curtis, daughter of Janet and Tony, was sitting with her husband, Christopher Guest, a couple of tables away. I had never met her, so DiAnn urged me to go over and introduce myself. So I walked up to Jamie Lee and said, "I broadcast the Mets games, and I used to play baseball. My name is Ralph Kiner, and I dated your mother." I expected her to look at me with puzzlement. Instead, she leapt to her feet and threw her arms around me, and exclaimed, "Daddy! I've been searching for you all my life! At last I've found you!" I don't know how anyone can be that quick. I looked over at DiAnn, and she was already counting on her fingers to see if it was possibly true that I was her father. Coincidentally, Jamie Lee looks very much like my daughter, K.C. But DiAnn added up all the years and months, and there was no way possible.

Soon after that, DiAnn and I were flying across the country. During the flight, the stewardess handed me a note that said, "Mom says you're behind in child support payments. Send money!" We hadn't known that Jamie Lee was aboard. Another time she sent us some pictures from an old snapshot album that her mother had given her. They were photos of Janet and me that had been taken in 1951. She included a note from Janet saying, "It's been a long time, hasn't it?" Maybe I did make an impression after all.

Before my first marriage in 1951, I lived in the off-season in Alhambra with my mother. But I would go to Palm Springs with a friend whose parents had a home there. I went for the fabulous climate, to escape the smog in L.A., and to play golf, which I had started playing in 1946–47 when I joined a club in Alhambra. The other attraction in Palm Springs was celebrities. Palm Springs was the only place where I'd see them on the street.

The Hollywood crowd began coming to Palm Springs in the winters beginning in the forties. Before that it was a desert full of sagebrush, cactus, and sand, the last place any sane person would go to get away. What originally drew celebrities all the way from L.A. were two big illegal gambling places, which I'm sure were run by the mafia. But that was before actors Charlie Farrell and Ralph Bellamy opened the Racquet Club, a tennis facility with bungalows. It became wildly popular with the Hollywood elite, and not just those who played tennis. Among the guests were Spencer Tracy (who spent all winter there), Barbara Stanwyck, Robert Taylor, Gene Autry, Bob Hope, Cary Grant, William Powell, Henry Fonda, Humphrey Bogart, Jack Benny, Bette Davis, Jane Russell, and Howard Hughes. Supposedly, it was where Marilyn Monroe celebrated New Year's Eve in 1948.

The unofficial social director of the club was Mousy Powell, William Powell's wife. Powell was a big baseball fan and from Pittsburgh, so we had a lot in common and became good friends. Charlie Farrell had been a handsome leading man during the twenties and early thirties, starring in both silent movies and talkies, and would find new fans during the fifties as Gale Storm's father on the popular television show *My Little Margie*. (He also would be the mayor of Palm Springs for seven years.) When I married Nancy, he gave us a lifetime membership. When Farrell died in 1990, my membership was revoked, which made me ask, "Whose lifetime, his or mine?"

Among the many other celebrities I met at the Racquet Club, as a bachelor and then as a married man, was Jack Benny. He was a kind, very funny person, who was responsible for the funniest line I ever heard on the radio. I've never forgotten the first time I heard that classic bit in which a mugger with a gun demanded of Benny, "Your money or your life." The mugger grew impatient when Benny, who pretended to be a skinflint, gave no response, and he asked Benny why he was taking so long. Benny said, "I'm thinking! I'm thinking!" It still makes me laugh. I doubt if Benny remembered watching me play baseball when I was a teenager during the late thirties at Gilmore Field, but I certainly remembered it, so it was a special treat to meet him and talk to him as a peer.

Celebrities who played tennis flocked to the Racquet Club and its competitor, the Tennis Club. But at the time Palm Springs still had no eighteen-hole golf course. So I "roughed it" on its one nine-hole golf course, O'Donnell's, which is also where Crosby, Hope, and all the celebrity golfers who came there played. I'd have matches with Bing, Bob, or whoever else was around.

I got to know Crosby really well in the winters when we played a lot of golf and I started playing in his tournament. I discovered that he was a pleasant man to be around when he wasn't moody. He could be as affable as you would want and then for no apparent reason become very quiet and reserved. He was different from Hope in that he was extremely introspective and usually preferred being alone and reading a book to being in front of an audience.

Crosby had been a caddie as a kid and became a great golfer. He had a 2-handicap and often shot in the 60s. He was the club champion at numerous golf courses, including Lakeside Country Club in Burbank, winning five championships there. He was obsessed with the game and kept a bag of balls and clubs at Paramount. Between scenes, he practiced hitting golf balls into a rug that was suspended high in the air.

When Hope and Crosby played together, they were funny but very competitive. They even had gone at it when they played a series of exhibitions during the war to promote the sale of war bonds. They were friends so there was no squabbling, but you could tell they wanted to beat each other. Bing hated to lose. If you ever beat him, which wasn't easy, he'd say, "Let's go play the whiskey route." That meant repeating the last two holes till he got his money back. We'd play $5 Nassau. Despite the small bets, he tried his best to win, so they were tough games. He was fun to play with because he really loved golf.

On the other hand, Hope was very difficult to play with because he always wanted to have an edge. When you begin a game against another player you compare handicaps and figure out how you can make an even game of it. Hope didn't want an even contest, so for several holes you'd have to negotiate his handicap with him to get a game that would produce a winner and loser. When he had the chance, Hope liked to play for big money, maybe $5,000 a match. He was a very good 4-handicap player and won lots of money from hustlers by outhustling them.

There always had been a lot of hustlers and oddball golfers hanging around Crosby and Hope. One character was named Tom Montague, who played in the first Crosby tournament. Montague was an extremely strong guy who could tear telephone books in half. He had a gimmick: he'd play golf with a baseball bat, rake, and shovel—and beat you. When Crosby first played him, he didn't know who Montague was. The first hole Montague made par with his three unusual props, and Crosby just walked off the course, saying he wouldn't play anyone like that. Montague never let reporters write anything about him when he made an appearance, but his picture was taken once and carried across the country by the Associated Press. It turned out there was a warrant out for his arrest and he was taken back east in custody. Crosby and Hope both stood up for his character and got him out of whatever jam he was in.

Another legendary character was Alvin "Titanic" Thompson, an infamous golfer and cardsharp in the East. One of his gimmicks was to walk onto a course with beat-up golf clubs and a bag that was stolen. He'd get into a game and bet whatever small amount the other three men always wagered. So he'd win $15 to $20 or so. But he'd say he didn't want their money, and would tell them to just hold on to it and he'd be back the next day and give them a chance to erase their small debt. They thought that was very generous because they knew he wouldn't have the same luck two days in a row. The next day they would double the bet. And somehow he'd pull out another victory. This would happen for two or three days. The kicker was that he'd still insist he didn't want the money, and to prove it, he'd promise to return the next day and play them left-handed, for double or nothing. The men jumped on that bet. The problem was he was *better* left-handed. That's how he made his money. He was a mythical figure. (Titanic would bet on anything. In the Polo Grounds, he would buy a ticket downstairs and order a bag of peanuts. He'd open the bag and then bet the stranger next to him that he could throw a peanut into the upper deck. There's no way you can throw a peanut that far because it's too light. But he'd insert a lead peanut into the bag that he could throw into the upper deck. So he'd collect the bet from the unsuspecting patsy.) It's little wonder that he had to be on the move. There was no television then, but his reputation preceded him. Incidently, Titanic, who got his nickname because he claimed to have survived the sinking of that infamous oceanliner, was the model for the Damon Runyon character called Sky Masterson, played by Frank Sinatra in the movie *Guys and Dolls*.

Occasionally, on an invitation from Crosby, Hope, Forrest Tucker, or another celebrity, I'd play the eighteen-hole course at the Lakeside, across from Warner Bros. It was *the* place to play in Los Angeles, along with Bel Air (where Howard Hughes once landed a plane), the Los Angeles Country Club (where Crosby lived and sometimes played because his father was a member), and Hillcrest, which had many Jewish members, some in the movie industry. Crosby and Hope were members at Lakeside. So were Stan Laurel and Oliver Hardy, who was the better golfer of the two. W. C. Fields had been a member before his death on Christmas 1946, and everyone still talked about him. He was a character who certainly drank as much as they said he did, including on the golf course.

Errol Flynn was also a member at Lakeside. Once Flynn was making a picture at Warner Bros., and while on a break he came in and ordered lunch, which consisted of a few drinks. An amateur golf champion named Roger Kelly was eating lunch there and went over to Flynn. Roger had a nice wife, but she didn't like his drinking, so he had recently quit. Roger asked Flynn how he could drink and not get in trouble when he reported back to the set. And Flynn explained, "They have a new whiskey and no one can smell it on your breath. It's called *vodka*." So the light went on above Roger's head, and, thanks to Flynn, he started to drink again.

I was told that once for a match when he was partnered with Sam Snead at Bing Crosby's Clambake, Roger showed up in the morning, teed up his first ball, and fell flat on his face. Snead threatened to walk off. Roger struggled to his feet and said, "Sammy, I'll tell you what I'll do. I will play you $100 a hole and $100 a drive." Snead thought he had a chance to make a lot of easy money and agreed. Roger beat the hell out of him. Roger was a great player at a time when even the best golfers were probably better off working a regular job than playing on the pro circuit. He made a good living as a well-known and well-liked attorney. Later on, he became the president of Lakeside and quit drinking entirely. Then he couldn't play golf a lick.

Among the most colorful characters at Lakeside were the caddies. They had names like Jerry the Junkman, "One Beer" Spivens, Staggering Haggerty, George "Scorpie" Doyle, and Stinky, who always dressed in the best boulevard style, even on the course. Scorpie, who often caddied for priests, would go to Palm Springs in the winter once there were eighteen-hole courses. Bob Hope, who slept in spurts, would wake up in the middle of the night and call Scorpie to walk with him around the airport and talk.

Johnny Dawson, the National Amateur Golf champion, realized that a lot of golfers at Lakeside would come out to Palm Springs in the winter if there was a club with an eighteen-hole course. He came up with the novel idea of putting up an eighteen-hole golf course and selling lots for houses right there on the grounds. He wanted to buy land in Palm Springs but couldn't do it there because it was all Indian property and only short-term leases were available at that time. So instead he boldly purchased 100 acres 15 miles away in Rancho Mirage, where no one lived and, he was warned, there was the real possibility no one would come to play golf. The Thunderbird Country Club turned out to be a brilliant investment. The course was challenging and gorgeous; electric carts were introduced for the first time anywhere (making the sport accessible to countless people around the world); and lots for houses were sold at very reasonable rates. So I decided to build a house right there, with the course outside my door.

I was a bachelor when I made my house purchase, but I married Nancy after the '51 season, and we moved into it together. I was a charter member at Thunderbird, as were Bing Crosby and his best friend, Phil Harris. Crosby, ever the loner, built the only house on a hill above the course. (It is directly across the street from where I live today.) Harris and his wife, Alice Faye, built their house off the seventh hole, not far from mine on the eleventh.

I hadn't met Phil until we became neighbors, but I knew he was the only person Crosby was really close to, and that included Bob Hope. They'd known each other since 1925; they played golf and, being outdoorsmen, went on hunting and fishing trips together until Crosby's death. Phil and I became fast friends because he was a baseball fanatic, and we would hunt—mostly for quail and duck—and play golf together, including at Crosby's tournament.

At the Crosby National Pro-Am, a pro and one amateur played the three rounds together, the first at Cypress Point, the second at the Monterey Peninsula Country Club, the third at Pebble Beach. One year, Crosby teamed Phil with pro golfer Dutch Harrison. They were in the running for the title going into the seventeenth hole of the final round, which was unlikely because Phil was a high handicapper. But he was a good putter, and he sank an unbelievable 80-footer. He had to putt it over the rough because of the contour of the green. Scorpie Doyle was Phil's caddy, and when he was asked how long the putt was, Scorpie replied, "If I owned that much property on Wilshire Boulevard, I'd be a billionaire today." After making the putt, Phil said to Dutch, "You're on your own now. Take it from me, cuz I'm out of here." They went on to win the tournament, and Phil rewarded Scorpie $2,500 for his work. (The best I ever did were two fourth-place finishes, once with Pittsburgh pro Lew Worsham, who had won the 1947 U.S. Open, and the other time with Bud Ward, who was playing in his first professional tournament and won his first professional money ever.)

Phil was an interesting guy. He was born in 1906 in Linton, Indiana, but grew up in Nashville, the son of a musician. He began his own show business career as a drummer, forming his own band in 1931. When I was in high school, we'd go to the Biltmore Bowl and dance to his music. I also saw Phil and his band performing at the 1939 World's Fair in San Francisco. During the early thirties, Phil began appearing in films and on radio, at first with his band and later as a comedian and dramatic actor. In 1941 he married Alice Faye, who preceded Betty Grable and Marilyn Monroe in the line of 20th Century Fox's blonde bombshells. Phil teamed with Alice on popular radio shows of the forties, including Jack Benny's program, on which Phil was a regular, and they had their own show from 1948 to 1954. They had two daughters (named Alice and Phyllis—strangely, Alice looked like Phil and Phyllis looked like Alice), which was why Alice essentially retired from motion pictures at the height of her fame. Although older, their kids would become close to ours, Michael, Scott, and K.C. (Kathryn Chaffee).

Ironically, when I was growing up, Alice Faye was my favorite actress. I thought she was the greatest thing around. My suspicions were confirmed that her appeal on screen was a reflection of the nice person she really was. Once we became neighbors, she spent a lot of time with Nancy and me. She was a very quiet person who stayed in the background, which you almost had to do with Phil because he was projecting all the time. Anyone who saw her musicals or heard her on the radio knew she had a marvelous voice, but we could never get her to sing, even at parties, only dance. She never went with Phil into L.A. except when they were working, probably to distance herself from show business. She was content to hear him on the radio.

Phil was marvelous on the radio, particularly in his side-splitting exchanges with Jack Benny. There is no doubt Phil was the funniest person I ever met. He was bursting with stories and one-liners. Things would come out of the blue. For instance, when we were talking about Elizabeth Taylor in the midfifties, he said, "Eddie Fisher being married to Elizabeth Taylor is like trying to stop the Super Chief with a Zippo lighter." Of Jim Garner's temper tantrums on the golf course, Harris joked, "His putter's got more air time than the chief test pilot at TWA." When he heard that Randolph Scott, a very good golfer and good friend of mine, had built a house that overlooked the L.A. Country Club but was being denied membership because it excluded actors, Phil cracked unsympathetically, "If they'd seen any of his pictures, they'd know he is no actor." That was one of the lines he used all the time, and Scott couldn't help but laugh.

When Phil himself tried to join the Lakeside Country Club, he was turned down. He was told the reason was that he was Jewish. Harris was livid, claiming he wasn't Jewish but part Indian. In fact, he had a Native-American name, "Wonga," which people who knew him would call him. He told them, "I tried to join Hillcrest, which is a Jewish club. And they turned me down in one minute. You guys took *two weeks* to turn me down, and I'm not even Jewish."

I also was a target of his barbs. For many years he told the story of watching me play in Wrigley Field, after I had been traded to the Cubs during the 1953 season. I was playing left field, Hank Sauer was in right, and the center fielder was the speedy Frankie Baumholtz. The story goes that Hank and I made Baumholtz famous because we were so slow that he had to cover practically the whole outfield. When we met up after the game, Phil told me there was a little lady sitting next to him and every time I'd have to field a ball hit near the left-field line she'd yell out, "Throw it to third, Ralphie! Throw it to third." Meaning that because of my speed, it was a sure double and possibly a triple. Bob Hope could deliver lines, but he had writers. Phil was spontaneous. His nonscripted stories and remarks on the radio and in social situations were unbelievably funny.

Phil Harris' importance in my life is that he focused my attention on making light of things even when working in a high-pressure business. I watched how people reacted to the amusing things he said and realized there's always room for laughter. He helped develop whatever wit I had, and indirectly that helped me when I became a broadcaster. On the air, I have always been inspired to tell stories and play up the humor in the game because he changed my thinking.

Phil made a fortune picking up real estate in the Palm Springs area, at $500 to $1,000 an acre. So did Dean Martin. Bob Hope? He bought California. Hope was a member at Thunderbird but had a house in the old-town area. Later he built a house that was as big as an airplane terminal, which he'd use for his big parties and to host his golf tournament. I didn't get to know Martin very well, though I'd met him and Jerry Lewis when they broke in their hit act at the Copacabana in 1947. Both were pretty good golfers, though Martin was more serious about it. They would make a movie called *The Caddy* in 1953, in which Martin played a pro golfer, and several big-name pro golfers turned in cameos.

There was another comedy team at Thunderbird in the early days, Lucille Ball and Desi Arnaz. I first met then in about 1952 or '53, when *I Love Lucy* had made them national sensations. They came to Thunderbird to consider moving there, and Nancy and I invited them to dinner. While Lucy helped Nancy in the kitchen, Desi and I talked and had a few drinks in the living room. By the time the women emerged from the kitchen, Desi was a little drunk, and Lucy was mad at me about it. They did end up moving to Thunderbird, and over the next few years we had dinner together often and our kids grew up with their children, Desi Jr. and Lucie. Lucy was quiet and introverted—the opposite of Desi, who was quite gregarious. He and I played a lot of golf together (Lucy never played) and became close friends. I used to laugh when he'd try to say Pittsburgh: because of his Cuban accent, it would come out *Piss*burgh.

The Thunderbird Country Club was so successful that a rival club, Tamarisk Country Club, soon was constructed nearby. It scored a coup when Ben Hogan agreed to be its club pro. He agreed to do it because at the time even the most successful professional golfers made only about $30,000 a year. Baseball players had much more stature. I thought Hogan was a bit taciturn but a nice man, despite his lack of friends. I'd go to parties with him and his wife, Valerie, and discovered he was much more social than he was reputed to be.

I played with Hogan. He'd practice a lot with different clubs and different distances. He'd have someone shag the balls for him and field the balls with a catcher's mitt on one bounce. He was so accurate that the kid would have to move only a step or two each time. He had tremendous concentration. Once Claude Harmon, one of Hogan's few close friends, was playing with him at Augusta. At the famous par-3 hole, Harmon made a hole in one. As they were coming off the green, heading for the next tee, Hogan said, "Claude, that's the first time I've ever had a two on that hole." Harmon looked at him and said, "Ben, I just aced the hole! And you didn't even say anything, like 'Nice shot!'" Hogan had been concentrating so much he didn't pay attention to what Harmon did. I figured I'd ask Hogan to give me a golf tip, so I asked him the right way to cock the wrist. All he'd say was, "You just cock it."

I once played with Hogan in a foursome at Thunderbird. We asked him what we'd play for. Hogan suggested that we play a $10 Nassau, meaning $10 on the first nine, $10 on the back nine, and $10 on the overall match. I said, "Fine. What do you want to play at?"

He said, "I'll play at scratch."

I said, "You've got to be kidding. You have got to be at least a plus-5."

He said, "That's the way it is."

I said, "OK, but you then have to come down to Phil Harris' alfalfa field and hit off my pitching machine, and I'll play you at scratch hitting a baseball."

I had screwed Phil up by turning up the velocity to 90-mph pitches, and I wanted to do the same thing to Hogan, but he wouldn't go for it. As it turned out, we played golf at scratch; we lost and paid up.

The other great golfer of the era, Sam Snead, also came to the area quite often to pick up extra cash. Snead wouldn't play anybody unless there was at least a $100 bet. He thought anybody who wanted to play with him had to fork up at least that. He'd win 99 percent of the time or more. If he lost, he'd pay the $300 or $400 with a check. He knew full well that the guy would never cash it because he'd want to show his friends Snead's autograph, proof that he beat Sam in a match.

Golfers had been popular with Hollywood stars ever since Bobby Jones made a series of instructional films with them in the early thirties. After that, numerous stars played in their spare time. They wanted to get to know the golfers and pick up pointers. On the other hand, I never gave advice on hitting to celebrities. You couldn't take Jack Benny out on the baseball field and teach him how to hit against Ewell Blackwell. But in golf you compete against the course and yourself, so anything you learn from a pro can be put to good use. (And even if you should play against a pro, it can still be an even game because of handicapping.)

Celebrities also welcomed tennis players to the Palm Springs area. They couldn't compete against a great tennis player, but they hoped he or she would impart some wisdom that they could put to use when they next faced one of their celebrity peers. In 1951, I played doubles at the Racquet Club with Dick Savitt as my partner, just after he had won at Wimbledon. I remember it vividly because I hit a hard serve that struck him right in the back of the head. He went down to the ground in a hurry. I thought I had killed him. I didn't, but he never won another Wimbledon.

Ginger Rogers was thrilled to play with Nancy as her partner, because it was the rare opportunity to play with a champion. Bob Prince, the Pirates' announcer, and I challenged them to a male-versus-female match on the court at Ginger's house in Beverly Hills. They beat us badly. It was no contest. Nancy was the fourth-best female player in the world at that time— the only time I beat her was when she was pregnant—and Ginger was a good athlete, so Bob and I didn't have a chance. Ginger quoted that famous line of hers: "I don't know why Fred Astaire is acclaimed as being the greatest dancer; I did everything he did, only I did it backward and in high heels."

Thunderbird, Tamarisk, the Racquet Club, the Tennis Club, and some newer resorts contributed to a real estate boom throughout the whole area, from Palm Springs to Rancho Mirage and beyond. Many celebrities chose to reside and play golf and tennis there in all but the extremely hot summer months. At the time there were only a few other athletes who spent time with celebrities. I was the only baseball player on the West Coast to do so because I just happened to be the only one to live near Palm Springs. I played a lot of tennis, including against Hank Greenberg when he visited, but most celebrities I met were on the golf course. I didn't feel I was pushing myself on them—many would seek me out because they had a real liking for baseball and didn't have the chance to meet many players.

Other than Crosby and Hope, the best golfers I played with included Bob Sterling, Bob Wilke, who made a living playing outlaws in Westerns, and

Forrest Tucker. Sterling, who would achieve some fame on the television series *Topper*, was a very good player. He had his own course at one time. Tucker was an excellent golfer; he was even the club champion at Lakeside in a year Crosby didn't win. I played quite a bit with him, including in tournaments. He was a big, burly guy with a strong personality, kind of like the comic soldier he would later play on the TV series *F Troop*. He was a real character; he was also a fairly big drinker, and often drank while we played—which was fine with me because he could hold his liquor. Years later I ran into him at the airport in Atlanta and he wasn't well. He told me that his doctor had limited him to one drink a day, so he was now pouring his daily vodka into a large milk bottle instead of a glass.

James Garner and Jack Lemmon came in a bit later. Jim was a terrific golfer, although he was probably the only celebrity I played with who couldn't control his temper—fortunately, it was always directed at himself. Jack wasn't a good player and had the frustration of *never* making the cut in the Crosby golf tournament. He tried for 35 years. There was a running joke about it. Phil Harris quipped, "Lemmon has visited more bunkers than Eva Braun."

Frank Sinatra had built a home in the old-town area, using the architect I would use, Stuart Williams. About a year after I moved to Thunderbird, he built another house at Tamarisk, and I got to know him really well. He was single at the time and was dating Anita Ekberg. He always had a lot of people around him, even in his house. He was mercurial when he drank, but at other times he was a nice guy and I really enjoyed being around him. Supposedly, he always resented that he couldn't play golf like Crosby and Hope, but he was a decent player. I played in the original Frank Sinatra Celebrity Invitational in the sixties. He was involved with this tournament for a very short time, maybe one year; but then he started up his still-existing tournament that is now being run by his widow, Barbara. Sinatra and I had dinner several times and usually talked baseball. He was a tremendous, knowledgeable fan and became close friends with Tommy Lasorda, who became the Dodgers manager in 1976. (One year, Rick Sutcliffe was left off a playoff roster and charged into Lasorda's office. He started hurling chairs around. Then he threatened to throw one at Lasorda's treasured signed picture of Sinatra that was hanging on the wall. Tommy grabbed it and pleaded, "Please don't break the picture! Please don't break the picture!")

I played a lot of golf with Randolph Scott, who was a member of Thunderbird but didn't live there, and Hoagy Carmichael, who did have a home at Thunderbird. One celebrity I really had a good time playing with was Johnny Weissmuller, the Olympic swimming champion who made it big in Hollywood playing Tarzan for about 20 years. He was about a 7-handicap, so we were evenly matched. He was a tough competitor who didn't lose a

Working on my preseason form during spring training in 1953.
Photo courtesy of AP/Wide World Photos.

Our close friend and a frequent visitor in Palm Springs, former Olympic swimmer Esther Williams.

Here I am with Pirates general manager Branch Rickey in Havana, Cuba, before the start of the 1953 season.

At home in Palm Springs during the winter of 1953. I'm reading a statement to the media during the heated labor negotiations that off-season. The Yankees' Allie Reynolds and I were the player representatives in that historic pension fund dispute with owners. Photo courtesy of AP/Wide World Photos.

Golfing in Palm Springs with some of my regular partners (from left): Phil Harris, Desi Arnaz, me, and Bing Crosby. Those are two of the first electric golf carts ever made.

Signing a ball for a young fan before the All-Star banquet in Pittsburgh a few years after I retired from playing. I've always felt that players should do their best to make themselves accessible to the fans. Photo courtesy of AP/Wide World Photos.

A visit with then–Yankees manager Casey Stengel in the dugout at Ebbets Field on October 1, 1952. My season with the Pirates had ended, but Casey and the Yankees were about to open the World Series against the Brooklyn Dodgers. Photo courtesy of AP/Wide World Photos.

With Hank Greenberg after I'd found out that I had been elected to the Hall of Fame in January 1975. Photo courtesy of AP/Wide World Photos.

Receiving an honor before a game in Pittsburgh in 1975. From left are David Reed, Edgar Speer, Danny Murtaugh, me, Stephen Olenick, Frank Mills, Joseph Drummond, and Mike Kornick. Photo courtesy of AP/Wide World Photos.

In the press box at Shea Stadium before a Mets game in 1985, the year before we went all the way. Photo courtesy of AP/Wide World Photos.

The Pirates recently honored me with this bronze sculpture before Opening Night at PNC Park, where it now has a permanent home in the left-field rotunda.

Here's the Kiner clan during the ceremony dedicating the sculpture in Pittsburgh. At left is son Michael with wife Maria and baby Nancy; daughter Kathryn (K.C.) with husband Robin Freeman and their two sons, Chase and Kyle; myself and DiAnn; and son Scott with his daughters Lindsay and Shawn.

DiAnn and me at the Hall of Fame in the summer of 1996.

Another Hall of Fame moment.

swimming race over a 10-year period before he retired. I teased him that the women of the time swam faster than he did when he set all his records, and he'd go into a whole explanation of how the women weren't racing under the same conditions he was.

Esther Williams used to tell me about how after her Olympic swimming experience, she and Weissmuller swam together in Billy Rose's Aquacade in New York. After each show ended, they had to swim underneath a structure to get out of the pool, and she had a hard time getting through each time without Weissmuller pulling her suit off.

I got to know Esther well. She was a fun, unpretentious L.A. girl and a super athlete. She was married to Ben Gage, a big guy who worked in radio in Chicago. One night, Nancy, a male friend of mine, Esther, Ben, and I went out to dinner to a nightclub called the Chi-Chi. We came back to the house at about 2:00 in the morning, and the next thing I knew, Esther jumped into the pool naked. My friend had so much to drink that he went directly to bed. I tried to wake him up so he could take advantage of the scenery, but I couldn't do it. The next morning I told him about it, and he was so angry I hadn't wakened him that he didn't talk to me for about a month. He said, "You should have tried harder."

At one point, Esther was engaged to Jeff Chandler. He was a big baseball fan and a good friend of Bob Prince's and would come to a lot of our games in Pittsburgh. According to Esther's autobiography, she decided to call off the wedding plans the day he called her upstairs and she found him wearing her clothes. I guess he was more intent on wearing them than she was.

The postwar period was a golden era for both movies and baseball. The studio system was still active, though it would be dissolved in the near future; television was coming in, and fans could finally see the faces of ballplayers. The line between entertainment celebrity and baseball celebrity was diminished. The legendary Hollywood stars and baseball players were still alive and, in most cases, active in their professions. Glamour was at a high level. And this was most evident, perhaps, at the pro-am golf tournaments.

In 1958, the Crosby National Pro-Am expanded to 72 holes and became one of the first PGA Tour tournaments to be nationally televised. After playing in it about 10 years, I gave up my clubs for a microphone and became part of the broadcast team for several more years after that. The network, not Crosby, hired me. Bing served as the color man for his tournament. One year Lindsey Nelson and Bing were driving around in a cart to cover the golfers at the different holes. It was not unusual for it to be wet and rainy, and Lindsey got stuck in the mud. The two men looked at each other. Lindsey told me later, "I knew right then that the guy who would get out of the cart and push it out of the mud wasn't going to be Crosby."

Bing Crosby died, as he would have wanted it, after completing a round of golf, at La Moraleja Golf Club, outside Madrid, in 1977. He had a heart attack. It was as great a loss to the golf community as it was to the entertainment world because he and Bob Hope did more than anyone, including the professional golfers themselves, to promote and popularize the sport they loved. I still treasure the times I played with him and at his splendid tournament. His tournament lost its luster after his death, and, sadly, his name was removed from the tournament's title in 1986. Today it is called the AT&T Pebble Beach National Pro-Am.

Bob Hope's Chrysler Classic still existed under that name through 2003, when Hope died at the age of 100. Always defensive about his fortune, he contended to the end, "Golf is my profession; I tell jokes to pay greens fees." Hope's tournament is the exception to the rule. Almost all the other Crosby-inspired pro-am events hosted by Dean Martin, Danny Thomas, Sammy Davis Jr., Jackie Gleason, Andy Williams, Glen Campbell, and others disappeared and are now mostly forgotten.

The golden era of golf and Hollywood faded away. I was fortunate to have been in the right place at the right time and to have had the right credentials and right friends to have played a part in it.

Other than playing in an occasional celebrity golf tournament or hosting visitors in the Mets' broadcast booth, I don't mingle with current celebrities. I don't know who most of them are. Unfortunately, there aren't many old-timers around anymore.

When I married Nancy Chaffee in 1951 it was considered big news because it involved two public figures. Although it wasn't on the level of DiMaggio and Monroe, it received media attention similar to when Leo Durocher married Laraine Day and football hero Bob Waterfield wed Jane Russell. It was covered by Pathe News for movie theaters, and everyone wanted eyewitness accounts from guests like Hank Greenberg, Bob Lemon, and tennis champion Jack Kramer. However, no one wanted to talk to a muscular young man nobody recognized. When Eddie Mathews was called up by the Braves the following year, he informed me, "I was at your wedding." "But we didn't send you an invitation," I said with confusion. "I didn't need one," he shrugged. "It was a big event, so I snuck in."

Now, when star athletes get married or when an athlete weds a major entertainer, no one seems to care. For instance, David Justice's brief marriage to Halle Berry got very little coverage. Boston shortstop Nomar Garciaparra's sudden engagement to soccer star Mia Hamm is probably still a secret to most sports fans. And when Derek Jeter, perhaps baseball's most popular current player, dated Mariah Carey, perhaps the most successful current female pop singer, it got less press than when baseball bad boy Bo Belinsky dated movie hellcat Mamie Van Doren 40 years before.

The reason for so much complacency is television. Because of so much exposure, sports figures and other celebrities no longer have *mystique*. This is not to say that fans don't still think they lead glamorous lives and admire them to an astonishing degree. But fans no longer think celebrities exist in a totally different world from their own. Unlike in my day, baseball players and entertainers are no longer part myth, part mystery. They are now familiar to anyone with a TV, fixtures in their homes. In fact, ballplayers are now merely TV stars, similar to soap opera actors whose characters' trials and tribulations are watched by viewers on a daily basis. Because ballplayers make appearances on various series (usually playing themselves), in commercials, and on talk shows that also have entertainers as guests, the line is further blurred between them and other celebrities. Television has the power to lump together the ballplayers, singers, movie stars, television actors and personalities, and everyone else who appears on the tube in a celebrity hodgepodge. As a result, no one retains their glitter or glamour.

Only with this generation have baseball stars come to be equally known, equally liked, and equally paid as entertainers. And the entertainers don't seem to care. Just like in my day, they admire ballplayers as much as, if not more than, people in their own fields, but now some are actually putting on uniforms and swinging bats. For instance, Garth Brooks, Tom Selleck, and Kevin Costner are among those who have worked out with major league teams at spring training. Others have played in celebrity baseball and softball games with the pros; some have participated in celebrity-ballplayer hitting events during All-Star Weekend. Once again, there is little distinction between the ballplayer and the entertainer.

With increasing frequency, ballplayers use the media to get free publicity. When they attend a concert or sporting event, they get the best seat in the house and are inevitably shown on television. Movie and television stars do exactly the same thing. Billy Crystal can frequently be seen at Yankees games, Jerry Seinfeld shows up at Mets games, countless stars attend Dodgers games, and so on. Similarly, both athletes and entertainers are seen at televised football and basketball games and boxing matches.

When a star wants to promote something, he often heads directly for the broadcast booth. My old partner Lindsey Nelson said, "Baseball is baseball and we don't need to see actors on our broadcasts." He didn't want to do it. But if games are dull, it doesn't hurt to talk to somebody who is well known and interesting. The Mets were one of the first teams to televise all their games, and celebrities took advantage of the opportunity to get exposure. Every time we'd play in L.A., we'd have someone come on the air. You don't want to be talking to somebody about their movie or show when the winning run is coming around third, but usually it works out fine. I always enjoy it if the guest is someone like Billy Crystal, who is a great ad-libber. When I've never heard of the celebrity, I'm less enthusiastic about a conversation.

Danny Kaye, who was a great baseball fan and once a part-owner of the Seattle Mariners, would often come up to the booth when we were in Los Angeles to say hello. I looked forward to that because he was an interesting, funny man. In addition to being a multitalented performer, Kaye was also an exceptional cook who was best friends with famous French chef Jacques Pepin. Once Dodgers broadcaster Vin Scully, whom Kaye frequently visited in the booth, invited him over to his house to cook a meal. Vin told me it was the greatest meal he ever had. But it took Scully two weeks to clean his kitchen because Kaye was the messiest cook he'd ever seen.

Well, if Kaye were still alive, he could cook in my kitchen any time. And if Ginger Rogers was up for a game of tennis or Esther Williams a swim, I wouldn't object. And if Lou Costello or Jack Benny wanted to talk baseball, I'd be happy to oblige. And if Crosby, Hope, and Harris wanted to rise at the crack of dawn to play golf with a former baseball player, I'd be more than willing. I've never been someone to dwell on the past, but it would be great to relive an experience or two from when the golden eras of baseball and the movies overlapped and some remarkable people crossed my path.

Chapter **8**

Ralph Kiner, **Broadcaster**

When I went to high school, I had no aspirations to be a broadcaster. I wanted to be a ballplayer, and if that didn't work out, I was going to be a sportswriter, because in the movies they were high-class guys who got to meet everyone. The only reason I took a class called "radio speech," which proved to be a fortunate choice, was the same reason I accepted ridicule to be the only boy to take shorthand: there were a lot of pretty girls in those classes.

Although I didn't think I'd ever talk on the radio, I wanted to play on it someday like the Pacific Coast League players. There were two local teams, the Los Angeles Angels and Hollywood Stars, but it was difficult for me to see them play because I was short of money and had no transportation until I scraped together $75 to buy a 1919 Model A Ford in my senior year. So radio was my only real contact with professional baseball. On Saturdays, they would have live broadcasts of the Angels and Stars' home games or studio "re-creations" off ticker tapes of road games. I loved those radio games, much more than I would televised games. My imagination took me to great places. Radio broadcasters also used their imaginations, especially when they did the re-creations.

Re-creations were brilliant theater that resulted from teams not being able to afford costly telephone line charges. A Western Union operator in the other team's ballpark would send Morse code to the studio in the home city. The single broadcaster would take a coded description off the ticker tape and embellish it, and someone else in the studio would incorporate sound effects. When there would be a hit ball, the broadcaster might choose to say it was a sizzling line drive, which would prompt the effects person to use a wooden mallet to mimic the sound of a wooden bat smashing the ball. Depending on the real outcome of the play, the engineer raised and lowered the volume of recorded crowd noise. Of course, when someone homered, there would be a huge cheer. Every pitch was an exciting short story, partly fact and partly fiction. We could hear the tape ticking in the background, so we knew games were being re-created, but we'd still get lost in the broadcaster's words and feel we were at the park.

Re-creations were vital to the popularity of America's pastime for several decades, but they were mostly forgotten until Ronald Reagan became president and he recalled nostalgically that before he became a Hollywood actor during the late thirties, he did re-creations of Cubs games. Like all broadcasters, Reagan sweated through technical glitches. He would tell the story of having to stall one day when the tape broke while a batter was at the plate. While he waited to find out what really happened, he had the batter hit six minutes' worth of foul balls—each of which were fought over by fabricated kids in the stands.

There were other kinds of distractions during re-creations that tested the ability of broadcasters to improvise. My onetime partner Lindsey Nelson told the story of a broadcaster who was having an affair with the receptionist at the studio. He was taking a chance because she was married to the town sheriff. One day he was breezing through the ninth inning of a re-created game when he noticed that she was standing at the window to the broadcast booth. She was frantically holding up a sign that read: "He found out about us!" The broadcaster announced there was a fly ball to left field, and before that ball came down, he jumped up, grabbed his jacket, exited the closest door, and skipped town.

Although I grew up idolizing Babe Ruth, I didn't really become a fan of the major leagues until I was in the seventh grade and the 1934 World Series between the St. Louis Cardinals and Detroit Tigers was broadcast. The first national radio transmission of a Series wouldn't be until a year later, so I assume it was a re-creation. Oddly, the games I remember most in that classic seven-game Series were the ones I couldn't listen to because I was in school when they were played. Our teacher wouldn't allow a radio in the classroom, but I found out what was going on from Ruth Bobkin, the woman who looked after me while my mother was working. Her husband Bob and teenage son Robert were the ones who started me playing baseball as a young boy, and they lived in a house I could see from a classroom window. She listened to the games and would come outside and whistle from her porch to get my attention. Then she'd signal me with her hands— the right hand was Detroit, for whom I was rooting, and the left hand was the Cardinals, who won the Series—and from the number of fingers she held up, I could tell the score. She'd do this every inning. I still loved the Pacific Coast League, but that's how I got hooked on the majors. After that Series, more major league games were broadcast into the area. I still remember sitting close to the radio every Saturday and listening to Hal Berger's exciting re-creations.

Harold Arlin, who worked for KDKA in Pittsburgh, had broadcast the first major league game on the radio, between Pittsburgh and the visiting Phillies, back in 1921, but baseball on the radio was still in its infancy during the thirties. Of the pioneers in the medium, surely the one who had the most impact was Red Barber. In 1934, Cincinnati Reds general manager Larry MacPhail hired him off a college radio station to do a number of live home games and re-creations of road games on the Crosley-owned station. (Powell Crosley was the owner of the Reds.) A year later, Barber broadcast the major leagues' first night game when the Reds hosted the Phillies at Crosley Field and President Roosevelt threw a switch at the White House to turn on the stadium's lights. In October, when the first World Series was broadcast nationwide, Barber was the commentator. He also was behind the mike for the first nationally *televised* baseball game, between the Reds and Dodgers at Ebbets Field, when NBC did an experimental broadcast in 1939. By that time he was a fixture on World Series broadcasts. He was always prodding Gillette to hike the broadcasters' pay for the Series because they were getting next to nothing and being exploited as much as the players were.

When Larry MacPhail moved to Brooklyn in 1938, he took Barber with him. The Dodgers, with the Kentucky-born Barber becoming the most popular voice in the borough, were the first team on the radio in New York. MacPhail broke the agreement between the Yankees, Giants, and Dodgers not to broadcast games; they had believed fans would just listen to their favorite teams and not want to pay to see them in person. They had missed the boat because exposure leads to more people going to games. (Similarly, when television came along, most teams were reluctant to broadcast home games.) The two other New York teams would follow the Dodgers' example. Then in 1946, the Yankees became the first team to broadcast all their games live. That was my rookie year, and seven years after the Cubs had become the first team to broadcast all their games, half of them being re-creations.

Beginning in 1940, Barber did the World Series with Mel Allen, an emerging talent. Allen got his job as a Yankees announcer when Arch McDonald's previous partner made the mistake of saying "Ovary Soap" three consecutive times while doing an on-air commercial for Ivory Soap. By the early fifties, Allen, who quickly became the lead broadcaster for baseball's most dominant team, was as famous as Barber.

For Series games, Barber followed the orders of Judge Landis to report only what the players, managers, and umpires did and analyze *nothing*. He maintained that style in his local broadcasts for the Reds and, beginning in the late thirties, the Dodgers. Because of his influence, play-by-play men for decades to come would limit themselves to reporting and avoid observations and opinions. Included were the two true poets of the profession, Ernie Harwell and Vin Scully, future broadcasting giants who learned their craft while sharing the booth with Barber in Brooklyn. Harwell soon moved across town and briefly worked with Russ Hodges on Giants games before finding a permanent home in Detroit; Scully became the "Voice of the Dodgers" after Barber had a contract dispute with the team and joined Allen in the booth of the rival Yankees in 1954. While Harwell and Scully would continue to broadcast for their respective teams into the 21st century, Barber's tenure with the Yankees ended in 1966, two years after Allen's firing. He was let go, oddly enough, because he was uncharacteristically outspoken on the air, pointing out that the Yankees, who had fallen into last place only two years after being in the World Series, had attracted only 413 fans to one game. Although Barber would stay in baseball, his career in the booth came to an end.

Broadcasters with strong personalities like Red Barber (Dodgers), Mel Allen (Yankees), Rosey Rosewell (Pirates), Russ Hodges (Giants), Bob Elson and Jack Brickhouse (Cubs and White Sox), By Saam (A's and Phillies), Arch McDonald (Senators), and Harry Caray (Cardinals) became part of the lives of their listeners. They were welcomed into their homes every day, as good friends. Most of them were "homers" who used "we" in regard to the team, just as the fans did. All had catchphrases, and most had homer calls that became part of their fans' vernaculars. Best of all, they created thrilling images of players and plays and, before there was television, cultivated the romance of baseball.

Of course, television changed baseball broadcasting. For years when there was a ground ball to short, fans wouldn't know if it was only an average play. No longer could broadcasters make every play sound spectacular. If a guy didn't make a great catch, the broadcaster couldn't tell the fans watching at home that he did. Television made everyone more critical of how the game was played.

Players, in general, had a mistrust for anyone in the media, but for the most part they didn't fear broadcasters. In Pittsburgh, for instance, they were much more wary of reporters, because many of them would take their cues from the owners and rip them in the press. We thought broadcasters were neutral in their allegiances and tried to win their favor so they'd say something nice about us. In New York, each team's number one broadcaster would interview one of us before a game and they'd play it afterward. Some teams had live postgame television shows. You could make 50 bucks for an appearance, so it was important to be asked on. The hosts were always friendly and tried to make the players feel comfortable in front of the cameras. Most players were delighted television came in. It looked like a very good source of income, and it also gave us exposure we never had before. I know I was recognized more, particularly because of All-Star Games. Players in the World Series got the most exposure, especially after the Series was televised from coast to coast beginning in 1951. I never got the benefit of that.

I always was fascinated by the workings of the media, and I jumped at the opportunity to be part of it once I became famous for hitting home runs. After the 1947 season, I was asked by both a Pittsburgh newspaper and a Pittsburgh radio station to send back reports from the World Series between the Yankees and Dodgers. It was the first Series I ever saw, and I did it in style with Hank Greenberg. We went to the game in a limo, had great seats, and ate a picnic lunch that was made by Lindy's. And when we walked on the field, the New York and Brooklyn fans recognized both of us and cheered. I had a ghost-writer for my daily column of observations called "Kiner's Liners," which ran in the *Pittsburgh Press* throughout that historic seven-game Series. But it was the real me on the radio. I did a postgame report with Pirates announcer Bob Prince from a New York studio, and it was sent back to Pittsburgh. We were kind of stuck there on our own, and Mel Allen came down after broadcasting the game to be on with us and give us material. To do that in the middle of the whole darn thing for no money showed what kind of guy he was. What also was great about Allen was that he was an unstoppable talker, so I didn't have to come up with many questions.

Doing that radio show was fun, and I was eager for new opportunities. In 1948, the Pirates played an exhibition game in Washington, and Bing Crosby and Bob Hope were there doing a national radio show and decided to use me in a sketch with Dorothy Lamour. She came home with a package and I was supposed to say, "What's in that package?" But I said something like, "Boy, you really pack a mean package." Maybe I was distracted by her exotic looks, but it took me five or six takes to get that line right. I had only three or four lines to deliver, but acting wasn't my world and I wasn't too good at it. That might explain why my friends Crosby and Hope never asked me to appear in their movies.

As I became better known, Bob Prince got me a few radio commercials, as a favor. I also did national print ads for Chesterfield and Wheaties, and a local one for Braun Bread. In Pittsburgh, Isley Ice Cream used a life-size statue of me for promotion.

The first television show I ever did was Merv Griffin's morning show. I went on with my wife Nancy in the early fifties, before Merv made zillions of dollars. I was in New York playing ball, and Nancy was a champion tennis player, so he asked us both to be guests. I didn't tell him that I saw him sing with my favorite band, Freddy Martin's, when they played at the Coconut Grove at the Ambassador Hotel. Nancy and I also were substitute cohosts on a television interview program in Los Angeles during the off-season. We took over for Los Angeles Rams receiver Elroy "Crazylegs" Hirsch when he went on vacation. The half-hour show was sponsored by Union Oil, the company that provided Walter O'Malley with an enormous loan that allowed him to move the Dodgers to L.A. in 1957. We would give instruction, like how to hit a baseball or serve a tennis ball, and interview in-studio guests.

I was probably the first ballplayer to have his own TV show *during* the season. It played on a Pittsburgh station Sunday evenings at 7:30. We'd play doubleheaders on Sunday, but there was a 7:00 P.M. curfew in Pennsylvania, so Bob Prince, who ran the show, and I managed to get to the downtown studio on time. All we needed was a police escort from Forbes Field. No problem. They even used sirens. We'd then race up the stairs and do the show. It was on live, but we'd include prerecorded tapes of such bits as Brooklyn's Roy Campanella showing viewers how to catch. Ray Scott, who became a Hall of Fame football announcer, handled the commercials. I did one with him for Braun Bread, although I didn't know how to sell a product. Scott would ask, "Ralph, what do you think of Braun Bread?" Clearing my throat, I'd muster all my thespian skills and deliver my line, which was, "Well, Ray, Braun Bread is one of the best things I've ever had, and it has really helped me hit home runs." It was terrible. That might have been the most primitive show ever on live television.

Game shows were in vogue, and I was invited on a few in New York that were shown nationally. They were fun to do. In the summer of 1952, I was on the television version of the longtime radio hit *Information Please*, hosted by Clifton Fadiman. Viewers submitted tough questions to a panel of two regulars and the guest, me. It was intimidating because they had intellects on that panel—Franklin P. Adams, who in 1908 penned "Tinker-to-Evers-to-Chance," and John Kieran, who in 1927 began to write the first bylined sports column in *The New York Times*. That show wasn't rigged, but I'm sure they picked questions I might get right. Fortunately, I had been a flyer in the navy and remembered a few things about celestial navigation. On *What's My Line?*, the panelists had to guess who I was. I was playing for the Chicago Cubs by that time, and I was dressed up as a bear! Anything to be on television.

I still didn't think of becoming a baseball announcer, but without knowing it, I was putting together good credentials. I had made numerous guest appearances on a variety of television and radio shows, pitched products, done studio work, and even had my own shows.

After my playing career ended in 1955, I became the general manager of the San Diego Padres. To increase revenue, I sold a package of 10 Saturday afternoon games to television for a small fee. I couldn't afford to pay a broadcaster, so I did them myself. That was the first broadcasting I ever did. I didn't get into analysis at all. Nobody did back then. It was simple: "Ground ball . . . one out." No verbs needed. It was a new experience, and I enjoyed it. I thought we did a pretty good job although we were on a shoestring budget. We wanted to get exposure and it worked. People would watch the Saturday game on television and come out Sunday for a doubleheader.

When the Dodgers and Giants moved to the West Coast, that was the death knell for the PCL. Thanks to some insensitive number-crunching by Walter O'Malley's puppet, Major League Commissioner Ford Frick, we received peanuts as compensation for their infringement on our territory. Four PCL teams had to relocate, and the others struggled badly. Seeing that the league's days were numbered, I resigned as GM of the Padres in 1960. I didn't expect O'Malley and Frick to sabotage my next business enterprise as well. Bill Veeck and Hank Greenberg, who at the time were running the White Sox, had the rights to the L.A. area for an American League expansion team in 1961, and I was set to be in the front office of the new team. We had signed a radio and TV contract with KMPC, which Gene Autry owned, so we were ready to go. But then Frick flew out to L.A. to meet with O'Malley, and they changed the ground rules for owning an L.A. franchise. Veeck and Greenberg were told they would have to pay damages to the Dodgers and be a tenant in Dodgers Stadium. O'Malley wanted L.A. all to himself, and Frick tried to help him. Veeck and Greenberg decided there was no way to operate in O'Malley's privately owned ballpark, and they withdrew. When they pulled out, Autry and his station were already in place, and that's how the Singing Cowboy got the Angels. But I was out of a job.

When the Pirates got into the 1960 World Series, I got a phone call from my old friend Bob Prince. He was going to announce the Series with Mel Allen on television, and he asked me if I'd be interested in doing a postgame interview show with him for the games played in Pittsburgh. I said I would. My show was sponsored by Mellon Bank, one of the biggest banks in the world at the time. The Series opened with two games in Pittsburgh and came back for the final two games, including the fantastic seventh game in which Bill Mazeroski won the Series with a home run. I couldn't get Mazeroski or the other players on the air because we were in a studio, so we looked around for people who were indirectly involved with the Series. When Russ Hodges walked by, for instance, we shanghaied him and had him on the show. Curt Gowdy, the Red Sox announcer, was in town, so we also pulled him into the studio. We always found someone.

In addition to being a great announcer with a deep voice that Pirates fans loved, Bob Prince was a real character. He was unlike anyone you'd see nowadays, or back then for that matter. At one end of the baseball broadcaster spectrum was Red Barber, an ordained minister who was very straitlaced and had no sense of humor. At the other end was Bob Prince. He was crazy. He'd do anything. When I had just joined the Pirates in 1946, he worked out with the team and took grounders. Our hard-nosed manager Frankie Frisch intentionally broke his thumbs by hitting him hard grounders.

That didn't slow him down. He once jumped out of a third-floor window at the Chase Hotel into a swimming pool. He drank a lot but was sober when he bet Pirates first baseman Dick "Dr. Strangeglove" Stuart that he could dive into the pool from the window. Prince was a good swimmer and diver, but he had to dive out the window and past some wires and over the diving board. He risked his life for $25. Fortunately he made it. That escapade was written up in a story about him in *Sports Illustrated*. When his wife, Betty, read the story, she chastised him, "You know you're crazy, and I know you're crazy, but does the whole world have to know?"

Prince didn't know it at the time, but that World Series assignment he got me was a big break, leading to my career in broadcasting. It opened doors, so I never had to apply for work. Because of television and the arrival of instant replay, teams were hiring an increasing number of former players to serve as analysts. I was offered a spot doing sports on a television news show in Pittsburgh. I turned that down. Gabe Paul, the Reds GM, asked me to broadcast Reds games on TV with Frank McCormick. While I was considering that, I was offered the job of radio play-by-play man and commentator for the Chicago White Sox. I accepted the Sox job because of my friendship with Hank Greenberg, who was Bill Veeck's partner and vice president with the team. He was the one who put me in contact with WCFL. By this time, I was thinking that broadcasting might be a good way to prolong my career in sports. I always had self-assuredness, and thought if I tried it and it didn't work, I'd just move along and try something else.

My job description at WCFL in Chicago was pretty weird. The station had air time to fill up in the afternoons, so I'd do two games each day, unless I was on the road with the Sox. When the Sox were home in Chicago, I'd go to the radio station and do re-created games by myself between two other major league teams, and then I'd go to the ballpark and do a Sox game live with Bob Elson. When there were no games, I'd have to do a radio disc jockey show, playing music and talking sports. I buried that experience in the recesses of my mind, but recently I suddenly remembered that I had hosted perhaps the worst radio show of all time. My defense for why I was so lousy was that I had no idea what I was doing. I could bluff my way through Bing Crosby or Glenn Miller, but otherwise I was lost. It wasn't rock 'n' roll, but I didn't know who I was playing. WCFL was a major fifty-thousand-watt station that went all over the country, so everyone heard me.

I also broadcast games under fire, without anyone helping me. I learned the most doing re-creations, because I really had to work to fill in the story. Say there was a single to right field. I'd make it a line drive or bloop hit. But then after I put the man on first, a correction might come through on the tape saying there was nobody on base, and then I'd have to figure out how to get him off it in a credible way. Sometimes the tape would break down and nothing would come across. So until the ticker tape started up again, I'd have to come up with a reason for the delay—"This storm came unexpectedly! The grounds crew is rolling out the tarp!" I had to make things up in a hurry, and sometimes I sank and sometimes I swam. It was a great experience, and I was proud to begin my broadcasting career following the tradition of all the great broadcasters who did re-creations. That's how I learned to be a broadcaster, more than from working with Elson.

Bob Elson, a funny-looking man with straight black-gray hair, was the big broadcaster of the day in Chicago and would end up in the broadcasters wing of the Hall of Fame. He really came to prominence when he conned his way into the good graces of Judge Landis years before so that he could broadcast World Series games. Elson was very popular with the fans, and I got along with him, but he was pompous and demanding. In fact, his nickname was "Commander." He was called that because during the war he was in the navy, although I think he was stationed in Chicago. Elson was the king of the name-droppers and a shill for restaurants, bars, and other businesses in the area who weren't our sponsors. One of the things he'd do is pretend to spot the owner of a place he liked to frequent, and he'd end up getting free drinks or meals for giving it a plug on the air. Many broadcasters did that at the time, but Elson was the least subtle.

In addition to broadcasting games, Elson had a lot of irons in the fire. He had a show where he'd grab celebrities who were changing trains in Chicago while on their way from New York to L.A. Before they climbed aboard the Twentieth Century Limited, he'd interview them. He had another show in the Pump Room at the Ambassador Hotel and interviewed celebrities there. He also talked to players on his live news show at the studio. He was known for asking a question and then leaving the booth while the player gave the answer, and the abandoned player would have to babble on till Elson returned. I don't know why a player never gave a one-word response to teach him a lesson. Once someone hired a girl to come in and do a striptease in front of Elson while he did his live show. He liked good-looking girls so much that he forgot what he was talking about. It's too bad things like that don't happen anymore.

Before my second year of broadcasting with the White Sox, Veeck and Greenberg sold the team. So I signed a new deal with the Sox's new general manager Ed Short. Prior to the 1962 season, I was one of the broadcasters for the nationally televised Bing Crosby National Pro-Am Golf Tournament. My job was to interview players as they finished their rounds. I'd been doing that for a few years, and I would eventually also do Bob Hope's tournament and several others. While I was at the Crosby tournament in northern California, I got a call from George Weiss, the onetime GM of the Yankees who was now running the expansion New York Mets. He asked me if I'd be interested in broadcasting Mets games on both television and radio with Lindsey Nelson and Bob Murphy. With Greenberg and Veeck gone from Chicago, this offer really appealed to me.

As luck would have it, Lindsey also was on the team of broadcasters for the tournament. I had met him the previous year when I was in Milwaukee and he was in town doing the *Game of the Week* on TV. I liked him instantly. So I immediately asked his advice on whether to accept Weiss' offer. He told me, "Take the job." He confirmed what I already knew, which was that New York was a great place to be as a broadcaster. But he really swayed me when he pointed out that because the Mets were a new team, we wouldn't be replacing any broadcasters for whom the fans felt attachment. I was still a relatively inexperienced broadcaster, so what he said made me feel less pressure.

I told Weiss I would love to come to New York. Getting out of my contract with the White Sox would be no problem, but there was still one minor hurdle. Weiss informed me that I had to get the approval of someone named Norm Varney. He was the account executive for J. Walter Thompson, the firm that was representing Rheingold beer in its sponsorship deal with the Mets. (Rheingold paid $6 million for five years of commercial time on Mets games on WOR-TV, which was more than Joan Payson had spent on the entire team—meaning she was already making a profit.) Weiss told me that Varney was going to watch the golf tournament and judge my performance.

Knowing I was being scrutinized, I did interviews on the eighteenth green the next afternoon. So there I was having a quick, straightforward Q&A with golfer Gay Brewer, who was leading the tournament. Suddenly, the producer decided to liven things up by pushing Phil Harris—who always played in the tournament—in front of the camera while we were talking. Phil was a close friend, so his sudden appearance didn't throw me for a loop, but I knew him well enough to be cautious of his quick and often wicked wit. So I asked a safe question, "Phil, you know Gay Brewer, don't you?" And he answered, "Yeah, he's a fag wine maker from Modesto." Remember, this was 1962! Bing Crosby was watching on TV and almost fell out of his chair. I didn't know how Norm Varney reacted. I would have no recollection of what I said afterward, but somehow I got out of the interview in a hurry.

When they cut away, I said to Phil, "Why the hell did you say something like that?" He replied, "Well, we were only on a short time, so I had to get their attention." I snapped, "You certainly did that." Fortunately, there were no repercussions. *And* I was hired by the Mets. Maybe they figured that if I could handle that, then I could handle talking to the Mets' first manager, Casey Stengel.

Recently I was playing golf with a guy named Herzog. We were talking about broadcasting and golf in the old days, and he started laughing and said, "I worked with 3M when it sponsored the Crosby Pro-Am. I don't remember who the poor announcer was, but I've never forgotten that when he asked Phil Harris if he knew Gay Brewer, Harris responded, 'Gay Brewer is a fag wine maker from Modesto.'" As I went into my preshot routine, I said, "I can tell you who that poor announcer was. It was *me*."

I was the third and final person George Weiss asked to be part of the television and radio broadcast team for the Mets' inaugural 1962 season. Lindsey and Bob Murphy had already signed on, though I'm not sure in what order. I hadn't met Bob before, but I knew his older brother Jack, who was a popular sports editor with the *San Diego Union* and would be responsible for bringing the San Diego Chargers to the city. Bob had broadcast Red Sox games with Curt Gowdy and then had been the number one announcer for the Orioles. He and Lindsey had worked together before, for "the Old Scotsman" Gordon McClendon, re-creating baseball games for Texas-based Liberty Broadcasting. From 1957 to 1961, Lindsey called the *Game of the Week* for NBC, and some people thought he was foolish to give up a network job to broadcast the Mets locally. By that time he had already won several Sportscaster of the Year Awards and was as big as they come in the business, in baseball and football, so it was really a coup for Weiss to acquire his services.

Lindsey, Bob, and I took pride in that we were going to be the broadcasters for the team that was bringing National League baseball back to New York. When the Dodgers and Giants left for the West Coast after the 1957 season, they ripped out much of the fabric and soul of the city. Brooklyn fans were so devastated that many swore that they would never watch baseball again. The Mets unabashedly borrowed their colors from the departed teams—blue from the Dodgers and orange from the Giants—and tried to revive the fanaticism. It had seemed out of whack that there had been no National League team in New York for four years, and the Mets' arrival restored order. The Mets came into being because of my onetime nemesis Branch Rickey, who announced the formation of the Continental League, a competitive major league for the 1961 season. That scared the majors into expanding to Los Angeles and Washington in the American League in 1961 and Houston and New York in the National League in 1962. My guess is that Rickey received an enormous payoff to disband his league and allow four of his cities to be incorporated into the majors. That was probably his intention all along.

Before the Mets' first exhibition game in St. Petersburg, Florida, Weiss called together his new broadcast team. We sat in a small room in the hotel waiting for him for about 15 minutes, making small talk. Then he came in and sat down. And nobody said anything. Everybody just sat there. Then he got up and said, "You're professional broadcasters, you'll do a good job!"

And he left. That was the total sum of the input he ever gave us. Nobody said anything more to us about our broadcasting for years.

The three of us had minimal discussion about what the nature of our broadcasts should be. That allowed Lindsey and Bob the freedom to continue to broadcast as they always had and for me to develop my own style, which would center around my insight as a former player about the game on the field and my knowledge of baseball's past. However, we did decide right away that none of us would be "homers." We wanted to be different from Yankees broadcasters Mel Allen and Phil Rizzuto, who, as a sure indicator of their home team bias, referred to "Ballantine Blasts" only when there were Yankees homers. If we had to refer to "Rheingold Roundtrippers"—which, thankfully, we never did—it would be for *both* teams. Almost all broadcasters were "homers" because their teams wanted them to draw fans to their stadiums, but we decided to be objective because we knew many visitors to New York would be watching or listening to our games, and they wouldn't necessarily be Mets fans.

We did a lot of socializing that first spring. We did only radio from Florida, and we'd drive from the ballpark to the Colonial Inn, which had been chosen as team headquarters because it accepted black players. There we'd take another lesson in Stengelese from the Old Professor in the pressroom and then go to dinner together, usually with Rheingold's liaison Al Moore. More often than not, we'd wind up in a piano bar. Lindsey and Al, a former New York Giant who became a close friend to the three of us, knew all the songs.

After we came to New York for the season, Bob and I lived at the Manhattan Hotel in the heart of the city for $5 a day. Mets coach Rogers Hornsby tried to get us to move out where he was, at the Concourse Hotel in the Bronx, and pay only $3 a day, but we stayed put and would go to and from the Polo Grounds together. Lindsey was living out in Huntington, Long Island, with his wife and two daughters, so the only time we saw him during homestands was at the park. By the time Shea Stadium opened in Flushing, Queens, in 1964, Bob had moved to Huntington too, and he and Lindsey traveled to the park together, while I went alone from my apartment on New York's East Side.

On the road the three of us stayed at the same hotels as the ballplayers. When we had free time, we'd go our separate ways—one reason is that I was the only one who played golf—but we always ended up meeting after the game. Later we'd return to the hotel and maybe spend a few hours listening to Casey Stengel at the bar. If we saw him at the bar on nights we wanted to get to sleep, we'd sneak around back like three schoolboys trying to avoid their headmaster. If he spotted us, we knew he'd talk to us until morning. Casey would never go to sleep, which is the reason he was often seen snoozing in the Mets dugout during games. Once at 3:00 in the morning he cornered me in the elevator and wouldn't let me off. He just kept talking, and I couldn't get away even to use the bathroom.

Lindsey was self-sufficient but liked our company and probably spent more time with Bob and me than anyone else ever. He was well read and intelligent and a great raconteur. Lindsey told us many fascinating stories about his time in the war. He was a captain in the army and took part in the invasions of North Africa, Sicily, and Normandy. He fought in the Battle of the Bulge and was at Remagen Bridge when the American and Russian forces met. He befriended William Westmoreland, who was then a battalion commander of artillery. He also became close with Ernie Pyle, the famous war correspondent, and sent his own reports of the war over the wires. Lindsey didn't tell us only of battles but of venturing into towns and drinking—and these tales could be quite hilarious. People who didn't know him didn't realize how much fun he could be out of the booth.

As free and easy as he was when out socializing, Lindsey was strictly the professional when at work. He was never late in all the years we worked together, and he was meticulous about everything, including keeping all his books and notes in the booth in perfect order. Unlike me, he wasn't a storyteller on the air because he wanted viewers to focus only on the game. I don't want to give the impression he was dry, because Lindsey was anything but that. He was witty and enthusiastic, and fans loved to listen to his great voice—smooth, with traces of Tennessee.

Lindsey had as much fun as Bob and I did that amazing first year. On Opening Day, memorably, he interviewed Casey Stengel prior to the game and asked him to introduce the players. Casey, who called Lindsey "Miller" and the Mets' two pitchers named Miller "Nelson," gave long introductions of the players at each position, and it was evident he was stalling while he tried to remember their names. For instance, he'd say, "Our third baseman used to play for the Dodgers and he has a plate in his head and his name is Don Zimmer." And he couldn't remember the name of the right fielder and kept talking about how he played for the Pirates and the Reds and finally he said, " . . . and if he starts hitting like he did with Cincinnati, he'll ring a bell—and that's his name, Gus Bell." It turned out Casey spoke nonstop for 23 minutes, while Lindsey patiently stood there with the microphone in his hand and a bemused expression on his face. He dared not interrupt to ask *another* question!

Casey was a wonderful character who had a different take on everything. For instance, when Hobie Landrith was the Mets' first draft choice, Stengel explained, "If you ain't got a catcher you get all passed balls." A year later, after a Met batter homered down the short foul line at the Polo Grounds, Stengel said, "Ain't that somethin'! Just when my fellers learn how to hit the ball in this park, they're gonna tear the thing down." Casey was a memorable guest on the first *Kiner's Korner*, my live postgame television show. When he got up to leave, he neglected to unhook the microphone that was around his neck and pulled down the entire set. It wouldn't have been so bad if the show had been over, but we still had to come back from commercial and finish.

Stengel was the Mets' greatest attraction, the person who tried to take the focus off his struggling players as the losses piled up, but there were a number of stunts that pleased the fans who flooded into the Polo Grounds. One involved the Mets' mascot, a beagle named Homer who had been trained by Rudd Weatherwax, the trainer of Lassie. Homer did a lot of tricks, including back flips and holding a banner in his mouth that read "Let's Go Mets." As a result, he got as much fan mail as any player. Bob Murphy even interviewed him while Homer sat on his lap in a hilarious television moment. On "Miss Rheingold Day," Lindsey called him out from the stands. Homer was supposed to run around the bases, but when he got to second he shot straight across the diamond to home. That was like the Mets players had been running the bases all year, and the fans loved it. (Homer was retired after the year to the home of Al Moore, who was surprised to discover that the educated dog wasn't housebroken.)

The Mets opened the year with a loss on April 11 and didn't win until their 10th game. At one point, Stengel admitted he worried his new team would finish the season at 0–162. He wondered, "Can't anybody here play this game?" As they continued to lose at a record pace—they would finish 40–120—and in every way imaginable, we made another conscious decision, which was to not hide the fact that the Mets were inept at times. We weren't going to be condescending, just honest. As it turned out, the Mets' poor play was what made them so endearing to their fans, especially to those bitter toward the two best teams in the National League, the San Francisco Giants and the Los Angeles Dodgers. As Lindsey so aptly said of the Mets: "They were the last age of innocence. They played for fun. They weren't capable of playing for anything else."

That year the Mets began to challenge the champion Yankees at the gate, and our ratings on WOR closed in on theirs on WPIX. It was exciting. I think our broadcasts were so popular instantly because it was apparent to the fans that the three of us in the booth really got along. There was no clash of egos and no one pulled rank. It could very well have been that Lindsey was the number one man, Bob Murphy number two, and me, the newcomer, number three. But it didn't work that way. We were all equals. Nobody lobbied to be on television more, so every game, we shared time in the television and radio booths. So that there would be discussion about instant replays, there were always two of us doing TV. For *Kiner's Korner*, I'd go down to the studio at the end of the eighth inning, while one of them did television and the other radio. (Five years later, when Lindsey began doing Notre Dame football on Saturdays, Bob and I would split time on TV and the radio.)

In a business that always has been extremely competitive and territorial, and where paranoia often crushes relationships between partners, we remained cordial and cooperative, and the fans appreciated it. We called good games and were fair and impartial in our interpretations. If players used poor judgment or umpires made a bad call, we were obligated to point it out—but then we'd move on rather than being overly critical. We could have done the same types of broadcasts today.

In our second year on WOR, we changed from black and white to color. This coincided with our passing the Yankees in ratings. What gave us an added perk was a little star power. Fans tuned in to see what jacket Lindsey was wearing. Lindsey was inspired by the station's switch to color to shed his conservative image by wearing hideous sport jackets with all kinds of colors and designs. His jackets became his trademark, so he kept accumulating them until he had about 350 in his collection. On road trips I would frequently browse through men's stores, and when I came upon anything outlandish I would recommend it to Lindsey. If its look made your eyeballs bulge, he would buy it. As Andy Rooney said, "He's the only friend from my army days who dressed better then than he does now." For the rest of his career, Lindsey was known for his flamboyant apparel. Fittingly, he donated a particularly gaudy jacket to the Baseball Hall of Fame when he was inducted into the broadcasters' wing in 1988.

Nelson's jackets obviously didn't bring much luck, because the Mets suffered through ghastly seasons in the early years of the franchise. But it didn't matter, because the well-meaning but bumbling slapstick players who entered the Mets' wildly spinning revolving door—the baseball equivalents of the Keystone Kops—were never less than entertaining. If they had been a good team that we expected to win, it wouldn't have meant as much when a brash young left-hander named Tug McGraw bested Sandy Koufax in a game in 1965, claiming the Mets' first victory over baseball's best pitcher. Koufax had thrown the first no-hitter against the Mets during their initial season, and that had been a thrill to watch despite the Mets painting a picture of futility.

Another thrill was the NL's first perfect game, which the Phillies' Jim Bunning threw against the Mets on Father's Day two years later. That happened during the first game of a doubleheader, so I wanted to interview him between games. My producer Joe Gallagher couldn't get him to come on at first because he wanted money—he'd get $1,000 for going on *The Ed Sullivan Show* that night—but he convinced Bunning to do it by telling him the interview would be telecast back in Philadelphia. I spoke to him behind home plate. As we talked a woman ran out of the stands and ran up and put her arms around Bunning. Afterward, Bob Murphy asked Lindsey, "Was that his wife?" Lindsey said, "I certainly hope so." It did turn out to be his wife, but you never know.

The Mets always seemed to be part of history. In '65, the Reds' fireballing right-hander Jim Maloney threw 10 innings of no-hit ball against the Mets in another nail-biter. It was at Crosley Field, and Reds announcer Waite Hoyt came into our booth while his partner was doing the play-by-play. He said accusingly, "I heard you mentioned on the air that Maloney's throwing a no-hitter." We said that was true. He said, "You can't do that! You'll jinx him!" We told him, "He can't hear the broadcast, so how can it jinx him? And we owe it to our audience. If someone turned on in the fifth inning, doesn't he have to be told there is a no-hitter going on? Otherwise, he might turn off the game."

We always had subscribed to that theory. We'd tease each other during commercial breaks about not mentioning a possible no-hitter, but then when it seemed like the pitcher had a real shot at it, we'd talk about it on the air. That was something the three of us had decided to do, and to this day Mets broadcasters will constantly remind fans if nobody has gotten a hit. Hoyt went back to the booth, and I think he did talk about it. I don't know if he blamed himself when Maloney lost the no-hitter in the eleventh inning, as well as the game on a home run by Johnny Lewis.

Victories against pitchers like Koufax and Maloney were the highlights of entire seasons. I joked that the Mets hired me because they looked at my background with the Pirates and saw I had losing experience. The Mets never had a winning record for even a day because it was customary for them to have an early season losing streak that began on Opening Day. They lost all their openers until finally one was rained out. It kept raining for all three games of that series. That was the best start the Mets ever had.

It didn't always rain, so many memorable things happened. Roger Craig pitched well and lost 24 games. Hot Rod Kanehl made the team because Stengel liked his hustle in spring training when he climbed over the outfield fence to retrieve a home run by the opposing team. Richie Ashburn was given a boat for being the team's MVP in its disastrous first season, and it sank on its maiden voyage. Jimmy Piersall smashed his 100th career homer and ran around the bases backward, prompting Stengel to get rid of him because "there's only room for one clown on this team." Marvelous Marv Throneberry was called out for missing first base while circling the bases, and when Casey protested, his coach Cookie Lavagetto told him not to bother because Throneberry didn't touch second base either. It is a story familiar to all fans of Mets lore. My comment about the player who swung like Mickey Mantle and hit like Mickey Mouse was, "Marv never made the same mistake twice. He always made different ones."

Clarence "Choo-Choo" Coleman was a backup catcher and one of the symbols of those awful early Mets teams. He distinguished himself by hitting the Mets' first spring training home run in 1962, but Stengel was more "impressed" by his work behind the plate. Casey remarked that Choo-Choo was very fast at running to the backstop to retrieve passed balls. Choo-Choo probably took that as a rave. For some reason, my producer on *Kiner's Korner* wanted him as a guest. I was afraid to have him on because he wasn't at all conversational, and when he did talk he called everybody "Bub." My producer got me to agree by having a second guest there, Roger Craig. So Coleman was brought on and I decided to start out with the simplest question I could think of because the first question is imperative to set the tone. So I asked, "Choo-Choo, how did you get your nickname?" I expected him to say he liked trains as a kid, or something similar. His response was, "I don't know, Bub." I'm thinking, "Oh, boy, where do I go now?" I then asked, "What's your wife's name, and what's she like?" His curt response was: "Mrs. Coleman, and she likes me, Bub." With that, I turned to Roger Craig. That still stands as the shortest interview in all the years of *Kiner's Korner*.

Stengel, Throneberry, and Coleman weren't around when the Mets moved to Shea Stadium in 1964, although Kanehl would hang around for one more year. But the losing continued and attendance kept increasing. Fans started bringing banners to the park, which was unusual back then. We would shoot the banners so the fans at home could see. George Weiss came down one day and said, "I don't want any more shots of the banners. It's not baseball." So we stopped doing it, but then it was decided it was part of what took place at Mets games and the banners were shown again. That's how Banner Day started and became a Mets tradition. Among the most memorable banners were "To Error Is Human, to Forgive Is the Mets" and "The Mets Are Like Fine Wine, Always in the Cellar." When the Mets had a showdown with the Yankees in the annual Mayor's Trophy Game, the guards at Yankee Stadium were ordered to confiscate all the Mets banners so they wouldn't be seen on television. Although they were returned after the game, Mets fans were enraged and the rivalry between the two organizations intensified.

Those first few years were so much fun, on the field, in the stands, and in the booth. One time I set the booth on fire. It was in Houston. Bob Murphy and I were doing the telecast, and I was smoking a cigar. We were getting reports on other games being played that day on ticker tape, and we'd tear it off, read the information on the air, and then throw the tape on the floor. All of a sudden Murphy was jumping up and down and stomping on the floor. An ash had landed on the paper and it was ablaze, with flames and smoke, the whole shebang. Bob's dance saved the day.

All the twists and turns and fun and games culminated in the New York Mets' 1969 championship season, the greatest year of all. The Mets were awful since their inception, having never finished better than ninth place in the 10-team National League. But suddenly the team that was formed in '62 turned the corner and went 100–62, and then they swept the heavily favored Braves in the first NLCS and took four out of five in the World Series from the team that was regarded as the best in baseball, the Baltimore Orioles. (At the time, the stunned citizens of Baltimore were still smarting over the Colts' humiliating defeat by the underdog New York Jets in Super Bowl III.) There has never been anything like it. Even when the Angels won in 2002, having been more than 40 games behind the year before, it was nothing like what transpired with the '69 Mets, who were given something like a 100-1 chance to win the championship when the season began.

So many strange things happened, and in the booth we'd just look at each other and shake our heads and think, this can't be. For example, the Mets won both games of a doubleheader from the Pirates by the score of 1–0, and both runs were driven in by the pitchers, Jerry Koosman and Don Cardwell. How unusual is that? In a historic game, the Cardinals' Steve Carlton struck out a then–major league record 19 batters, but the Mets still won, 4–3, because the overmatched Ron Swoboda touched him for a pair of two-run homers.

The oddest occurrence of the season was when a black cat suddenly appeared on the field during a crucial Mets-Cubs confrontation. It walked in front of the Chicago Cubs dugout and eerily stared at their manager Leo Durocher, and then it haughtily pranced under the stands. How could a cat do that on cue? What great television that made! The Cubs had been running away with the pennant—the Mets were down 9½ games in August—but after the cat incident they went into a horrendous tailspin. Meanwhile, the Mets kept winning and passed them by and never looked back. There was a 20-game swing! It was like a movie script, and the honest, spontaneous enthusiasm of everyone caught up in what was happening in New York can never be duplicated.

Tom Seaver was the driving force among the players, always pushing the team to be better than they thought they were, never letting them settle. He went 25–7 and deservedly was selected the National League's Cy Young Award winner. Always smart and articulate, he was gracious enough to come on *Kiner's Korner* a few minutes after he lost a no-hit bid on a single with one out in the ninth inning by Jimmy Qualls, a Cubs utility player. His wife, Nancy, was there crying because it had been such an emotional night and had ended with disappointment. But Tom took the loss of the no-hitter in stride and said the important thing was that the team won a big game over the Cubs. I would never forget that show.

Seaver lost the opening game of the World Series, but he rebounded with a 10-inning 2–1 victory in Game 4, as the Mets won the final four games while yielding only five runs to the powerful Orioles. The Series was as improbable as the season and contained many memorable, often bizarre, moments. In Game 3, Tommie Agee hit a leadoff homer and later saved five runs with two seemingly impossible catches. In Game 4, J. C. Martin was hit by a throw while running inside the base line on a bunt play; when the ball eluded the Orioles fielders, the winning run scored. In Game 5, Cleon Jones was awarded first base because Gil Hodges pointed out to the umpire that there was shoe polish on the pitched ball. Light-hitting Al Weiss hit a big score-tying homer late in the final game, his only homer at Shea Stadium all year. One game earlier, defensive liability Ron Swoboda made a miraculous game-saving catch while sliding on his belly and face in right field. (Casey Stengel had once said of Swoboda, "He will be great, super, even wonderful; now if he can only learn to catch the ball.") Only Hollywood could concoct such a thing, but if you saw the movie, you'd say it couldn't really happen.

I had never been to a World Series as a player, but it was such a thrill to follow a team that did make it and then be able to broadcast the Series on the radio. The 1969 World Series was the highlight of my broadcasting career. Vicariously, I experienced my first championship, and at long last I got a ring.

After 1969, which was an unbelievable year, every year, even the Mets' pennant-winning 1973 season under Yogi Berra, paled in comparison. But I did enjoy 1973 because any time you broadcast a winning team it's fun—although for much of that year, we didn't realize we were broadcasting a winning team. The Mets won only 82 games, and it took a tremendous surge at the end of the season for them to squeak by. Their motivating force was Tug McGraw, whose "Ya gotta believe!" became the Mets' rallying cry. You'd see banners with his words all over Shea Stadium. Converted into a reliever, McGraw was a fun, good-natured guy who enjoyed being in the spotlight. He had a great attitude that explained why he was a great closer: "Ten million years from now, when the sun burns out and the Earth is just a frozen iceball hurtling through space, nobody's going to care whether or not I got this guy out."

The Mets had a real shot to win the World Series against the defending champion A's, but they fell short by losing the final two games. I worked the Series for CBS radio with Jim Simpson, as I would do a few more times. In the last game the Mets had a good chance to win even going into the seventh inning, so the producer sent me to the Mets locker room in case they did. There would be champagne and burning eyes and ruined clothes, and so on. So I was standing in there waiting to see if the Mets came from behind and I would be called on to do interviews. It so happened that Willie Mays, who was finishing his career with the Mets and had a terrible Series in which he lost balls in the sun, was taken out of the game early. He came into the clubhouse, which was empty but for one attendant and me with the camera crew. Years ago I'd seen a movie called *The Picture of Dorian Gray*, and Willie Mays reminded me of the tragic title character. He looked like the oldest man in the world. When I played against him in the early fifties, I had never seen any player with more excitement and joy for the game of baseball. But it was all gone. Standing there after the last game of his career, he was a sad sight. When it was apparent the Mets were going to lose, I got out of the clubhouse as soon as I could. I felt an era was over.

After the 1973 season, the Mets went downhill and had many horrible ballclubs. Broadcasting their games became tougher. We hadn't minded when they lost their first six seasons, but once they were champions in 1969, we couldn't feel that way anymore. We didn't become "homers," but we wanted the Mets to win because that meant there would be more fan interest. When you have a good ballclub, the joy is contagious and goes through the whole organization. When you have a bad club, it has the opposite effect. It's twice as hard to broadcast for a bad team because you have to be honest and point out all the mistakes. And management, which doesn't like you to do that because they're losing money, can become supercritical of you rather than of the team.

The lean years took their toll on all of us, including Lindsey, who also suffered the loss of his wife in 1973. By the late seventies, it seemed likely that one of us would break up our team. I thought Bob Murphy was the best candidate because his old team, the Red Sox, was offering him a broadcasting position. I thought the time was right for him to move on because he was having an antagonistic relationship with M. Donald Grant, the Mets' chief executive. Grant had represented Mrs. Payson in the beginning days of the franchise, but he had stayed out of the broadcasting. He gradually acquired more power, and when she died in 1975, he stepped in, representing her two daughters. I became skeptical that he knew anything about Mets fans when he said he didn't want to schedule Saturday afternoon games because that was when fans in the New York area would be off watching polo. That showed the kind of circle he was in. That was one of the silliest observations I ever heard from a baseball executive—it was like when the talent scout wrote his studio boss that the little-known Fred Astaire could "dance a little"—but this was the same guy who would trade Tom Seaver to the Reds for four players of marginal talent.

Grant was very difficult to get along with, and when he had an occasional "adult beverage," he was even less pleasant. Grant needed somebody to knock down, but he didn't get on Lindsey's case because of Lindsey's great stature as a broadcaster, and he didn't get on mine because he admired me as a ballplayer. So he took out all his complaints on Bob Murphy and gave him hell. They once got into a verbal battle during a game. Grant called Bob out of the booth during a commercial break in the late innings. Murphy didn't like what he said, and they became confrontational. They were going at it head-to-head, when Murphy said, "Do you want this game to go back on the air?" Grant said, "Certainly I do." "Well, I have to go back or nobody will be talking." It was only when Bob brought up his job offer from Boston that Grant got off his back. Bob would have left otherwise.

By 1978, I also considered leaving. Peter O'Malley called me and asked if I'd be interested in working for the Dodgers because Jerry Doggett was retiring. I said sure, and I interviewed for the job. It boiled down to two candidates. They gave the job to Ross Porter. That was the best thing that ever happened to me. It wouldn't have been the same with another team.

So Bob and I stayed, and before the 1979 season, Lindsey suddenly announced his retirement. I found out from George Steinbrenner at a cocktail party for the Howard Cosell Golf Tournament in Palm Springs. He came up to me and said, "Do you know your partner left?" I said, "Which one?" He said, "Lindsey Nelson retired." I exclaimed, "You've got to be kidding!" Lindsey had never indicated he was going to quit. Two weeks later he signed with the San Francisco Giants. I was surprised and sad because I knew it meant one of the best chapters in my life had been closed. Lindsey, Bob, and I had been together for 17 years, the longest run for any three-man announcing team in history. Once Lindsey left the Mets we didn't really stay in touch, although I did see his daughters once or twice. When he died, neither Bob Murphy nor I attended his funeral. I guess that may sound strange because for so many years we considered ourselves family. That had just been in another time.

In the early eighties, I was assigned to just do television and Bob was assigned to do just radio. Bob never complained to me about it, but I'm sure he was disappointed because television gives you more exposure. I didn't see it as a demotion. I really believe it was done because Bob was better than I was at radio play-by-play.

There was a revolving door to our booth after Lindsey left. Several broadcasters came through and were my partners on television. Fortunately, there were only a couple I didn't enjoy working with during that period (and for my entire career). One partner was extremely nice, but he'd do a radio broadcast on TV, and I hated that. He was too descriptive about weather and the sun and everything else, and he never stopped talking. If the play-by-play man doesn't give you a chance to make your points, you can't have a good broadcast. Good ones will make a statement and then let you talk. It has to be a natural conversation. Sometimes it just doesn't work. For instance, the play-by-play man can continually ask questions about things that have nothing to do with what's going on on the field. Then the analyst is put in a bad spot because he doesn't want to be rude to his partner but knows they should be talking about the game. Equally bad is when he asks questions that are impossible to answer or will take too much time to answer properly, and the analyst is left out on a limb.

It wasn't until Tim McCarver was hired by the Mets in 1983 that things settled down in the booth. As the first former-player-turned-commentator who really got into baseball strategy on the air from pitch to pitch, McCarver was very instrumental in changing the role of the analyst on baseball broadcasts. Having hung up his catching gear only three years before after a lengthy career, Tim imparted the wisdom he acquired down on the field while playing baseball's most cerebral position. In his 16 years in our booth—during which time he also began doing national network games—Tim did as much to make Mets fans knowledgeable about the inner workings of baseball as I did to teach them the history of the game. And he did it with unbridled enthusiasm and humor intact. We would both take turns doing play-by-play and color, and through our on-air conversations and debates, we inspired viewers to consider all possibilities.

Tim and I worked well together because we didn't always agree. I liked to take the situation on the field and advance it to the point where viewers could see the options. Tim, who could have been a great major league manager, was more likely to say, "You can't do this and this; you *must* do this." His belief tended to be that there were several options *until* you thought about it and realized you should rule out every option but one. He was often adamant that there was *the* right thing to do. That was fine with me because that led to good back-and-forth. McCarver learned how to play baseball in the St. Louis Cardinals' tradition, so he talked about the importance of manufacturing runs, particularly the all-important first run of the game. He'd expertly discuss the best ways to move runners into scoring position with less than two outs, based on who the batters were and the pitcher's stuff. He'd bring up sacrifice bunts, other productive outs, the hit-and-run, and so on. Then, perhaps to get his goat, I would suggest that the best strategy was to just hit the little round ball over the fence.

I think the broadcast team of Kiner, McCarver, and Steve Zabriskie was part of the reason that the fans became reenergized and ratings and attendance went back up. Another factor—the real one, of course—was that the Mets team on the field also came back strong in the eighties, with such colorful and talented players as Keith Hernandez, Gary Carter, Darryl Strawberry, Lenny

Dykstra, Mookie Wilson, Ray Knight, and pitchers Dwight Gooden, Ron Darling, Sid Fernandez, Bob Ojeda, and Jesse Orosco leading the way. In 1986, the Mets had one of the best teams of the past twenty-five years, and when they beat the Red Sox in the World Series, I got another championship ring. However, by that time, the networks had their own commentators in place to do the Series, and I was on the outside. I found it strange broadcasting for a team all year and then not doing it in the postseason. I was part of the action, but then I wasn't allowed to be there for the payoff. It's hard to take when you should be rewarded for all the bad years.

The World Series had always been special to me, dating back to that 1934 Series. In 1945, when I was in the navy, I listened to the Series in the early morning hours while in Hawaii. As mentioned, in '47 I attended my first Series, writing a column and doing a postgame show; and in '51, I was back again as a spectator when the games went from coast to coast for the first time. When I wasn't at the fall classic as a columnist, broadcaster, or fan, I watched on television. Nancy and I would have game parties with hors d'oeuvres and drinks, and we'd all gather around the TV. In fact, to this day I have watched almost every inning of every World Series since 1951. I love baseball, so watching baseball's biggest event is always a treat, but I would prefer broadcasting it, especially if the Mets are participants. To not be part of the broadcasting team in 1986 or 2000, when the Mets lost in five games to the Yankees, was disappointing.

In 1986, I could have used the distraction because that was a difficult time for me. I had recently experienced the most awful single moment in my entire broadcasting career. Back in 1985, Hank Greenberg started complaining of a bad back and kept going to doctors who couldn't find anything wrong with him. It turned out to be cancer of the kidney. Of course, his wife knew, and maybe his kids, but he didn't tell anyone else, even me. Although we stayed in touch by telephone, he'd always have an excuse not to see me. So in 1986, I was unable to visit him as I always did during the Mets' two annual trips to Los Angeles. I was concerned, but his relatives insisted that he was well other than a bad back and had become a hermit only because he wanted to work on his memoirs. I suspected they were hiding something, but I had no idea how sick he was.

On September 4, 1986, I flew into Boston with the team to broadcast a charity exhibition game between the Mets and Red Sox, the two teams that would meet in the World Series. Our bus broke down at Logan Airport, so everyone frantically hailed taxis or hitched rides to Fenway Park. That whole day was disorienting, so at first it didn't sink in when news about Hank came over the wires during a commercial break. Then it hit me and hit me hard. In shock, I went back on the air and said, "I've just heard the worst news I've heard in my life—Hank Greenberg has just died."

Since then Hank's name has come up numerous times during my broadcasts. That has been fine with the producers and directors who have done the Mets games since the mideighties on local channels and cable. That's fortunate because when David Hill became the head of Fox, which currently owns the rights to the *Game of the Week*, the All-Star Game, and the World Series—with Joe Buck and Tim McCarver as its top team—he told his announcers, "I don't want you to talk about dead guys." His remark was in the paper, so I talked about it on the air. I said, "Baseball is based on dead guys"—meaning Babe Ruth, Ty Cobb, Hank Greenberg, and so on. Baseball is so great because you can relate the present to the past. I will bring up what happened when I played baseball in the forties and fifties if it relates to what is happening in the game I'm broadcasting. I'm sure Hill was trying to attract kids to baseball without scaring them off with history lessons, but the players of the present are part of a tradition; baseball didn't start when they were born. Football and basketball haven't the same identity. Lindsey Nelson once said that baseball announcers are really like disc jockeys—they'll play records and talk about the players' backgrounds, like anyone would do with Sinatra, Crosby, or Fitzgerald. He was right—that's how baseball should be broadcast.

There are two ways to broadcast. For the network, you can be more critical and point out all the things you know aren't being done correctly because you don't have to worry about a home team audience. When you're broadcasting locally for a team, as I do for the Mets, the majority of fans are Mets fans and don't want to hear bad things about their players. They might not have done well, but they don't want to hear them knocked. Being an ex-player, I have to point out what they did wrong and what they should do, especially when a play in question is being replayed on the TV. You have to give your insight on why something happened or didn't happen. You have to point things out, but it's important not to dwell on something done wrong—you say it and get it out of the way. If you don't say it at all, however, you will get criticized by the media for trying to protect a player so the fans won't get mad at you.

On national television, you can also delve more into the strategy of baseball because viewers aren't necessarily just rooting for their team to beat the other. They may be watching two teams they don't know much about and want to know what the two managers who are pitted against each other might be thinking. Not rooting for a particular team, they are more inclined to want to learn about baseball. That's why Tim McCarver is an ideal choice to be the analyst for these games.

Tim does get criticism from the media and fans on occasion when he points out things that are negative. But if you're paying guys who are experts, why wouldn't you want them to voice their opinions? People overreact. Some fans actually criticize analysts for being opinionated. But why else are they hired? And they criticize us all for being biased. As I discovered when I did the national broadcast for the 1969 World Series, fans always think you favor the other team. It's a common reaction. They say, "Why did he bring that up? Why is he talking about *our* guy blowing a six-run lead?" They don't want you to dwell on the key play of the game if it cost their team a victory. It's a no-win situation.

One thing that hasn't changed is fans assuming that what broadcasters say is fact and not opinion. That's why players don't want broadcasters to say anything negative about them. One of the problems was that until recently players didn't hear broadcasts—I never heard a live broadcast when I played, so I didn't hear anything said about me and didn't want to. It would be players' wives who would tell them what was said about them, and they didn't always get it correct. When the players would hear their wives' interpretations of what was said, they would get angry.

Today, players listen to television feeds in the dugout. Once Fran Healy and I were broadcasting a game in which the Mets had the lead in the ninth inning and their manager, Bobby Valentine, made a defensive switch in left field, replacing Benny Agbayani. The replacement made a great play on a hit down the left-field line and threw to second base to hold the batter on first. Healy said, "It was a good thing Valentine made the change." And I agreed it had been a good move. Agbayani heard what Fran had said and got all over him. Fran explained that he wasn't putting down Benny but praising the fielder who took his place. Of course, Benny was no great fielder and it was a good move. You get feedback from sensitive players. That would have happened in the old days, too.

I've never had a player complain to me about what I've said, although I have strongly questioned their play at times. I would say quite naturally that Roberto Alomar, who played poorly for the Mets in 2002, shouldn't be bunting with a man on second because he was needed to drive in runs. I'd go down to ask him why he bunted, and he'd say, "Because that's the way I play." That's no answer. It was a bad play, with no justified reason for it happening, and you have no choice but to tell fans about it.

In the eighties, Tim would question on the air why Darryl Strawberry would stand in one spot in right field. When lazy or insecure outfielders make a home in one spot, players yell, "Move around, you're killing the grass." In fact, Darryl wore away the grass, and that small yellowed area was called, derisively, "the Strawberry Patch." Tim wouldn't just criticize Strawberry's lack of mobility from the safety of the booth, but would talk to the Mets' manager, Davey Johnson, about it. He'd ask, "How can you let Strawberry stand way out of position and not move him around?" Johnson's answer was, "I don't want to fool with his *comfort zone*." Johnson figured his top slugger would let a few balls drop, but he'd hit a couple of home runs to make up for it.

We have had no trouble talking about umpires in the booth. We've come a long way since Judge Landis picked broadcasters and told them, "I don't want you criticizing my umpires or saying anything derogatory about the game or you won't work again." It's human nature to not want to be criticized in front of millions of people. But as a broadcaster, you have to point out bad calls to have any credibility, and you must praise the umpires when they make difficult calls correctly. If it's a really bad call, you have to explain how difficult the call was to make. You have to give the umpire some credit because it's amazing they are right on so many plays, including the most difficult to call—slides into bases.

I will talk about an umpire being too arrogant. A player will challenge an umpire, and if the umpire challenges him back it starts real problems, including umpires being shoved. If they don't lose their cool, the problem is usually solved. When umpires want to get back at the players, then there are problems. I don't think broadcasters have any obligation to umpires to make them seem better than they are. We don't deal with umpires personally, and I don't know the majority of them. I haven't had angry feedback from umpires, although I know McCarver has.

I've also been fortunate that fans haven't jumped on me. The only thing I have been criticized for are malaprops and saying some things that defy logic. When you say thousands and thousands of words, you are going to make mistakes, I don't care who you are. They usually happen when you stop listening to yourself. The director may be saying something in your headset while you are trying to carry on a conversation. When the director comes through in your ear it breaks your concentration.

So later you find out that you told the listeners, "On Father's Day, we again wish you all Happy Birthday"; or, "The Hall of Fame ceremonies are on the 31st and 32nd of July"; or, "Solo homers usually come with no one on base"; or, "If Casey Stengel were alive today, he'd be spinning in his grave"; or, "Darryl Strawberry has been voted to the Hall of Fame five years in a row." I admit they are funny, too.

One game during Tim McCarver's first year with the Mets, I introduced him by saying, "And here's my partner, Tim MacArthur." Tim knew right away that I'd mixed up his name with America's WWII hero, Douglas MacArthur. He laughed and corrected me, saying his name was Mc*Carver*, and I deadpanned that what I said was close enough. As we went to commercial break, I stated, "MacArthur once said, 'I shall return,' and we'll be right back after this . . ."

When Gary Carter debuted for the Mets in 1985 after being acquired from Montreal during the off-season, he won the opening game with a dramatic home run in the tenth inning against the St. Louis Cardinals. And I introduced him by saying, "Now up to bat for the Mets is Gary Cooper." Here's my excuse: Glenn Close sang the national anthem that day, and I was thinking about the baseball movies *The Natural,* in which Close played Robert Redford's love interest, and *The Pride of the Yankees,* which starred Gary Cooper. Gary was a great sport about it. He came on *Kiner's Korner* afterward and introduced himself to me as Gary Cooper and even signed a picture to me, "Gary Cooper Carter."

Once at the beginning of *Kiner's Korner* I even forgot my own name . . . temporarily. Obviously, names have figured into many of my malaprops.

In a game in which the Mets were playing horribly, I got handed a note from our new sponsor, American Cyanamid. And I said, "We'll be back after this word from American Cyanide."

Fortunately, my most repeated quote was a good ad-lib, not a malaprop. It was a comment I made about a very gifted outfielder for the Phillies: "Two-thirds of the earth is covered by water. The other third is covered by Garry Maddox." Another quote that has been attributed to me is, "Home-run hitters drive Cadillacs and singles hitters drive Fords." That was actually first said by my Pirates teammate, pitcher Fritz Ostermueller.

In the beginning I was sensitive when people called attention to my gaffes because I wanted to be perfect, and not saying what I intended bothered me. When I realized I couldn't be perfect, I stopped worrying about it and shrugged it off. At least my verbal misplays added humor to the broadcasts, which is usually a good thing. I think there are a lot of opportunities for humor that are missed by the current generation of broadcasters. Too much airtime is instead filled with the reading of statistics, an easy crutch of uncreative announcers. We get volumes of stats in the booth. I don't mind relevant stats, but do fans really want to know that the batter is hitting .225 against lefties when the sun was only halfway up in the sky? It's unreal. Too often the screen is so cluttered by numbers and useless information that you can barely see the players.

While many producers rely too heavily on graphics, I do appreciate much of the advanced technology that enhances today's broadcasts at a time when baseball is competing with other sports for high ratings. Numerous cameras and sophisticated sound equipment placed all over the stadium come into play, so viewers might feel they are right there on the field of action. And tapes of plays that just happened, shot from different angles and at real time and in slow motion, can all be run before the next batter receives his first pitch.

Back when we started broadcasting the Mets, we were proud of instant replay, but the replays had to be done at the downtown studio, and they actually took about 90 seconds to appear on the screen. On *Kiner's Korner,*

I'd say we were going to take a look at Willie Mays homering against the Mets during the game, but the guy downtown heard wrong so we'd show Willie McCovey hitting a home run. Then I'd have to say, "Due to technical difficulties . . ." Now we don't run into such troubles because we have tape machines in the ballpark and they can run back the images you want instantly. It makes for a smoother broadcast.

Broadcasting is easier today because there are so many more options than when managers just played the game by the book. It's more fun to discuss strategy now that managers are basing their strategies on instincts, common sense, knowledge, and intelligence. They aren't predictable, which can lead to interesting discussions in the booth.

The hardest thing about broadcasting today is that there are so many more players in baseball with foreign names. You have to really work to pronounce them right, with the right inflection and accent. Also, when discussing the individual players, you have to take into consideration that the habits and styles of foreign players are different from those of American-born players and may factor into their performances. But there is nothing that's impossible to handle.

Most shows on television today have two plots instead of one, and baseball broadcasts are becoming like that, with multiple storylines. But I should warn those people who want to make baseball fit exactly into the rest of television that it's much different from anything else, and that won't work. Unfortunately, producers and directors are from a new generation that is into high technology and speed, and they want to have a number of elements going at the same time. They are trying to put more things in than they should, and it can be a real distraction. If I'm telling a story about Cubs manager Dusty Baker and my director is shooting someone in the Mets bullpen, won't I come across badly if I don't forget all about my story and comment on the visual? So by doing too much, the impatient director has ruined my story to go to another story too quickly.

I'm there only for the game. I'm on the side of baseball. My ideal game to broadcast would have no commercials and few graphics, be on Saturday or Sunday afternoon with the temperature about 80 degrees, and be played on natural turf. And there shouldn't be too much talking in the booth. But there would have to be more cigar smoking. We aren't allowed to smoke anymore; it's against the law. So after every 15 games or so, someone will complain about my smoking and the next game a guard will come to the booth to make sure I haven't lit up a cigar. As I wait for him to leave, I miss the old times.

During the early years with the Mets, I worked with one-year contracts. So for about five years, I never really knew from year to year if I'd be rehired. The Mets had approval of the announcers, but I'd have to deal with a representative for J. Walter Thompson and with our sponsor Rheingold

Beer. Then, when they were sure I was a keeper, they began offering me contracts with varying numbers of years. Now, I have one-year contracts again, so I hope they're not trying to tell me something.

It certainly is a source of pride that I've been with the New York Mets for 42 years. In 1962, I couldn't conceive of working with the Mets for more than 40 years or doing *anything* that long. Until Bob Murphy retired after the 2003 season, he and I were together with the Mets all that time, in the same city. My favorite baseball announcer, Vin Scully, has been with the Dodgers in L.A. even longer, and he does solo broadcasts. That won't happen again. When Ernie Harwell retired, he said, "If I were coming up as a broadcaster today, I'd never be hired." Bob and I are the same. Scully, too. Our style of broadcasting is different from that of the new commentators. Now they think the louder you talk and the more you scream, the better it is. I prefer the old style of broadcasting in which you talk to the guy sitting next to you as if you were sitting together in the stands. But that isn't what they want. They want noise. Recently, I was telling Fran Healy that eventually baseball broadcasts won't have play-by-play men and analysts. It will be just visuals and computerized sounds. I wonder what kind of conversation that will be.

Chapter **9**

The Future, **Then** and **Now**

I 'd bet that if you ask every professional baseball player what they dreamed of becoming when they were kids, 99 percent will say they are living that dream. But if you follow up with a question about what they want to do after this brief part of their lives is over, almost the same percentage will shrug and say, "I have no idea." They might even add, "I haven't thought about it yet." A few may express some vague notions of staying in baseball in some capacity, of perhaps managing, coaching, or teaching baseball somewhere, but for the most part ballplayers don't want to burden themselves with worry about the end of their youth and the idea of mortality.

While players are in uniform, they don't think about much other than playing ball and making a living doing it. They don't particularly care about who owns the ballclub, who the commissioner is, or even, in most cases, who their own manager is. And they don't pay much attention if someone else in baseball is threatening to hit 74 homers, or some rookie sensation in the other league has won 20 straight games, or baseball is making plans to expand to Ethiopia. They may turn on ESPN, but you'll rarely catch them watching CNN or C-SPAN or perusing the daily newspaper. It takes a lot of hard work and concentration to succeed as a professional ballplayer, and the smart ones, oddly enough, focus almost entirely on themselves and their teams. They just want to swing the bat or throw the ball. From my own experience, I know that only at the end of their careers do players start thinking about what they will do for the rest of their lives. I always felt I could succeed in some profession outside baseball once my playing career ended, so I didn't worry about it. Luckily, I never had to prove I was right.

Ballplayers who last as many as five years in the big leagues are fortunate, so it would make sense for every professional player to be better prepared for a second career. Present-day major leaguers have, of course, the advantage of making high salaries, even as rookies. So even if their careers end abruptly, they should have enough savings to tide them over for a year or two while they search for an ideal job in or outside baseball or go back to get their college degrees. In my era, almost all ex-ballplayers had to find work immediately because they had little money stashed away. Having modest ambitions, many—foolishly, I thought—went directly home after they retired from baseball rather than remain in the cities where they had fame. Those who had taken off-season jobs in their hometowns during their careers now thought it was safer to accept their employers' offers of permanent employment than to seek something more lucrative where they played ball. They disappeared from the center stage.

Few players from my era had any real business sense. That could come only with experience, but most business ventures that came our way were of the get-rich-quick variety. Every year we all were asked to be part of a couple of "surefire" schemes, or were seduced into lending our names to some silly business opportunities that went belly-up. We hoped to duplicate Ty Cobb's success when he loaded up on inexpensive stock in Coca-Cola and made a fortune. Some players beat the odds. I did well with a sporting goods business that I went into in 1948 with former major leaguer Max West, who was also from Alhambra. I lent my name and he did the work. I eventually sold him my part of the business. Stan Musial went into partnership with restaurateur Julius "Biggie" Garagnani, and their Stan and Biggie's Restaurant became one of the most popular steak houses in St. Louis; also through his association with Biggie, Musial made a mint by purchasing hotels and restaurants in Florida. The equally charmed Yogi Berra purchased some land in Florida that was seemingly worthless—other jittery players sold their lots the first chance they got—until Walt Disney wanted to build Disney World right on that spot.

A number of players acquired bowling alleys and restaurants; Roy Campanella had a liquor store; Al Lopez went into the oil business in Texas and got rich. I also went into the oil business in Texas with Bob Prince and his brother Seton. I was sure I was going to be rolling in dough when the first three of our seven wells came in—but before we popped the tops on the champagne, they all went dry.

When I started making money I invested in long-term life insurance—which was a can't-miss proposition because policies were so cheap at the time. Unfortunately, I was so intrigued by the future of television that I cashed out and used all that money to buy into a UHF station in Pittsburgh. John Galbreath, the owner of the Pirates, and Bob Prince also had pieces of the action. Because it was a UHF station, viewers needed to purchase a special device to hook onto their television sets, so we had virtually no chance of attracting a large audience. However, we believed that when local television expanded and they needed new VHF stations, they'd come running to us because we were already established. Having Galbreath involved seemed to give us an inside track on getting a regular channel. But it didn't happen. I thought it was a logical idea at the time, but our enterprise went under, as did most of my ventures with Prince. Those players with the Midas touch were the exceptions.

Because most players of my day didn't think much about their own futures, one wouldn't expect them to contemplate the future of baseball. Probably because of my work for the pension plan, I was one of the few to wonder about what would happen to the game with the passage of time. But I did it only on occasion and without much prescience.

I assumed that the Players Association would maintain the higher status players had achieved when we got them the pension plan, a minimum salary, and a percentage of TV revenues, but I didn't predict it would become a full-fledged union during the midsixties, when Marvin Miller became its chief executive. And I never imagined how much the players would gain as a result. For example, at the end of my career, I never thought agents would represent players during contract negotiations. The idea of a player ever making $20 million a year, or even $1 million, was preposterous. It never crossed my mind that players also would make tremendous money from product endorsements and licensing deals with baseball card, glove, bat, and other companies. Or that there would be a huge market for our autographs.

I couldn't even have hallucinated that ballplayers would be granted free agency. But the Dave McNally–Andy Messersmith case in 1975 determined that veterans would become free agents if they played without a contract in the option years of their original contracts. Free agency plus binding salary arbitration swung the pendulum of power away from the owners to the players. No one I ever talked to as a player rep or played with fathomed that players would someday be in control of their futures. But through the union, it became an entirely new ballgame. With the exception of integration, the termination of the reserve clause was the greatest change in baseball history.

At the time I retired in 1955, I realized that integration of Major League Baseball was a successful endeavor and would continue until all 16 teams had African Americans on their rosters. I was surprised that it took another four years until Boston became the final team to sign a black player, but after that I expected integration to speed up. I didn't foresee the increased popularity of the NFL and NBA, which, beginning in the sixties, would compete successfully with MLB for the best African-American athletes. Today, teams average only two or three African Americans on their 25-man rosters, which isn't much better than it was five decades ago. However, an increasing number of black players from Latin-American countries are making a major impact on the game and on baseball's social structure. Baseball made the mistake of expanding at the same time owners found themselves unable or unwilling to recruit African Americans, but the game reached a high level again when it began to pursue Latin-American players in a big way. Players from the Dominican Republic, Mexico, Puerto Rico, and other Spanish-speaking islands and countries are found throughout baseball.

Of course, I was aware that baseball was beginning to open up to Cuban and other Latino players during my era, but I couldn't have forecast the rate at which they have been coming to the majors in the past decade. Nor could I have predicted how global the majors have become, with players from as far away as South Korea, Japan, and Australia. I had no idea Japanese players would be so good. Neither did Commissioner Ford Frick, who after touring Japan in 1953 said the Japanese Leagues were the equivalent of Class A in America. It's clear that with the startling success of starting pitcher Hideo Nomo, reliever Kazuhiro Sasaki, and outfielders Ichiro Suzuki and Hideki Matsui, more Japanese Leagues stars will be courted by American teams.

Perhaps in the not-so-distant future there also will be major leaguers from China, Russia, and Africa. Internationalization is needed to keep the game strong, which is why I know MLB will continue to chase after foreign athletes and sponsor baseball schools and camps around the world. I think MLB may eventually follow the lead of the NFL and set up an off-season league in Europe, perhaps to develop players and surely to popularize the game and get more people playing it there so a television market can be created. They are even considering playing regular-season baseball games in Europe. In 2003, the attendance-challenged Montreal Expos, who got a reprieve on being moved or contracted, played 22 regular-season "home" games in Puerto Rico. MLB will continue to think globally, but it shouldn't take for granted that it will find enough good (and cheaper) players elsewhere to fill up rosters. It's also important to aggressively go after the best athletes in the inner cities and stop losing them to other sports.

With the integration of African-American stars during the late forties and fifties, the major leagues improved significantly. Finally, at the time the best athletes gravitated toward baseball, the best players of both races and the best Hispanic players filled the 400 roster spots. I was optimistic that there would always be an enormous talent pool and that the players themselves would become better. But I had no idea that the record book would be left in tatters because the game on the field would change so much.

The sacred, seemingly unbreakable records that dated back to Babe Ruth and Ty Cobb have been supplanted for obvious reasons: players are much bigger and stronger, ballparks are smaller, balls are livelier, bats have more torque, repeated expansion has diluted good pitching, and teams play eight more games each year. Baseball has evolved and progressed as it should, but the old records have been a major casualty. Players used to talk about which records would never be broken. Right at the top of our list were Babe Ruth's 714 career homers and Lou Gehrig's 2,130-consecutive-game playing streak. Without ever hitting 50 homers in a season, Hank Aaron passed Ruth's mark in 1974 to move to the top spot in the record books, under the "old rules." Less legitimate is his final total of 755 homers, which he reached by spending two more seasons in the American League as a designated hitter—a bad concept that nobody thought of in my day. On the other hand, there is no way to discredit Cal Ripken Jr.'s record of playing 2,632 consecutive games at shortstop or third base from 1981 to 1998. It is truly one of the most astonishing achievements in baseball history, made even more difficult by the longer seasons. Aaron's record is in serious jeopardy now that several players are capable of hitting 50 homers a season—and Barry Bonds, Sammy Sosa, and Alex Rodriguez seem to be on pace to do it. But Ripken's iron-man mark appears as out of reach as Gehrig's used to be.

The only significant long-standing post-1900 records left that I don't think can be broken are Cy Young's 511 career wins, Johnny Vander Meer's two consecutive no-hitters (1938), Jack Chesbro's 41 victories (1904), and Ty Cobb's .367 career average. It will take a major effort to pass George Sisler's 257 hits (1920), Hack Wilson's 191 RBIs (1930), Earl Webb's 67 doubles (1931), or even my seven consecutive homer titles, but there's a chance those records won't stand the test of time.

It has been more than 60 years since Joe DiMaggio stroked hits in a record 56 consecutive games and Ted Williams became the last hitter to go over the magical .400, when he batted .406. Even when I started my major league career in 1946, five years after their feats, I didn't think DiMaggio's streak would ever be broken. He was fortunate to set it when there wasn't much national coverage. Now the added pressures of the media would make a 57-game hit streak unapproachable. Everything has to fall in place. Say you come up to the plate for the last time in a game and haven't had a hit. Then you will have to be really lucky to get one because you will be at the mercy of pitchers who know you'll be swinging at balls outside the strike zone. When Pete Rose set the modern National League record with hits in 44 straight games in 1978, at the age of 37, he complained his streak ended because he wasn't pitched to.

Somebody will hit .400 again, although probably not as high as Rogers Hornsby's 1924 mark of .424, the best post-1900 batting average. I'm surprised it hasn't happened already. Rod Carew, George Brett, and Tony Gwynn came within a few hits of doing it. It's true that gloves are so much better that you're bound to be robbed of a few hits during the course of a season, but current hitters benefit from artificial turf, shorter fences, rabbit baseballs, better bats, and a smaller percentage of good pitchers. Also, I think the amount of protection they can wear under their uniforms gives them an extra advantage because they no longer have to fear the knockdown pitch. So it's possible.

Whoever approaches one of baseball's most cherished records will experience intense media scrutiny. It is really amazing how much attention major sports stories receive today, and it will only get worse for the potential record breaker. As a player at the time television was just coming in—when newspapers signified "media" to most of us—I was one of the few who even realized that TV had the potential to have a major impact on our sport, as well as on society. That's because I lived near Hollywood and spoke to many people who were convinced the new medium was much more than a novelty. That's why when I was negotiating to renew the pension plan, I insisted that players receive a high percentage of television rights for the World Series and All-Star Game instead of a flat fee.

I anticipated that pay television would come in eventually because it was a hot topic of conversation in California. Walter O'Malley planned his relocation of the Dodgers in Los Angeles in anticipation of that revenue—a world-altering idea that hadn't seen the light of day yet. Television broadcasts were so primitive in my era that I never could have foreseen MLB's current national contracts with News Corp.'s Fox and Walt Disney Co.'s ESPN for an estimated combined value of $3.3 billion over six years. I never could have predicted that teams would broadcast all their games across the country on "Super Stations," or that teams like the Yankees would own their own cable networks, or that there would be 24-hour television sports channels—along with 24-hour sports talk-radio stations.

I can say with confidence that not one person in my era—it was unanimous—even suggested that Major League Baseball would find its way onto the Internet. We'd heard of computers, of course, but none of us believed we'd ever actually own one ourselves someday—that was science fiction—and be able to watch or listen to games in progress. Yet today, computer owners can listen to games being broadcast locally all over the country, or watch games by picking up the feeds of the local television broadcasts. In 2003, more than one million people signed up for the league's audio service and approximately twenty-five thousand subscribed to the television service in its first year. MLB.tv broadcast more than one thousand games, and the average subscriber could watch as many as 45 games a week, paying by the game, month, or season. Nationally televised games were excluded, and all teams were blacked out in their local markets with the exceptions of the Montreal Expos, Toronto Blue Jays, and Kansas City Royals, who asked MLB.com to offer some of their games that weren't televised in their markets.

Interestingly, Major League Baseball says there is significant demand for games outside a team's home market because, as its surveys show, about 50 percent of a team's fans don't live in the area. The league expects many business travelers to sign up, and in-room connections are already becoming a selling point for hotels. If MLB's prediction proves true that people will start watching games on their computers at work, I would think we will see an increase in weekday afternoon games, which I would welcome.

Major League Baseball hopes its webcasts will increase broadcast revenues and stimulate interest in the game without further saturating the market. In the old days we considered ourselves lucky if there was one baseball game on the radio or television on a given day, so the proliferation of games today on television, locally and nationally, is mind-boggling. In fact, there are so many other sports and baseball games on local and national television each week that televised baseball games rarely attract a large viewership anymore. CBS, ABC, and Fox are projected to lose $5.5 billion combined on baseball, football, basketball, and other major sports contracts between 2000 and 2006. My explanation for the lower ratings is that the habits of this country have changed tremendously. Now there are too many diversions for people to watch baseball as they once did. On weekends in particular, people are out and about, not sitting in front of their sets. They may be taking their kids to their weekend soccer games or other sports or activities, or playing a sport themselves. So hardly anybody is home.

The escalating popularity of golf has really cut into televised sports on Saturdays and Sundays. It's the one game you can play till you're dead. There are 40 million people playing golf, and when they aren't playing on the weekend, they are watching it on television. So baseball, the other warm-weather sport, is the sport that suffers, in TV ratings and attendance.

You can't compare ratings for baseball now with other eras, because other activities weren't always so readily available. Television revenues remain, particularly at the local level, the single most significant factor in baseball's economic picture. The quality of baseball teams and the solvency of entire organizations depend foremost on whether they are located in big or small television markets. Surely television has been the decisive factor whenever there has been talk of expansion or franchise movement during the past 55 years, and that will continue to be the case.

It seems strange, then, that television wasn't even a consideration when the first franchise shifts in 50 years took place near the end of my major league career. At that time, attendance determined the profitability of most teams. Other than in New York and Chicago, local radio and television broadcasts were primarily vehicles to inspire fans to go to the ballpark, and they didn't contribute much to a team's assets.

The first franchise shifts after 1903 involved the Boston Braves, the St. Louis Browns, and the Philadelphia Athletics. All three moved because they played in cities where there were also teams from the other league that cut sharply into their attendance figures. The Braves were the first to vacate, in

1953, resettling in Milwaukee. Their bold move had major implications for baseball's future because it made other owners of financially strapped teams think about moving their franchises, too.

Everyone thought it was wise for the Braves to leave Boston, which belonged to Red Sox fans; the town that was famous for beer was a potentially successful home because the minor league Brewers had drawn well there under Bill Veeck. As it turned out, the Braves had a great young team, with Hank Aaron, Eddie Mathews, Joe Adcock, Del Crandall, Johnny Logan, Billy Bruton, Lew Burdette, and the slightly older Warren Spahn, and they drew like crazy in the early days. It wasn't until the original Washington Senators moved to Minneapolis–St. Paul in 1962 that Milwaukee's attendance began to suffer. Then people from or close to Minnesota stopped going to Milwaukee to see the Braves play. In 1966, the Braves would relocate again, to Atlanta. At the time, Atlanta wasn't a big city, but there was a tremendous population to draw from, without any competition in the area. Atlanta has grown considerably, so it's strange that attendance today isn't higher than it is. It's certainly not due to the lack of success.

Despite Bill Veeck's ingenious promotions and his signing of the ageless Satchel Paige (who at 46 became history's oldest All-Star in 1953), the St. Louis Browns had trouble attracting fans as the second tenants in Sportsman's Park. Veeck considered moving the Browns to several cities, including Baltimore and Los Angeles. But the American League owners refused to give him permission to relocate and he was forced to sell the team to a Baltimore syndicate headed by the city's mayor. With Veeck out of the way, they immediately approved the Browns' move to Baltimore for the 1954 season. The franchise's 52-year history came to an inglorious end.

The Philadelphia Athletics, which at times had been a great, proud franchise, had fallen under hard times after WWII, so in 1955, they packed up and headed to Kansas City. The city had a strong baseball tradition with the Monarchs of the Negro Leagues and the Blues, the Yankees' farm team. The fans rolled out the red carpet for their first major league team, but soon grew impatient because they weren't used to a losing ballclub. The Kansas City Athletics couldn't escape the second division or rid themselves of the tag of being the de facto farm club of the Yankees, having supplied them with numerous promising players in one-sided trades, including Roger Maris and Ralph Terry. Like the Braves, the A's would move for a second time, when their money-conscious owner Charles O. Finley took them to Oakland in 1968. The Kansas City Royals began play in 1969.

At the time I retired, I believed more franchise shifts were a distinct possibility. In fact, I thought that some other struggling team might heed Horace Greeley's advice and move all the way to the West Coast. Prior to World War II, an earlier Browns owner, Harrison Barnes, intended to move his team to Los Angeles, but his plans were derailed with the attack on Pearl Harbor. I don't think his timing would have been good, but after the war, an immense population surge made L.A. an ideal city for a major league team. Vincent X. Flaherty, who wrote for the *L.A. Examiner*, tried for years to bring in major league baseball. Unlike those who saw L.A. as a college football town, Flaherty pointed to the success of the Los Angeles Angels and Hollywood Stars.

I didn't think a team would move to L.A. in the near future, or I might not have settled in as the GM of the San Diego Padres. And I never pictured the Brooklyn Dodgers and New York Giants leaving their homes after so many years and being transplanted in Los Angeles and San Francisco. That possibility was as unlikely to me as someone in a space suit swinging a golf club on the moon. When I played, I couldn't imagine there would no longer be the Brooklyn Dodgers or New York Giants. No one thought that would ever happen—especially their loyal fans. For one thing, I thought only franchises that were losing money moved—and the Dodgers were extremely profitable. When both National League teams left, it was a real disaster for New York. In particular, the mystique and romance of the Dodgers persisted. Many of their fans were so upset that they never watched baseball again. Others took to rooting for the underdog Mets in 1962, as did deserted Giants fans.

Like almost everyone else who loved baseball and cared about its traditions, I would have preferred that the Dodgers and Giants had stayed put because of their loyal fans and that two other teams had moved west. However, only Dodgers owner Walter O'Malley realized that a team could make a killing in Los Angeles. O'Malley let it be known as early as 1953 that he wanted a new park in Brooklyn that could hold fifty-two thousand fans (twenty thousand more than Ebbets Field), was located close to subways and major roadways, and had ample parking to accommodate fans who had moved to Long Island. The place he had in mind was the crumbling Fort Greene Meat Market. He asked Robert Moses, the city's Washington-appointed Slum Clearance Commissioner, to condemn the site and give him the land for next to nothing. Moses refused, offering him instead land on the edge of Bedford-Stuyvesant. This time O'Malley was the one who said no, and then he shocked the city by saying he was moving his team to California.

O'Malley has been accused of wanting to leave because his attendance was too black and Brooklyn was too black. Supposedly, Jackie Robinson was opposed to the move and because O'Malley didn't want him to stir up the players or bring up the race issue publicly, he got rid of the iconic Brooklyn Dodgers player in the cruelest manner, swapping him to the archrival Giants for oft-traded pitcher Dick Littlefield. Robinson retired rather than play for the enemy, and his voice was conveniently silenced while the Dodgers played out their final season in Brooklyn and then departed for Los Angeles.

The popular story is that the Dodgers moved because O'Malley couldn't get his new ballpark. I disagree. I think the major reason he did it was because he knew that California was on its way to becoming the most populous state, and he expected television, particularly pay-TV, to become a major resource for baseball. I think he didn't want to stay in Brooklyn even if a new ballpark was built for him because he knew he could become a whole lot wealthier out west. He wanted to set up an empire. O'Malley did make a tremendous amount of money in Los Angeles because of record-setting attendance and exceptional local television deals (although he didn't show home games for years), but he got a bad surprise when a public referendum passed that forbade him from putting the Dodgers on pay-television. No one ever mentions this, but more than 40 years later, the Yankees organization would swipe O'Malley's idea and form the YES Network. They would find financial success by camouflaging what is essentially pay-TV with the cable blanket.

O'Malley was vilified and compared to Hitler and Stalin for abandoning Brooklyn and moving the beloved team three thousand miles from Bedford Avenue and leaving behind furious and shocked fans. Lost was the fact that he had many good ideas and was a tough negotiator who made a helluva deal in which he got valuable property for nothing (although it didn't include the oil rights). He built a great ballpark with his own money and paved the way for the financial growth of baseball. As a business and a sport, baseball had to expand west, and he was the one with the guts to do it.

O'Malley didn't want to be isolated, so he convinced Horace Stoneham to take the Giants from Coogan's Bluff to San Francisco, so they could continue the rivalry between the two teams. The Giants had more reason to leave than the Dodgers because only six hundred forty thousand fans had gone through the turnstiles at the Polo Grounds the previous two years. O'Malley reminded Stoneham that the San Francisco Seals, Joe DiMaggio's onetime team, always drew well in the Pacific Coast League. He didn't point out to Stoneham that Los Angeles was far and away the better city for a new franchise and that it was possible for it to double or triple the attendance of a San Francisco team, as well as make far more money in television. But I'm sure Stoneham wasn't hard to sway. After all, he was the guy who once called off a game at the Polo Grounds because when he woke up one morning in the clubhouse office, he saw water cascading down the window. He didn't realize the stadium's maintenance men were simply washing windows.

The Dodgers and Giants moved west in 1958, not caring that they were destroying the Pacific Coast League in the process (and essentially putting me out of the GM business). Because the Dodgers started breaking attendance records—first in the L.A. Coliseum, where they drew more than ninety-three thousand for a "Roy Campanella Night" exhibition game in 1959, and then in

O'Malley's Dodger Stadium—I expected more franchise movement. But I didn't think of expansion, which had never been done in the modern era. However, it was necessitated when the major leagues wanted to kill off Branch Rickey's proposed rival league, the Continental League. So in 1961 and 1962, new teams were added for the first time in the history of modern baseball: the Los Angeles Angels, new Washington Senators, Houston Colt-45s (later the Astros), and New York Mets.

I was not in favor of expansion beyond 16 teams, but it had to happen, at least in a limited way. I didn't think baseball could go much beyond 20 teams and certainly not to the present-day 30 teams. Yet I did realize that expansion on top of the moves by the Dodgers and Giants made baseball a much bigger enterprise. Still, nobody could even guess how much it would change and in how many ways. Franchise moves and expansion certainly helped baseball grow, but at the same time they have led to as many financial problems that dog baseball as have free agency, escalating salaries, and long-term contracts. Despite the fact that their franchises go up in value, the majority of owners claim they are barely hanging on financially. Evidently, they didn't realize that when you buy a franchise you should know what you're getting. Owners that don't choose their locations wisely experience firsthand the huge discrepancies between teams that make money and those that don't.

When MLB started to add teams, the new owners liked the idea of receiving easy money to pay off the high salaries and didn't consider whether their new homes would be able to support major league baseball teams. As a consequence, while some newer franchises have been wildly successful, others have failed miserably. New teams generally have a terrific turnstile count for the first couple of years. Fans will usually wait a while for a new team to become a contender, but if it takes too long, their patience will run out. Once the team has success, it had better be a consistent contender after that or attendance will drop. Toronto, Florida, and, more recently, Arizona are teams that did exceptional business when their teams were world champions, but as they went down in the standings, so did the attendance figures. Fortunately, Florida made the postseason again in 2003, causing an attendance surge.

A winning team must have enough revenue to pay the escalating salaries of its best players and bring in high-caliber free agents. Because if a team loses its best players and top gate attractions and then falls in the standings, it might take years to win the fans back. People want to see a winning team and a winning attitude by the ownership. If an organization loses that confidence it will lose its customers. It's an enormous challenge for baseball to keep struggling teams alive and also give them the resources so they can contend with the richer teams—so far baseball hasn't been up to the challenge.

When moving franchises into smaller cities, owners have to consider that if they aren't going to be able to get a large television contract, they won't be able to compete. But there has been too much expansion and too many franchise shifts into territories that don't have large television markets or large enough fan bases to support baseball teams. Moreover, some newly arrived teams cut into the fan bases of other teams and are then surprised when there aren't enough fans or television revenue to share. For example, when Finley moved the A's to Oakland, both the Giants and A's suffered. It made no sense to start a team in Oakland when San Francisco was already there, because it's the same market. If the Oakland Oaks and San Francisco Seals of the PCL had to relocate after the Giants moved into the area, then why would another team do well there? (It wasn't until the Giants moved out of Candlestick and into their new Pacific Bell Park in 2002 that they began having attendance figures as high as the Dodgers had for years.)

When I became the GM of the San Diego Padres of the PCL in 1956, I did a 10-year survey of attendance in the league, from 1945 to 1955. To me, it made sense for a major league team to move to San Francisco because of the consistent success of the Seals and Oaks, who averaged more than one million fans a year, and the fact that the new team would help provide coast-to-coast baseball. It also made sense when they put an American League team in Los Angeles, because of the consistent success of the two PCL teams in L.A., the Angels and the Stars. A second team had at least a shot at success because there was a big enough market to draw from. It turned out to be too hard for a second team to break through because the Dodgers were so popular and the new team was relegated to being the second tenant in Dodger Stadium. But when the Angels moved 20 miles south to Anaheim and had their own ballpark, it changed the picture. There was always potential for the Angels to draw impressive crowds, and it finally happened beginning in their 2002 world championship season.

The biggest-drawing franchise in the PCL was Seattle, above the California teams. So that was a city I would have recommended for the majors. As it turned out, the first major league team there, the Pilots, flopped and fled to Milwaukee, where they became the present-day Brewers—one of the many small-market teams that struggle with attendance and haven't the money to sign free agents to become contenders. The second Seattle team, the Mariners, struggled mightily until they came up with some star-studded contending teams in the midnineties. Now, having moved from the Kingdome to fan-friendly Safeco Field, they stand as one of the few expansion teams that is profitable and competes year after year—although they couldn't afford to hold on to such high-priced superstars as Ken Griffey Jr., Randy Johnson, and Alex Rodriguez.

When I was asked if San Diego could be a major league city, I said I didn't think that idea had merit. We had drawn about four hundred thousand before the Dodgers' arrival, and that was about two hundred thousand less than the PCL's Angels drew in Wrigley Field in Los Angeles. The major problem is that we were bordered on the south by Mexico, the Pacific Ocean was to the west, there were mountains to the east, and the Dodgers were to the north, so the team could draw fans from only a small area. The San Diego Padres, using the same name as the PCL team, became a National League franchise in 1969 and would have the attendance difficulties I predicted, except on those rare occasions when they had contending teams. What did change was the population. San Diego proper grew from a half million to more than two million people and is still growing. If the Padres put together a winning team, they should be rewarded by a huge growth in attendance.

The Montreal Expos joined the National League the same year as the Padres and eight years after the original Senators moved to Minnesota and became the Twins. Both the Twins and Expos drew very well at one time, but when Commissioner Bud Selig stated he was in favor of contraction prior to the 2002 season, those were the two teams that he said he wanted to do away with. There wasn't much outcry in Montreal, where there is anemic attendance, but the passionate fans in Minnesota rebelled. Not surprisingly, the players union mounted a campaign to stop contraction, which would eliminate jobs, and members of Congress threatened to strip baseball of its antitrust status. As a result, Selig backed off, saying he'd bring it up again in a few years. The Twins may no longer be an endangered species because attendance went up in 2002 in response to a division-winning season for the ballclub. The Expos, which are now owned by MLB, are in a holding pattern until they can migrate to another city.

But where can they go? Washington, D.C., seems to have the inside track, but if you put a team in Washington for the third time, you will infringe on the Orioles and re-create the situation they had when the previous Senators teams moved to Minnesota and Texas, respectively. You also run into complications over television money, as there are in San Francisco and Oakland. When you put two teams in the same vicinity, they will have issues with attendance and TV revenues—it's hard for both teams to thrive. Besides, there is an old adage that says you should never put a team in a capital city. Why not? Because there are so many politicians there who never pay for their tickets, and most of the people there are interested in things other than baseball. Capital cities run on politics and lobbies; baseball cities run on business opportunities and manufacturing. That's why Washington, D.C., hasn't been successful. Places near industry are ideal because people there make enough money to go to ballgames. Washington doesn't have that.

I read that someone wants to buy the Montreal team and put it in Riverside, California, which is 60 miles from L.A. That won't happen because the Dodgers won't let a team cut into their territory. Indianapolis would take away from Cincinnati, and you'd be robbing Peter to pay Paul. If you put a team in Memphis, you will cut off attendance to Cardinals games. Charlotte is a possibility, but is there television money? You don't want another small-market team. You don't have to have a huge population, but you need to draw from outlying areas. For instance, Cincinnati isn't a huge city, but there are many towns around it, like Dayton and Columbus, so they pull from about 10 million people. Would Charlotte have such a fan base?

Portland is far enough away from other major league towns, but it doesn't have the population to support a major league team. Travel to Honolulu would be too tough. Vancouver is too close to Seattle and it would have the same problem with the exchange rate that burdens Montreal and Toronto. Canada doesn't seem like a viable market.

Mexico City could do it based on population. But its economy is bad and the money exchange would create the same problems as in Canada. Monterey is a possibility, but a team there might hurt the Astros, who draw a lot of people from that location to their games. Puerto Rico was tested as the second home of the Montreal Expos, but it isn't the answer because of its small population. Most games don't sell out even though Hiram Bithorn Stadium has a small seating capacity.

I think Japan would be a good possibility if we had supersonic jets. It would be impossible as it is now because of scheduling.

Football has a vacancy in L.A., but there is no such city for a baseball team to move to. I think all the good places have been taken. I have no idea where you can put a team. So I'd either stand pat or, perhaps better, contract. I know contraction is not a popular idea with the fans or the union, but it's the best option for a team that is legitimately losing money and has no chance to turn things around. The solution is not to move to another city where, even if they build you a new stadium, there will be similar problems in the future. So many problems occurred because franchises were placed in cities that weren't capable of duplicating what went on in the bigger cities. Now they're paying for it. By moving franchises, as Commissioner Selig expects to do with the Expos, baseball is trying to cover a gunshot wound with a Band-Aid.

As of 2003 Montreal was the perfect candidate for contraction because it had no place to go and couldn't stay where it was. The team was not helped by its city, a French-speaking hockey town. When Montreal insisted that all the signs be French, they drove a lot of businesses out of the area, and businesses are what keep ballclubs going. Attendance was pathetic, partly because Montreal always had a hard time getting a television contract and a radio deal with an English-speaking station. Also, a team in Montreal will never be able to attract or hold on to talented players because of the Canadian exchange rate.

It's tricky figuring out which other teams should be considered for elimination because many teams that were troubled got a boost in attendance later, when they improved. Sometimes a team is in trouble primarily because of mismanagement, and the team has the potential to draw decent crowds. Some teams that are thought to be the best candidates to move or be contracted rise from the cellar when they are well managed and win. There once was minor discussion of combining Oakland and Anaheim into only one team. That seems particularly foolish because the A's now have strong attendance figures and Anaheim had a great 2002 season in which it drew more than 3 million fans as it went on to win the World Series. Still drawing extremely well, the Angels obviously overcame the problems of a small-market team, which is what they always have claimed to be. A small-market team? I'd like to know who did the census in that market.

When I played in Pittsburgh, we drew almost as many fans as Brooklyn did. That proved to me that the Pirates can draw if the organization is run properly. So it has upset me when I've heard talk about the franchise moving elsewhere. Pittsburgh was *the city* in my life. I realize that Pittsburgh makes only one-fifth of the television money that the Yankees and Mets get annually, but it would be disastrous to lose a great sports city like Pittsburgh because of inept management or poor performance. It is one of those cities that has proved itself in the past. The Pirates can draw fans if they have good teams. When they talked about moving, I wanted to say, "Just run the club better and you can stay."

Minnesota is a strange case. There is something phony about that situation. They have had good teams and have been able to draw at different times, although they don't have a large fan base. The owners would like to contract, and one fishy element is that they will pay a ton of money to the owner of a team that contracts. Twins owner Carl Pohlad apparently welcomed folding his $100 million franchise because he would have received $250 million from the owners. Minnesota's attorney general, finding the motives of Pohlad and the other owners to be suspicious, threatened to file a federal lawsuit against MLB, claiming the owners were illegally folding two teams to increase the market share for the rest. I think Bud Selig knew he wouldn't get the union to go along with the loss of so many jobs, so perhaps he brought up contraction only for leverage while the union and MLB were trying to hammer out a collective-bargaining agreement. Now Selig has placed the topic on the back burner for at least a few years—by the time it is revisited, he may have retired. Meanwhile, the Twins continue to win and draw well.

In Selig's defense, running baseball has got to be one of the toughest jobs in the world. Baseball economics are screwed up because the wrong people own most of the teams, and those are the very guys he is representing. Old-time owners were like movie moguls, who could be ruthless and cheap but loved movies. The owners of my day enjoyed baseball, and it was a hobby, not an investment. They usually made money, but if they lost a little it was a small price to pay for being in the newspapers. Now, instead of 16 owners, there are 30 owners, and getting 30 owners to agree on anything is almost impossible, especially when many have come in from the outside and don't comprehend that baseball is different from any other business. What works in the corporate world doesn't work in baseball. How do you keep track of 25 different kinds of contracts and balance budgets and work out television deals and figure out how to attract fans and put a winning team on the field? Now it's so complex that it would take a genius to figure out the solutions.

How can anyone make all 30 teams profitable or figure out how to bring salaries under control in a way that pleases both the owners and the union (and the players it represents)? At the same time, how can anyone achieve parity between big- and small-market teams, increase fan interest at a time of tremendous competition, and keep the quality of the game high? I can't see how to solve baseball's conundrums. So when I'm asked the first thing I'd do if I were running baseball, I quickly answer, "The first thing I'd do is resign."

However, I might jot down a few suggestions for my successor:

1. Contract bankrupt teams.
2. Tell owners to use financial restraint (and not use collusion to freeze out free agents).
3. Give owners the right to give contracts that are based on performances. This is a way to safeguard them from becoming paralyzed by long-term contracts for underachieving players, and even from giving them automatic raises each year. Do away with guaranteed contracts, except for those ended by injury. Salary without performance can't work for the owners. They should have some recourse if a player doesn't produce. The union would oppose this, but if the union won the war with the owners through arbitration, at least the owners might win this battle by taking the same route. An arbitrator with any common sense would not uphold a contract that gives raises to players whose performance level has dropped badly.
4. Keep youngsters, who are potential fans and potential players, interested in baseball, rather than losing them to other sports.

Even if it means building facilities and providing equipment for kids, it's economically advantageous in the long run.

5. Fairly distribute local television revenues of big-market teams to small-market cities with good fans and good teams—I would raise it to 60 to 40 percent, as we had in the PCL—because although teams are competitors, they are also partners who need each other.

6. Put in the collective-bargaining agreement that owners who receive money from distributed TV revenues and the luxury tax must use that money to acquire or develop players rather than pocket it. The money must be shared for the specific reason of creating competition, so the owners who get it should have to use it for that purpose. Teams need good players to increase attendance. Baseball has to find a way to let noncontenders keep their good players long enough for the rest of the team to improve.

7. If new stadiums are needed to keep teams in particular locations, work with the owners to come up with practical solutions. The success of San Francisco's new Pacific Bell Park, which was erected with private funding, may number the days that cities use public financing or bond issues to pay for stadiums to keep teams there. The new PNC Park in Pittsburgh was provided by the state, the city, and individuals, and for now a combination of all three may be the best way to go. A fair approach would be that the owner spends his or her own money to build a stadium if given free land.

8. Suggest that owners stop raising ticket prices when a city's economy is suffering and the team needs to hold on to its fans or even attract more. If fewer fans go to a team's games, fewer will watch their games on TV—and vice versa. There should be affordable tickets at every ballpark.

9. Show the postseason on free network television even if Saturday afternoon games on the network eventually are done away with.

10. If television broadcasts continue to be innovative, they could add interactive components to excite viewers. In that way, fans at home can select which players and what action they want on the screen at all times. They can choose camera angles and whether they want long shots, medium shots, close-ups, or split screens.

If the Yankees' YES proves to be successful, certainly other teams will follow suit. Texas has done well with television, which is one reason they have been able to pay for Alex Rodriguez. It would seem that if the Yankees are successful with YES, the Mets' Fred Wilpon would try to do the same thing. They have to come up with more money, and this move would cut out the middleman.

Mike Lupica, the powerful *New York Daily News* reporter, called YES "the network nobody needed," whose only purpose was to make a lot of money for the investors. If fans could continue to get games for free, then such networks wouldn't be needed or wanted. At the same time, owning networks may help some teams afford good players, so that would make the product better and perhaps keep ticket prices in check. Whether I'm in favor of organizations moving games from free television to pay-TV is beside the point—we can't really control it anyway, because it's an example of free enterprise.

Everyone debates the best ways to end the economic turmoil in baseball and prevent more work shutdowns or owners threatening to move their franchises to parts unknown unless their demands are met. Meanwhile, the game itself could use a little fine-tuning. I recently talked with Al Rosen, who is on a committee formed by Bud Selig to determine what can be done to improve baseball. He asked me for suggestions.

I told Rosen that the speed of the game is a problem. It has gone from a long game of two hours during the forties to four hours now. That's a big difference. You can eliminate things that have no action. For instance, no one wants a batter to step out of the box and take five or six swings or readjust his batting gloves. There is no real advantage to doing that. When we played, once we got into the batter's box and positioned our feet and got into our stances, we didn't want to get out. If umpires enforced a rule that said batters must stay in the box, that could save 20 minutes a game, especially if the umpires also make the pitcher throw the ball within the allotted time. There is a rule that with no one on base, he has to pitch within 20 seconds of receiving the ball. It's time that the umpires enforced it. Bill Veeck rang a bell after 20 seconds were up, but the peeved umpires didn't go along with it.

Catchers should be allowed only one trip to the mound in an inning. And a manager should have to take out the pitcher if he leaves the dugout for the first time. Once is enough.

When a pitcher is called in from the bullpen, there should be a cart ready. There's no reason he has to walk. He should have only a limited amount of time to get to the mound after being signaled or forfeit some of his eight warm-up pitches.

You have to allow pitchers to throw to first base as many times as they want to hold a fast base runner, although, as Tim McCarver says, "Speed slows down the game." Some pitchers will drive you crazy by throwing 10 times or more. But you can't limit the number of throws without giving the runner a tremendous advantage. However, I think it's legitimate to make the intentional walk automatic. Batters should just take first. The small number of times pitchers throw wild pitches isn't worth not trying to speed the game up. That said, I remember one time when Gerry Staley was walking me on purpose, and had the count 3–0, when he drilled me right on the back of the neck, on purpose. I was waiting for ball 4 and not paying much attention, and the next thing I knew, I was on the ground. The Dodgers' tough pitcher Ben Wade once gave Stan Musial an intentional walk by knocking him down with four straight fastballs.

You want rules that don't change the action but speed it up. You don't want anyone to delay the game on purpose. You gotta make it go. You can't eliminate commercials, but breaks should be limited to two minutes.

Other than speeding up the game, I have a few other suggestions for the commissioner, union, and owners to make the game better. I'd get rid of the DH. It accomplished what the American League wanted: it resulted in more scoring, kept great hitters in baseball long after their fielding skills had eroded, and caused controversy. But I think baseball, whether played by kids or adults, demands that all nine players in the lineup should bat and play the field. That would again put strategy back into American League games and eliminate the disparity between teams in interleague games.

Otherwise, I'd like to separate the American and National Leagues so that we restore the rivalry that once existed and make the World Series more special. As it is now, there are six divisions, and because of interleague play, there is little distinction between the teams in the two leagues. The two leagues should be separate and rivals. I don't believe in one-party government either. I'd go back to having presidents in each league—it was a mistake to move all power to the commissioner's office. Also, umpires should work in only one league. If you want all home-plate umpires to call balls and strikes the same way, you might as well install a robot. I prefer having the human element because that adds personality to the game. So I'd do away with QuesTec, the electronic system that has been intimidating umpires into trying to call the game as they think the league wants it, rather than how they see it.

Incidentally, the one time I wished there were no rivalry between the two leagues was when I visited Mickey Mantle's restaurant, on Central Park South in New York City. His restaurant was decorated with many nostalgic baseball photos and memorabilia, and I heard that the onetime American League star had put up my picture. I was curious, so I walked all around the restaurant searching for it. Finally I found it—on the wall in the men's room.

The All-Star Game, Arch Ward's creation, was great in the early days but 70 years later it is an anachronism. With interleague play, the All-Star Game is meaningless except for revenue. And the Lord knows, MLB wants revenue. The 2003 game, in which home-field advantage in the World Series was awarded to the winning league, was well managed and had more appeal than games in recent years—although the ratings weren't that much higher than usual. Despite Fox's promotion—"This time it counts!"—it was still an exhibition game in which the managers paraded as many players as they could in front of the fans. It still doesn't feel like it's part of baseball because it's not played like baseball, where the players who start are still in the game at the end. In 1950, several of us starters were still playing when it ended in the fourteenth inning, and that's what we expected before all those games when the NL president Warren Giles came into our clubhouse and told us how important it was that we beat the AL. Players today want to win, but they don't have the same intensity, which isn't surprising because they know that they will get only two or three at-bats. If there were no interleague play, the All-Star Game would have more credibility. But the only way to give it real meaning is to play it like a regular-season game, with most starters going the distance. Otherwise, awarding World Series home-field advantage to the champion of the winning league is just plain stupid.

I think the playoffs have been a good product of expansion. They have added excitement to baseball. However, after a 162-game season, teams should play a 4-of-7 first-round series, because the best of 5 isn't a true indicator of which team is better. Maybe someday the World Series will go back to 5-of-9, as it was at the beginning. Anything that will increase revenues should be looked into.

Finally, to make sure all players are on the same playing field, there should be mandatory drug testing. There's no reason in the world that players can't play baseball without using dangerous steroids, mysterious supplements, and addictive amphetamines. So many players claim they aren't taking anything that is illegal, but that's obviously not the case. We don't want it to be like it has been with pitchers who years after their retirements finally admit the suspicions were correct and they had indeed doctored the ball. This is much more serious. In the case of drugs, those who admit to it years later often have terrible health issues. We don't want such bleak futures for any players who made their contributions to baseball history.

When I was winning the seven consecutive home-run titles, I wanted very much to be in the record book, but I didn't think about my place in baseball history other than how it was right then. I didn't think about how I would be remembered in 20 or 30 years or in the 21st century. When I was playing, I never gave Cooperstown a thought. But after I retired and took note of my achievements, I realized that induction into the Baseball Hall of Fame would be the ultimate honor, a stamp of authenticity on my career. So, beginning in 1960, when I became eligible for admittance, I began a 15-year wait.

As the years went by and I was passed over, I didn't feel cheated, but I was definitely disappointed. I thought I had the credentials to be elected, but it was apparent that I was being denied for two reasons. First, I had played for only 10 years—of inductees, only Jackie Robinson and Roy Campanella had such brief tenures in the major leagues, and they had played beforehand in the Negro Leagues. Second, I never played in the World Series. My best finish was second place with the Indians in my final season. The Pirates never managed higher than fourth place and otherwise always finished seventh or eighth.

I remember with amusement the day I was finally selected in 1975. I was in my last year of eligibility with the writers before I'd be turned over to the Veterans Committee. So I wanted very much to go in then. But I didn't know how good my chances were. I'd finished second in the voting for five years, and normally a candidate got in after only one year in second place. I was at my home in St. Petersburg, waiting for a call from Jack Lang, the secretary of the Baseball Writers of America, to say whether I was elected. Of course, I was anxious, particularly because I knew that if I made it I would have to rush to the airport to make a flight to New York for the official announcement the next morning.

The phone rang! It was my second wife's mother. She wanted to know if I'd heard anything. I hurried her off the phone. Soon, it rang again. Again, it was my mother-in-law. She called a total of four times. Finally, I told her, "If you expect me to hear anything, you have to stop tying up the phone." At last I got a call from somebody else. It was Jack Lang, informing me that I had been selected. I barely made my flight and reached New York in time to meet the press. That's when it finally sank in: I was a member of the Hall of Fame.

The time came to fly to Cooperstown for the induction ceremony, so I chartered a plane for my daughter, K.C., and me to fly up from New York. The weather was terrible, and we couldn't land in Cooperstown. So we flew to the nearest airport, which was Albany, only to find its lights were out. However, we were able to land because of lights on the backup system. Then we had to get to Cooperstown, so we rented a car, got some directions, and took a quick look at the map to make sure we knew where to go. And then we headed the wrong way. We didn't see a sign that said Montreal until we'd gone a long distance. So we had some dinner on the road and turned around and went in the other direction. We finally arrived in Cooperstown at about 1:00 A.M, when the whole town had shut down. Meanwhile, Barbara, my second wife, and I were having one hell of a fight about tickets to my induction ceremony and everything else.

At least the ceremony went well. I was rewarded with a Hall of Fame plaque that reads:

RALPH MCPHERRAN KINER
PITTSBURGH, N.L. CHICAGO, N.L.
CLEVELAND, A.L. 1946–1955
HIT 369 HOME RUNS AND AVERAGED BETTER
THAN 100 RUNS BATTED IN PER SEASON IN
HIS TEN-YEAR CAREER. ONLY PLAYER TO LEAD HIS
LEAGUE OR SHARE LEAD IN HOMERS SEVEN
YEARS IN A ROW, 1946–1952. TWICE HAD
MORE THAN 50 HOME RUNS IN A SEASON. SET N.L. MARK
OF 101 FOUR-BAGGERS IN TWO SUCCESSIVE
YEARS WITH 54 IN 1949 AND 47 IN 1950.
LED N.L. IN SLUGGING PCT. THREE TIMES.

I gave my acceptance speech and things were looking up. But when fans were coming up afterward, a Chinese man who had trouble pronouncing the letter *l* said, "Congraturations on your erection!" I didn't know how to respond to that. So I'd say that except for being inducted into the Hall of Fame, that wasn't such a great weekend.

I make a point of returning to Cooperstown every year to help honor the latest inductees. I also serve on the Veterans Committee that selects players and executives for Hall of Fame induction who have been passed over by the writers. Among those I hope to see gain entrance in the future are Allie Reynolds, Al Rosen, Gil Hodges, Don Newcombe, Mike Marshall, Ryne Sandberg, Ted Kluszewski, Mickey Vernon, Marty Marion, Ken Williams, and three men who changed the game, Maury Wills, Bruce Sutter, and Marvin Miller. Regrettably, even the oldest Hall of Famers haven't seen many players who deserve consideration, including Negro Leagues stars. We have seen none of the players from the 19th century and early 20th century, so all we can do is go by their statistics and read what other players and sportswriters once said about them.

One person I don't think should be inducted into the Hall of Fame is Pete Rose, although there is no question he would deserve to be enshrined if *only* his performance on the field was taken into consideration. I resent that Bud Selig has tried to make him eligible for a vote by the writers and Hall of Fame members in order to please naïve fans. I have no personal grudges against Rose. He was always accommodating and friendly when I interviewed him. But from the day I first stepped into a minor league clubhouse as a rookie in 1941, I have been aware of the universal warning given to all players: there can be no gambling on baseball in any way, shape, or form. Every player who has ever played since the White Sox threw the 1919 World Series for money has been told there can't be gambling. If there's gambling and the integrity of the game is compromised, that could ruin the image of baseball. The evidence I have seen confirms Rose bet on games involving his own team. People are more forgiving today, but I'm from the old school, and I believe you have to live by the rules. Rose broke the one rule he could not break, as did Shoeless Joe Jackson and the seven other White Sox players who disgraced and almost destroyed baseball.

At one time I signed a petition saying Jackson should get in the Hall of Fame. I was coerced by Ted Williams, who was campaigning to get him in and pointing out that Jackson had been given a lifetime ban from baseball but was now dead. I wouldn't do it again. Since then, I have learned more about the Black Sox scandal and how Jackson was among those players who accepted money from gamblers to throw the 1919 Series. He had a great Series and supposedly tried to give the money back, but Sox owner Charles Comiskey wouldn't take it. I have sympathy for the ignorant Jackson, who couldn't write his name and would sit in hotel lobbies and pretend to be reading the newspaper. But anybody who damages the integrity of America's pastime should be severely penalized. Baseball is bigger than any individual. If Jackson were in the Hall of Fame already, there would be no way we could have him removed. The same holds true for Rose. In Rose's case, we already know what he did, so that should be enough to prevent the big mistake of letting him in. After finding out a retired bank president embezzled thousands of dollars, would you want to keep him in the Bankers Hall of Fame?

People who don't know baseball history, including members of the Hall of Fame, are the ones who push for Jackson's admittance. Similarly, it is people who don't understand the issues who think Rose should be enshrined. When fans turned against baseball after the strike of 1994, there was a lot of sympathy for Rose, who was a great and popular "people's player" and an ambassador for the game that had obsessed him all his life. Because he had been thrown out of baseball, they saw him as the victim of the same people whom they held responsible for ruining their game in other ways. They assumed his exile was another thing wrong with baseball, another way that baseball was slapping the face of the fans. But they weren't told the full story. They saw nothing wrong with his going to the racetrack or betting on football and losing hundreds of thousands of dollars. But they were never informed that as the manager of the Reds, Rose actually gambled on baseball, including on games involving his own team. He managed according to his bets, and fans don't realize this. When he accepted a penalty of suspension from Commissioner Bart Giamatti, he probably did it to escape major problems arising from a public hearing.

Standards should be higher instead of lower when you are a star like he was. I don't buy that he should be in the Hall of Fame as a player because what he did wrong was as a manager. I'd still keep him out. But it's a moot point. I have seen evidence that shows he was betting on games as a player as well. Rules are rules. You can't say a person is of Hall of Fame quality if he has bet on games and altered their results at any time.

There are issues more pressing than whether Pete Rose has his suspension lifted. There is the chance of more strikes, more lockouts, and more labor strife. Salaries may keep escalating and go through the roof. Big-market teams may become even more dominant, and small-market teams may claim bankruptcy. Baseball may eventually not be able to find a home on free network television—and if that happens, what will happen to salaries and TV revenues? And will security at ballparks become an even bigger concern? When a major leaguer in uniform is the one to knock over a mascot with a bat during a "sausage race," then you see how futile it can be to protect everyone in a ballpark.

Bill Lee, the iconoclastic former Red Sox left-hander, contended, "Baseball is the belly of society. Straighten out baseball and you straighten out the rest of the world." But it's not so easy. Yet, I'm optimistic about baseball's future. It's such a great game that no matter how many people try, no one can ruin it. I have no doubt that baseball will not only survive but will thrive well into the future.

As for me, at 81 years young, I am experiencing the best I could ever have hoped for. My personal renaissance began when I married my third wife, DiAnn, 26 years ago. My DiAnn has shown me that there is more to life than success in worldly matters. She has brought Christianity into my life, showing me the power of faith in Jesus Christ by surviving multiple myeloma (cancer of the bone marrow). My good fortune continues today because we have wonderful children and quite a few grandchildren and because I still have the privilege of broadcasting Mets games in what has been designated "The Ralph Kiner Television Booth" at Shea Stadium. If I were a guest on *Kiner's Korner*, I would say that my future is bright! I guess I'm old-fashioned because I love happy endings.

Index